The Political Economy of Telecommunications Reform in Developing Countries

The Political Economy of Telecommunications Reform in Developing Countries

Privatization and Liberalization in Comparative Perspective

BEN A. PETRAZZINI

Westport, Connecticut
London

Library of Congress Cataloging-in-Publication Data

Petrazzini, Ben A.
    The political economy of telecommunications reform in developing
countries : privatization and liberalization in comparative
perspective / Ben A. Petrazzini.
        p.   cm.
    Includes index.
    ISBN 0–275–95294–0 (alk. paper)
    1. Telecommunication policy—Developing countries.
    2. Telecommunication—Deregulation—Developing countries.
    3. Privatization—Developing countries.   I. Title.
    HE8635.P48   1995
    384'.068—dc20   95–7552

British Library Cataloguing in Publication Data is available.

Library of Congress Catalog Card Number: 95–7552
ISBN: 0–275–95294–0

First published in 1995

Praeger Publishers, 88 Post Road West, Westport, CT 06881
An imprint of Greenwood Publishing Group, Inc.

Printed in the United States of America

The paper used in this book complies with the
Permanent Paper Standard issued by the National
Information Standards Organization (Z39.48–1984).

10 9 8 7 6 5 4 3 2 1

Contents

Figures

Abbreviations

AD	Acción Democratica
ADEBA	Argentina Banks Association
ADS	American Depository Shares
ANC	African National Congress Party
ANTEL	Administración Nacional de Telecomunicaciones
ATUR	Automatic Telephone Using Radio
AT&T	American Telephone and Telegraph Company
BOT	build-operate-transfer
BT	British Telecom
C&W	Cable and Wireless
CANTV	Compañía Anónima Nacional de Teléfonos de Venezuela
CAT	Compañía Argentina de Teléfonos
CAT	Communications Authority of Thailand
CET	Compañía Entreriana de Teléfonos
CGT	Confederación General del Trabajo
CIC	Capital Issues Committee
CNC	National (Chile) Telephone Company
CNC	Confederación Nacional Campesina
CNOP	Confederación Nacional de Organizaciones Populares
CNT	Comisión Nacional de Telecomunicaciones
COPEI	Organización Política Electoral Independiente
CORFO	Corporación de Fomento a la Producción
CP	Conservative Party
CPE	customer-premise equipment
CPU	Centro de Profesionales Universitarios
CTC	Continental Telephone Company
CTC	Compañía de Teléfonos de Chile

CTCOY	Coyhaique Telephone Company
CTM	Confederación de Trabajadores de México
CTV	Confederación de Trabajadores de Venezuela
DAP	Democratic Action Party
DATRAM	Data Transmission Company
DBS	direct broadcast satellite
DEP	Directorio de Empresas Públicas
DOT	Department of Telecommunications
ECLAC	Economic Commission for Latin America
EGAT	Electricity Generating Authority of Thailand
ENTel	Empresa Nacional de Telecommunicaciones (Arg.)
ENTEL	Empresa Nacional de Telecommunicaciones (Chile)
ETMA	Empresa Mixta Telefónica Argentina
FCC	Federal Communications Commission
FDI	foreign direct investment
FOETRA	Federación de Obreros y Empleados Telefónicos de la Rep. Arg.
FOPSTA	Federación de Organizaciones de Personal de Supervisión
GATS	General Agreement on Trade in Services
GATT	General Agreement on Tariffs and Trade
GDP	Gross Domestic Product
IRI	Institute for Industrial Reconstruction
ISDN	Integrated Services Digital Network
ISI	import-substitution industrialization
ITT	International Telephone and Telegraph Corporation
ITU	International Telecommunications Union
JLP	Jamaican Labor Party
JTC	Jamaican Telephone Company
JTM	Jabatan Telekom Malaysia
KLSE	Kuala Lumpur Stock Exchange
LDC	less developed country
MAYCIS	Malaysia Circuit-Switched Public Data Network
MAYPAC	Malaysia Packet-Switched Public Data Network
MCA	Malaysian Chinese Association
MCI	Microwave Communications Inc.
MDC	more developed country
MFJ	modified final judgement
MIC	Malaysian Indian Congress
MITI	Ministry of International Trade and Industry
MNC	Multinational Corporation
MLp100P	main-line-per-100-people
MLpE	main-line-per-employee
MTC	Ministry of Transport and Communication
NAFTA	North American Free Trade Agreement
NEP	National Economic Program
NTIA	National Telecommunication and Information Agency
NTT	Nippon Telegraph and Telephone
NTTCP	Nippon Telegraph and Telephone Public Corporation
NZTC	New Zealand Telecom Corporation
OAS	Organization of the American States
ONA	open network architecture
PAN	Partido de Acción Nacional

PBB	Party Pesaka Bumipteran Bersatu
PBX	private branch exchange
PNP	People's National Party
PPP	Programa de Propiedad Participada
PPS	Partido Popular Socialista
PRD	Partido Revolucionario Democratico
PRI	Partido Revolucionario Institucional
PTD	Post and Telegraph Deparment
PTT	Postal, Telegraph and Telephone
RBOCs	Regional Bell operating companies
ROC	regional operating company
SAPT	South African Posts and Telecommunications
SCT	Secretaria de Comunicaciones y Transportes
SCT	Sociedad Cooperativa Telefónica
SIGEP	Sindicato General de Empresas Públicas
SHCP	Secretaría de Hacienda y Crédito Público
SOE	state-owned enterprise
SOTE	state-owned telecommunications enterprise
SPP	Secretaría de Programación y Presupuesto
STET	Societa Finanziaria Telefonica
STM	Syarikat Telekom Malaysia
STRM	Sindicato de Telefonistas de la República Mexicana
SWIFT	Society for Worldwide Interbank Financial Transactions
TELECOMM	Telecomunicaciones de México S.A.
TELMEX	Teléfonos de México
TMA	Telecommunications Managers Association
TOJ	Telecommunications of Jamaica
TOT	Telephone Organization of Thailand
UCD	Unión de Centro Democráctico
UDEP	Unidad de Desincorporacion de Entidades Paraestatales
UMNO	United Malay National Organisation
UPJ	Unión de Personal Jerárquico
UT	Unión Telefónica
VANS	value-added network service
VSAT	very small aperture terminal
YPF	Yacimientos Petroliferos Fiscales

Glossary

• *Analog*: Signal representations that bear some physical relationship to the original quantity, usually electrical voltage, frequency, resistance, or mechanical translation or rotation.

• *Bandwidth*: The width of an electrical transmision path or circuit, in terms of the range of frequencies it can pass; a measure of the volume of communication traffic that the channel can carry. A voice channel typically has a bandwith of 4,000 cycles per second. A TV channel requires about 6.5 MHz.

• *Binary*: A numbering system having only digits, typically 0 and 1.

• *Bit*: Binary digit. The smallest unit of information representing a signal, wave, or state as either zero or one. In an electrical communication system, a bit can be represented by the presence or absence of a pulse.

• *Broadband communication*: A specific transmission range, generally with a bandwith greater than voiceband. Cable is a broadband communication system with a bandwith usually from 5 MHz to 450 MHz.

• *Broadband integrated services digital network (BISDN)*: An integrated optical-fiber-based digital network in which the same switches and transmission paths are used to establish a simultaneous interface for a variety of services, including telephone, data, video, telex, and facsimile.

• *Byte*: A group of eight bits processed or operating together. A byte is typically the smallest addressable unit of information in a database or memory.

• *Central Office (CO)*: The local switch or junction point for a telephone exchange within a public network.

• *Centrex*: A telephone-company-provided service that gives business customers the ability to dial direct internally and externally without the need for a company-specific system, such as private-switch or branch-exchange systems. Some of its basic features include call transfer, conference calling, and call hold.

• *Circuit*: Combination of two channels that allows bidirectional transmission of signals between two points.

• *Channel*: A means of transmission based on wire, fiber-optic, radio, or other electromagnetic system used to establish a communication link between two points in one direction.

• *CT2*: A second-generation cordless telephone system in which power is boosted to give mobile telephones a range of several miles.

• *Digital data service (DDS)*: A dedicated circuit that transmits information between two or more points. It uses digital transmission at speeds of 2.4, 4.8, 9.6, and 56 Kbps. This service provides a higher degree of accuracy and reliability than analog circuits.

• *Fiber-optic*: Fiber-optic technology is a flexible ultrapure glass fiber the size of human hair that transmits informtion in the form of pulses of light. Fiber-optic services are differentiated according to the speed of the transmission.

• *Integrated services digital network (ISDN)*: A narrowband integrated digital network in which the same switches and transmission paths are used to establish a simultaneous interface for a variety of services, including telephone, data, video, telex, and facsimile.

• *Leased circuits*: A dedicated circuit made available at bulk rate to users requiring exclusive or continuous capacity for high-speed transmission.

• *Local area network (LAN)*: A telecommunications network (public or private) that grants services in an authorized local area, and interconnects with the public network to provide long-distance services.

• *Multiplexer*: An analog or digital device that allows a number of signals to share the same line.

• *On line*: When a user is actively connected to a network or computer system and able to interactively exchange comands, data, and information with a host device.

• *Open network achitecture (ONA)*: Standards that allow different telecommunications vendors to interconnect with a network.

• *Packet-switched data network (PSDN)*: An efficient data transmission system whereby messages are broken down into smaller units, or bundles, which are transmitted separately along the most direct route available, and then reassembled at their destination.

• *Paging system:* A radiocommunication technology used to send messages point-to-point in only one direction, generally with the purpose of sending a short message to mobile receiver.

• *Public switched telephone network (PSTN):* A telecommunications network used to provide service to the public in general. It does not include the customer premise equipment, local area networks, or private branch exchanges.

• *Private branch exchange (PBX):* A "dedicated" telephone exchange in an organization requiring multiple lines; offers features such as automatic call distribution and call waiting.

• *Private network:* A telecommunications network established by businesses (individuals or institutions) with their own hardware or through the lease of public network channels and circuits for intra- or interfirm communication.

• *Switch*: A process that interconnects telecommunications chanels or circuits to allow the transmission of signals.

• *Telecommunications network*: The infrastructure that provides channels and circuits based on cables and switches to conduct voice, data, or video signals between two points.

• *Value-added network (VAN):* Generally based on packet-switching technology, VAN networks provide services such as electronic mail, voice mail, and store-and-forward facsimile.

• *Value-added service (VAS):* Telecommunication services provided through private or public networks with computer-based information feature or performance.

• *Very small aperture terminal (VSAT):* A satellite-based technology using 4 to 5 meters dish antennas, used primarily for data transmssion.

The Political Economy of Telecommunications Reform in Developing Countries

Introduction

Puzzling and counterintuitive economic reforms are quickly spreading throughout the Third World. Less developed countries (LDCs) are opening their economies to market forces at a striking pace, despite well grounded and convincing arguments that structural constraints in the international system shaped Third World preferences for protectionism and state intervention (Krasner 1985). In the pursuit of a free market economy, the transformation of the political and economic role of the state has become crucial. Reforms such as privatization of state-owned enterprises (SOEs), liberalization of the economy, and reduction of state regulation are at the center of this historical shift in the organization of developing societies. Among the public services and state industries that are being restructured in most developing nations, one has emerged as the spearhead and showcase of a broader reform program: the telecommunications sector.

In the light of the increasing integration of the global economy (linked by a worldwide telecommunications infrastructure) and the simultaneous economic opening in many LDCs, telecommunications is now a fundamental prerequisite of any national or large-scale growth project in the developing world. As one of the few industries that cuts across and integrates social and economic activities, telecom holds a strategic position in the building of a dynamic and flexible national economy. The sector is central to the national and international flows of capital and commerce. This is specifically true because the merger of telecommunications and computers has radically transformed the role of communications technologies in the productive system. Information traveling across networks has become an invaluable asset for competitive production and trade success. High-tech telecommunications (telecom) systems are the gatekeepers of global trade and production.

As an international infrastructure, telecommunications is the "nervous system" of an emerging global information economy. The industry has progressively abandoned its limited point-to-point communication features to grow into a highly sophisticated "intelligent network" that carries valuable services and products in the form of information. Further, the sector is one of the largest and fastest growing in the world economy. Between 1992 and 1993 telecommunications was the fastest growing industry in the world with a 36 percent growth over the previous year.[1] By 1993 telecommunications was the industry with the second highest market value in the world after banking (Fig. 1).

This role of telecom in the world economy is manifested in the position in which telecom companies are ranked according to market capitalization—a telling indicator, because it reflects investors' fears and hopes. According to recent surveys the two most important companies in the world in 1993—based on their market value—were Nippon Telegraph & Telephone (NTT) and American Telephone & Telegraph (AT&T) followed by oil and financial businesses (Fig. 2). And while in 1994 AT&T moved to the seventh place, if one would reconstitute the company as it stands in most other countries in the world (i.e., as an integrated business providing both local and international services) the American firm would become by far the most valuable company in the world. Similarly, in LDCs the top firm according to its market value was Teléfonos de México (TELMEX), with telecommunications companies from Brazil, Chile, and Argentina ranked among the twenty-five most important (Fig. 3).

The key to this impressive growth is the fact that, in contrast to industry-specific innovations, changes in the telecommunications sector have significant direct multiplier effects across an unusually wide range of economic activities. However, despite the importance of telecom services for economic development, LDCs have traditionally remained untouched by the benefits of telecommunications. Out of the 670 million telephones in service in the world in the mid-1980s, 75 percent of them were concentrated in only eight industrialized countries. Seventy percent of the world's population living in LDCs had access to only 7 percent of the world's telephones. This uneven distribution of telecom resources was clearly reflected in the fact that the whole of Africa had fewer telephones than the city of Tokyo (Independent Commission for Worldwide Telecommunications Development 1984).

Mindful of this dramatic scarcity of telecommunication infrastructure and aware of the key role that telecom plays in economic development—but pressed by economic, fiscal, managerial, and technological constraints—many LDCs are struggling to move telecommunications from a second priority "public service," to a first priority "international trade tool."   Nothing better illustrates the changing perception in LDCs of telecommunications that the statement by Mexican President Carlos Salinas de Gortari, who asserted that "telecommunications will become the cornerstone of the program to modernize Mexico's economy" (Székely 1989, 81).

Figure 1

Leading Industries by Market Value (May 1994)

Rank	Industry	Market Value (billionsUS$)	Percentage Change from 1993
1	Banking	1,383.8	16.1
2	Telecommunications	641.8	10.0
3	Energy Sources	518.8	6.3
4	Health Care	509.1	-1.2
5	Utilities	463.8	-9.2

Source: Morgan Stanley Capital International (*Business Week*, July 1993 and July 1994)

Figure 2

Leading Companies by Market Value Worldwide (May 1993-1994)

Rank 1993	Rank 1994	Company	Country	Market Value (billions US$)	
1	1	NTT	Japan	140.52	128.94
2	7	AT&T	U.S.	82.40	73.87
3	2	Royal D./Shell	Neth./U.K.	81.59	91.93
4	5	Exxon	U.S.	81.35	7592
5	3	General Electric	U.S.	79.34	84.94

Source: Morgan Stanley Capital International (*Business Week*, July 1993 and July 1994)

Figure 3

**Leading Companies by Market Value in Developing Countries
(May 1993-1994)**

Rank 1993	Rank 1994	Company	Country	Market Value (billion US$)		% change from 93
1	1	TELMEX	Mexico	25.6	32.9	28
2	2	Korea Elec. Power	Korea	13.8	20.7	50
3	3	Cathay Life Ins.	Taiwan	8.0	14.5	80
4	4	Telebras	Brazil	7.3	11.2	52
5	5	Arg. Telec. Syst.*	Argentina	7.2	14.8	108
17	13	Telefónica de Arg.	Argentina	4.2	8.5	99
18	30	Teléfonos de Chile	Chile	3.1	4.4	41
21	28	Telec. Sao Paulo	Brazil	3.0	4.6	55
22	22	Telecom Argentina	Argentina	2.9	6.3	117

Source: Morgan Stanley Capital International (*Business Week*, July 1993 and July 1994)

* This is the value that ENTel would have had in 1993/94 if it had not been split in two different private companies.

THE PUZZLE AND THE CASES

In pursuit of this radical transformation, LDCs embarked on state reform programs. And, although state reform is viewed as a homogeneous trend throughout the Third World, a closer look at some of the countries in which reforms are most advanced reveals few commonalties. Regardless of shared goals, countries have followed very different paths to a free market economy. In the telecommunications sector, in particular, LDCs show today a range of policy models that cover a complex and diverse variety of combinations of ownership (public and private) and degree of competition (closed and open markets).

In the quest for a better understanding of the divergent reconfiguration of telecommunications systems in LDCs, this study analyzes the recent reform experiences of major countries of Latin America and Asia. The work concentrates on the privatization experiences of Argentina and Mexico; however, it also considers more briefly telecommunications privatization attempts in Chile, Colombia, Jamaica, Malaysia, Thailand, South Africa, Venezuela, and Uruguay.[2] The selection of cases is rooted in the fruitful similarities and differences that they offer for the study of the role of politics and economics in the transformation of telecom systems in LDCs. Most countries attempted similar telecom reform at almost the same historical period. Despite similarities in goals and timing, outcomes, however, differed markedly. More specifically, while most countries intended to privatize their state-owned telecommunications companies (SOTEs), some succeeded and others failed. Similarly, while liberalization was a widespread, shared target in most cases, only some succeeded and while others failed to meet their goals.[3]

The countries under study initiated a broad state reform program between 1987 and 1989 that made telecommunications a crucial, if not the key, sector in the process. In the four main cases, general guidelines for the restructuring of the telecommunications sector included transfer of SOTEs to private entrepreneurs, liberalization of markets, and reduction or elimination of state regulations. But telecom reforms are not the mechanical outcome of policy implementation. To the contrary, they are the product of complex and dynamic interactions among conflictive interests. As a consequence, the varied resolutions of these conflicts led to divergent outcomes in the success of SOTE privatization, and also in the likelihood and degree of market liberalization. Among successful privatizers, the convergence of political and economic factors also determined the extent of the reform. In other words, despite common initial goals, some countries were able to privatize while others failed to do so, and some were able to liberalize while others still have closed markets.

The governments of Argentina (1982–1987), Thailand, Colombia, South Africa, and Uruguay, for example, failed to sell their companies; but a later Argentine administration (1989–1990), and the governments of Mexico, Malaysia, Chile, Jamaica, and Venezuela succeeded in privatizing their national carrier. Similarly, some countries like Mexico, Malaysia, and Thailand were able to largely open their market to competitive entry, others such as Argentina and Jamaica still remain mostly closed.

In LDCs current telecom reforms and their divergent policy outcomes have clear political underpinnings. A long tradition of state intervention and politicized markets assured a pervasive role for politics. This study is an effort to unveil some of the political puzzles that underlie the various forms that telecom reform has taken in LDCs. The question that drives the research is, Why do countries with shared telecom reform goals and similar patterns of development achieve such different outcomes?

Although generally treated as a unitary process, the reform of telecom systems implies different kinds of transformations—such as privatization and liberalization—and, therefore, the involvement of different forces, actors, and outcomes. For analytical purposes, I will attempt to desegregate, whenever possible, privatization of SOTEs from the introduction of competition in the market.

In this study privatization is considered as the total or partial sale of shares of a SOTE to private investors.[4] Liberalization is defined as the lowering of entry barriers or opening the domestic telecom market to competition. Separating for analytical purposes privatization from liberalization allows us to explore more accurately: (1) Why some countries were able to privatize their

SOTEs while others failed to do so, and (2) Why some countries were able to liberalize their domestic telecom markets while others failed to do so.

The analytical separation of privatization and liberalization is rooted in the fact that, while clearly related, each process is different in nature and involves different interests and actors. Separating privatization from liberalization also offers better methodological tools to identify the political and economic forces as well as the central actors involved in each aspect of reform. Finally, when looking at the socioeconomic impacts of reform the analytical division between the two processes permits us to identify which reform effects are linked causally to the sale of the company and which to the opening of the market. The first section of the study is concerned with the effects of political and economic conditions and actors in the reform process and its outcomes: How and why did reforms succeed or fail? The last chapter, discusses the socioeconomic impact of telecom reform. Specifically, it looks at how early telecom reform outcomes affected various societal groups, such as users, labor, the state, service providers, and equipment suppliers.

UNDERSTANDING PRIVATIZATION OUTCOMES

In an attempt to explain why countries failed or succeeded in privatizing their SOTEs, the study argues that two elements are crucial to an explanation of divergent outcomes. The first is the relative autonomy and insulation of the state vis-à-vis political pressures, and the second, the degree of power concentration within the state apparatus. Evidence suggests that a low level of state autonomy and dispersed power concentration within the state is strongly correlated with likelihood of failure in the privatization of large public utilities. In other words, LDCs with highly controlled and vertically integrated political structures, such as Mexico and Malaysia, are more prone to achieve the privatization of their SOTEs than are those countries with a highly volatile and profuse power structure, such as Argentina and Thailand. In this way, the study points to the ironic fact that "dismantling" the state calls for the presence of a "strong" and autonomous state. The validity of these propositions is supported by studies that explore the politics of economic reform in other developing countries (Evans 1992, and Haggard and Kaufman 1992).

Although research on economic reform programs in LDCs points to the correlation between closed polities and successful implementation of adjustment policies, other studies of telecom sector in more developed countries (MDCs) reach exactly the opposite conclusion. In a comparative study conducted by Raymond Duch on the privatization and liberalization of telecommunications services in three MDCs (England, France, and Germany), the author concludes that pluralist, open political systems—such as England—are more conducive to reform than those based on corporatist-closed political structures—such as Germany (Duch 1991). The hypothesis rests on the notion that pluralist institutions "pose fewer barriers to new and unconventional interests that advocate policy change, while at the same time vested interests have less institutionalized protection against these challenges." Duch's argument runs counter to the conclusions of this study, which argue that in LDCs closed political systems are more conducive to reform than open-participatory ones. What might explain this difference is the source of pressures for reform. While MDCs have reformed mainly in response to the pressures of large business users (who were responding to the globalization and informatization of the world economy), changes in LDCs are generally initiated by the government as part of larger structural economic adjustment program (aimed at battling fiscal crisis and economic decay).

In MDCs the push for reform came from the outside of formal political institutions to the core of the state apparatus, and, therefore, the openness of the system to the participation of political actors became crucial. In a more closed system, like corporatist Germany, the penetration of outsider's demands becomes very difficult and the chances for reform are slim and move slowly. On the contrary, in England, pressures from concentrated groups with clear political agendas and considerable political leverage found a more fertile ground for reform initiatives. In LDCs those at the top of the political system pushed for reform, often against the interests of powerful political constituents (unions, the military, civil servants, local industries, and others), and this called for a closed and isolated policy-making process. In the cases in which the system was open to diverse and contradictory interests of various societal actors, programs to reform the state have failed in one way or the other.

UNDERSTANDING LIBERALIZATION OUTCOMES

Another puzzle to be explained is the success or failure of LDC efforts to liberalize telecom markets. While the variables of state autonomy and concentration of executive power offer important leverage to explain the fate of privatization attempts, they less well explain divergent outcomes of liberalization efforts. Generalizability of the hypothesis to explain market liberalization is challenged by the fact that countries with different political structures, such as Mexico and Thailand, share the achievement of some market liberalization, while countries with similar political profiles, like Argentina and Thailand, diverged in liberalization outcomes.

What instead emerges as a key explanatory factor is the status of the domestic economy at the moment of privatization and how investors assessed market prospects in each country. Attractive economic prospects in Malaysia, Thailand, and Mexico granted these countries bargaining tools, which were mostly absent in the gloomy Argentine case.

In economies growing at fast pace—such as Thailand and Malaysia—or with attractive potential markets—such as Mexico—governments face strong pressures from the business community to offer access to new telecom services at cost-based prices. Liberalization pressure is supplemented by the general inability of SOTEs to rapidly provide those services and with entrenched interest groups that have a lower economic and political stake in the liberalization of enhanced services. In the case of Argentina, economic factors adversely affected the privatization/liberalization process. The urgent need for foreign investment to jump-start a stagnant economy and the unattractive features of the local economy led the government to a complete sale of the SOTE, with a monopolic concession in most services that precludes the possibility of competition in the Argentine telecom sector for the next decade.

THE SOCIOECONOMIC IMPACT OF REFORM

After discussing cross-country policy variations, the final chapter analyzes and assesses early reform effects in various socioeconomic groups related to the telecom sector. The work concentrates on users of services, providers of services, equipment suppliers, labor, the state, and finally, for some Latin American countries, it explores briefly the impact of reform on the financial sector.

At this point it is important to bring to the forefront an issue that is central for an accurate assessment of the effects of telecom reform. SOTE privatizations' overwhelming fascination for students of telecommunication reform has led to an indiscriminate attribution—positive or negative—of the relationships of changes in the sector to the change of ownership. Without denying some important effects created by ownership transfer this study argues that changes in the sector are less driven by privatization than by fundamental changes in the underlying philosophy of the sector and the opening of the market.

In the past telecommunications systems in LDCs were rooted in a noncommercial philosophy that, based upon the principles of universal service, put forward the unquestionable notion that the provision of telephone, telegraph, telex, and other telecommunications services was a public duty of the government towards its citizens. Today these underlying notions have started to crumble and telecoms is viewed as a tradable service. This phenomenon can be broadly defined as the "commercialization" of telecom services. These changes in the basic principles that govern the sector underly most of the effects of recent telecom reforms—such as pricing policies, cross-subsidies, hiring and firing policies, network expansion, diversification of services, market liberalization, deregulation and reregulation. To put it more graphically, in countries in which companies are still state-owned, but have been corporatized and run on a commercial basis, the impacts of reform are very similar to those generated by SOTEs that have been privatized. It is also important to account for the fact that in the cases of privatization important reform effects were generated by the commercialization of services prior to the transfer of ownership to private investors.

After the change in the basic philosophy and accompanying commercialization of services, the lowering of entry barriers to domestic markets is probably the second most important factor in the reform processes. The accuracy of this claim is more clear when privatized SOTEs still run under monopoly conditions are compared with privatized companies that confront competitive markets. A good example to illustrate the point is the fact that while privatized firms enjoying monopoly protection have retained most of their labor force, privatized companies facing competitive markets have sharply reduced their personnel.

Besides discriminating between the impacts generated by privatization from those induced by commercialization or liberalization, it is important to keep in mind that, due to the variety of economic, social, and political changes that LDCs suffered in the 1980s, one should be careful to attribute causality solely to the sale of SOTEs, commercialization of services, or liberalization of markets. In the last few years the countries studied here have experienced major economic changes—such as structural adjustment programs, economic liberalization, decreased inflation, rapid growth of capital markets, new domestic and foreign direct investments, and repatriation of capital—that may have influenced outcomes in the telecom sector. For example, it is hard to tell whether the rise in the value of privatized firms' shares is linked to the change to private ownership or to the attractiveness and dynamism of the domestic economy, and, in particular, of the local stock exchange.

Finally, it is important to stress that this is not a theoretical work. It is, instead, a comparative historical analysis that uses theory to reach a better understanding of events in each country studied. In this regard, it does not seek "universal principles," nor does it try to understand historical processes in the light of neatly designed models. The research, instead, looks for causal connections that might offer theoretical insights potentially generalizable to other similar cases across time and space. For these reasons the study relies heavily on the methodological tools offered by comparative historical analysis.

NOTES

1. If we unbundle this measure by country, we find that among the nineteen countries reported in 1993, telecom service or equipment companies held the first or second position in thirteen of them—which places the telecom industry in the top of approximately 70 percent of the reported cases. In the following countries, for example, the dominant telecommunications carrier is the top company based on market value: Britain, Spain, New Zealand, Hong Kong, Argentina, Brazil, Chile, Mexico, and Malaysia. In Canada, France, the United States, and Sweden, telecom equipment suppliers are among the two top companies of the country. *Business Week*, 12 July 1993, 52.

2. The analysis concentrates on the case of Argentina because it offers the richest material to explore the accuracy of the hypotheses presented in this work. Mexico constitutes the second most important case, and other LDCs are included, mainly, to test the generalizability of the suggested hypotheses.

3. This study it is not an assessment of the virtues or defects of telecom reforms. It does not prescribe any policy for the sector, nor does it judge in any way the actions of governments. The notions of "success" and "failure" are linked to the initial goals each government had, and not to the author's personal view of the process. The work is comparative in nature and is basically concerned with an explanation of cross-country policy divergence.

4. Not all LDCs privatized their SOTEs in the same way. Privatization varies in pattern and scope in each case, and variation of privatization patterns is an event that should be explored. However, the task of this project is not to explore the

multiple faces of privatization, but to explain why certain LDCs were able to commercialize their SOTEs and introduce private investment and management, while others failed to do so.

1

Restructuring Telecommunications: A Transformation without Boundaries

Until recently, telecommunications (telecom) has been a rather arcane, obscure, and uninteresting field. In the last few years however, a technological revolution in conjunction with radical transformations in the international economy have brought telecoms to the center of the political stage throughout the world. Governments talk today about telecommunications, information infrastructure, and electronic highways much as they did about nuclear weapons, arms control, and foreign relations during the Cold War. This chapter briefly explores the principles around which the sector functioned until recently. It discusses some of the key forces that drove reform in more developed countries (MDCs), and it presents the differences in the reform process between MDCs and less developed countries (LDCs). It also describes recent events in LDCs telecom reform, and lays out the question around which this study is organized.

RISE AND DECLINE OF "NATURAL MONOPOLIES"

Decades of state-owned telecommunications led to an assumption that telephones have always been a public service owned and run by the national government of a country.[1] However, historically, in almost every nation around the globe, telecom services began as private, commercial business. Monopoly and the notion of universal service, which have dominated the sector for so long, were also absent at the industry's inception. In those early days telephone companies operated in a competitive, unregulated environment and targeted the most profitable areas. In LDCs services were not only private, commercial, and unregulated but, in most cases, were provided by foreign telephone companies.[2] Many of the patterns that characterized the early industry were progressively transformed in the first decades of the twentieth century.

Changes to the early competitive regime were rooted in persuasive economic, political, and social rationales. From an economic point of view natural monopoly theory suggested that telecommunications was an industry with clear economies of scale and, therefore, should be run as a monopoly (Sharkey 1982). Under economies of scale in telecom the cost of adding any additional customer drops as the number of subscribers increases.[3] A natural monopoly exists when the cost to one producer supplying all the market is lower than the cost for multiple producers supplying segments of the market. Considering that governments aimed at the highest possible network expansion for the least cost, it made sense to reduce the cost of providing services by establishing a monopoly. Economies of scope also supported the rise of monopolies. Arguably once a system is in place, it is less costly for the existing carrier to move upstream to new and related systems and services than for a third party to develop a new infrastructure to provide those services.

Furthermore, telecommunications required large sunk capital investments with long-term amortization. The existence of more than one company was thought to entail a waste of societal resources and would make it difficult for the dominant provider to recover initial investments, hindering its ability to commit new investments. Finally, the difficulties for interconnection created by the diversity of technical standards and protocols adopted by competing companies and resistance to interconnection were among the driving forces favoring the "one provider" solution.[4]

However, the existence of private monopolies offered incentives for monopoly pricing. To avoid this, some governments—such as the United States—developed a sophisticated mechanism to regulate the operation of the firm. Most others decided, for economic, social, and political reasons, that telecommunications services should be owned and operated by the state.

Political concerns reinforced the economic dimension of the monopoly. Telecommunications is a key resource in periods of domestic crisis or war, and governments were not willing to leave the control of the network in private hands. Issues concerning national integration and sovereignty were also related to the notion that a national, unitary network under state control was a great device in the pursuit of national integration and the consolidation of a national identity. An integrated network would function as a national communication web that linked people and institutions across regions and thus establish tighter social, political, and commercial ties within the nation.

To achieve these and other related goals governments established what became the core institution of telecommunications worldwide: Ministries of Posts, Telegraphs, and Telephones (PTTs). The mandate of PTTs was to achieve universal service (i.e., one telephone in every household).[5] A pricing scheme that relied heavily on cross-subsidies from long-distance, business, and urban to local, residential, and rural services was the means to achieve maximum expansion of the public network.[6] As sole providers of services nationwide, PTTs could manipulate prices and also shape national industrial policies for the telecommunications sector.[7] Monopsony in the equipment market granted government an important role in the development of a local telecom industry.

Collapse of the State as an Entrepreneur in LDCs

In the developing world the economic crisis of the 1930s, the rise of Keynesianism, and consolidation of import-substitution industrialization (ISI)[8] reinforced even further the intervention of the state in key sectors of the economy, and, in particular, in those (such as telecommunications) that were crucial to the development of a national infrastructure for industrial production.

Through implementation of ISI the state became regulator and protector of domestic markets and slowly took center stage in the productive process (Evans 1985). Private sector inability to fulfill certain economic and social functions crucial to national development, and states' willingness to bail out private-enterprise bankruptcies, led LDC governments to absorb functions that were traditionally conceived as belonging to the private sector. Furthermore, large loans poured into LDCs by international commercial banks in the late 1970s made the state the principal financier and guarantor of 80 to 90 percent of capital transfers to each country, overextending governmental economic functions (Frieden 1981). Within a few decades, what was initially viewed as the "engine of growth" in developing economies became a suffocating and paternalistic leviathan.

Functioning not only as regulators of markets but also as entrepreneurs, "overextended" states suffered from structural deficiencies that resulted in negative behavior by their agents (state managers, employees, regulators, etc.). State-owned enterprises (SOEs), for example, suffered from contradictory goals, ranging from profit maximization and efficiency to the fulfillment of welfare aims such as the provision of employment and subsidies to selected social groups. They functioned under the constant interference of the various ministries with oversight of the firms' operations. Social and political goals generally overshadowed arguments for economic efficiency. This dynamic led to relaxed—or even nonexistent—incentive and/or penalization mechanisms and an absence of effective measures of performance. These and a variety of other factors turned SOEs in the developing world into inefficient and costly operations, without clear benefits for society as a whole (Galal 1990, and Shirley and Nellis 1991).

The telecom sector evolved slowly in most countries. Despite this sluggish performance, SOTEs remained a profitable business. Companies were often used as cash cows for the subsidization of societal groups, rendering a low level of new investments, which in turn affected the updating and upgrading of the system's technology. Scarce investment also affected the expansion rate of the public network. Waiting lists for the connection of new services sometimes reached 50 percent of all lines in operation. Generally overstaffed and with few incentives to secure high productivity and efficiency, SOTEs failed to meet the demand for new, more reliable, and diversified telecom services. In sum, most national carriers were far from being model enterprises.

However, poor performance was not the reason for change. As a recent study carried out by the ITU shows, telecom restructuring in most LDCs is part of large economic adjustment programs driven by fiscal crisis and economic decline (Becher 1991).[9] During the 1980s most LDCs—and particularly Latin American countries—suffered a sharp deterioration of key economic variables: domestic savings and investments (mainly from public institutions) shrank or disappeared, inflation spiraled to unprecedented heights, wages dropped along with domestic consumption, and the unemployment rate grew.[10] The grim scenario of the 1980s is reflected in the negative per capita gross domestic product (GDP) annual growth rate of -0.8 percent that Latin America experienced between 1982 and 1988.

Along with general economic collapse, most countries suffered from serious fiscal constraints. In the effort to balance fiscal accounts, governments withdrew money from the few profitable state enterprises, and channeled it to more needy sectors of the economy. As a result, most SOEs suffered from very low investment rates. Infrastructures deteriorated further and quality and quantity of services lagged behind the growing demand spurred by modernization and development.

With few alternatives, governments adopted policy recommendations from international lending institutions and neoliberal economists from MDCs, who argued that economic failure in developing countries was due to ill-conceived domestic economic policies.[11] Blind adoption of ISI development, overregulation of the economy, excessive growth of the state, and a distorted financial system were presumably responsible for economic deterioration in LDCs.[12] The remedy for this illness was the deregulation of economic activities, the introduction of extensive competition in domestic markets, the increase of foreign investments, and, finally—crucial to overcoming fiscal deficit—an extensive privatization program.

Attracting private investment through privatization would not be an easy task. Lack of confidence in LDC governments led in the 1980s to a considerable drop in foreign direct investments and a transfer abroad of local private capital. Local governments signaled the seriousness of their efforts to introduce free market forces into their domestic economies by targeting telecommunications, a business with the potential for high profits.

But the demise of public utility monopolies—such as telecommunications— was not only the product of fiscal and economic crisis. Some LDCs also pushed reform because they saw in telecommunications a crucial tool for economic development.[13] The sector had undergone a profound technological change that affected its role in the economy and society. These changes raised questions about the legitimacy of natural monopolies, and nurtured the emergence of new ideas that pointed to the need for competition and private ownership in the sector.

Since the 1950s telecom has seen a rapid technological revolution that defied the status quo of monopoly/monopsony service delivery and equipment supply. Technological transformations appeared simultaneously with the expanding globalization of domestic economies and the increasing participation of information components in the production system (Wellenius 1989, 89). It is difficult to tell whether one of these changes pulled the other along. Did technological innovations lead to rapid "informatization" and globalization of economic operations? Did companies going global press for rapid development of information technologies? Most likely there was a feedback loop. Whichever way the causal arrow points, the convergence of both factors radically changed traditional patterns in the telecom sector worldwide.

Explosion of technological innovations in telecommunications technologies (such as fiber optics, private branch exchanges, multiplexers, packet switching, radio cellular systems, very small aperture terminals, new generations of satellites, etc.) and their merger with the booming world of computers and information systems disrupted the traditional conceptual basis and regulatory arrangements in which telecommunications services had been embedded for almost a century (Cowhey and Aronson 1989, 9). The mixing of regulated telecommunications technologies with the unregulated world of computers has not only challenged the ability of governments to protect telecom monopolies, but it also resulted in the rise of new customized service suppliers. From the margins of the public monopoly, the suppliers have slowly eroded the monolithic market control of dominant carriers. Technological innovations and fierce competition in the equipment market lowered the price of basic telecommunication to a degree that makes it affordable to large corporate users (Sinha 1991, 73).

As large corporate users went global in their operations, their needs for new customized and sophisticated services simultaneously grew. Telecommunications quickly became a major item in their budget.[14] High prices charged for long-distance and international services by PTTs—in their efforts to subsidize local network development—and the plummeting of telecom equipment prices both forced and enabled large corporations to build their own systems that bypass the public network.

Diversification of technologies, growing multiplicity of consumer needs, and inability of PTTs to respond to new demand led to firms that found market niches where economies of scale were not so clear. Further, lower equipment prices reduced high costs of sunk capital, giving credence to the idea that a second provider would not waste social resources.[15] In response to these developments, an intellectual movement articulated and systematized the new situation, offering persuasive arguments against the maintenance of telecom monopolies.[16]

The restructuring began with the liberalization of the equipment market, and it followed shortly afterward with the dismantling of absolute service monopolies. Due to the globalization of domestic economies and the increasing permeability of borders, for example, the reform initiative of a few MDCs affected the market profile of telecom service in other countries. As some countries dismantled cross-subsidies and introduced competition in VANS, the prices of telecom services for large users dropped, which induced the migration of large corporate users—who constitute the bulk of PTTs' revenues—to reformed markets that offered better opportunities. This process put increasing pressure in traditional PTTs to follow the reform path themselves.

Changes in the sector converged with political preferences supporting competition, deregulation, privatization, and free market policies in general. It did not take long for the traditional "natural monopolies" to crumple under the weight of the new economic and political trends. It led to privatization of SOTEs, liberalization of domestic markets, and the deregulation of the sector. First in the United States, followed shortly afterwards by Britain and Japan, and extending later to other countries around the world, telecommunications services began to undergo profound transformation.

But what do telecom privatization and liberalization really mean? What are their characteristics and effects? What do they imply for those related to the sector as providers, consumers, or regulators? The nature of private ownership and competition and the value that different social groups assign to the reforms will strongly affect the viability and extent of reform in each country.

RECENT REFORMS IN TELECOMMUNICATIONS

Recent telecom reforms worldwide have been dominated by three main events: privatization, liberalization, and deregulation.

- Privatization can be defined as "the transfer of commercially oriented SOEs, activities, or productive assets of the government to the total, majority, or minority private ownership or to private control" (Vuylsteke 1988, 1). From this point of view, privatization would include the public offering of shares, private sale of shares, sale of government assets, management/employee buyout, new private investments in a SOE, and lease and management contracts. The cases considered in this study consist mainly in a combination of private and public offerings of majority shares in the privatized SOTEs. Malaysia is the only case in which the company became a private business and floated only a small portion of shares in a public offering.[17]
- Liberalization is the lowering of entry barriers to all or part of a market, allowing third parties to compete with established— generally monopoly—providers of goods or services. In a liberalized telecom market, service providers are generally free

to set prices and determine service expansion and business strategies on their own. The countries explored here show a combination of liberalized and monopolic services. Most of them have kept basic services under monopoly for a number of years, while opening various other value-added and data services to competitive provision.

- Deregulation was originally conceived as a process through which governments would reduce their intervention in the operation of markets. The dismantling of legal controls would presumably provide the adequate condition for a healthy competitive business environment operating under market laws. In telecommunications, however, experience has indicated that achieving fair competition requires the reregulation of the sector. Countries today present a wide range in the degree to which they have deregulated and re-regulated telecom service operations.

Conceptually, privatization, liberalization, and deregulation are different. They can be carried out separately, they affect different aspects of the telecom sector, and they often involve a variety of different actors. However, in practice, they are closely linked; and any change in one of these policy areas will tend to affect the others. Timing in this regard is a key element in the dynamics between these aspects of reform.

The likelihood of privatization, for example, is undermined if there is already a high level of competition in the local market. The requirements of prospective private investors are generally high—to compensate for the risk of a competitive market—while the price paid for the company would be lower, and, if the market was not very attractive, there is a risk of not being able to sell the company. The likelihood of liberalization, in turn, is jeopardized if it does not precede privatization. In such cases, the government might forgo the possibility of opening the market in order to realize a successful sale—something common to Latin American telecom privatizations.

Privatization and liberalization generally have a strong effect on the degree and patterns of regulation. With the transfer of service operations to private hands under monopoly conditions, the state generally has to increase or create oversight and enforcement capacity in the sector to prevent predatory behavior on the part of the firm. If the market is liberalized, the regulatory agency will often face problems related to the tendency of the dominant carrier to crowd out new entrants, an event that would require more rather than less regulatory capacity.

Despite this close interdependence, there are economic and political differences among these reform initiatives. In economic terms, the liberalization of a market is a more relevant event than the privatization of a state-owned enterprise, and it has more lasting effects. There are also significant political differences among them. For most of the civil society, for example, the sale of a state-owned telephone company is a more controversial event than the lowering of entry barriers in a market. Privatization is a self-contained event in which the ownership of a firm is transferred from public to private hands. Liberalization of a market, on the other hand, is a more diffuse process occurring over an extended period of time. It lacks a single socially or politically dramatic event, such as the transfer of a public utility to private owners.

People generally recognize a private provider's responsibilities towards customers. Instead, they do not understand so clearly what may be the impact of market liberalization on the price structure of basic services. Moreover, liberalization will generally affect enhanced services, which in LDCs are still largely marginal making the issue less relevant than changes in the provision of basic services, which occurs with privatization.

For those closely involved in the provision of telecom services, such as unions, SOTE managers, state officials, equipment providers, and the like, the transfer of the state-owned company is also a clear-cut event that might threaten the continuity of benefits and privileges they previously enjoyed. Entry of new competitors into the market does not represent a similar threat. In sum, the privatization of a SOTE is a more contested and politically controversial event than is telecom market liberalization, and it stimulates more active participation of interest groups than does liberalization.

Finally, it is important to disaggregate privatization from liberalization to assess accurately the impact of each on the various actors related to the sector—that is, consumers, labor, the state, service providers, equipment suppliers, etc. Some of the issues that affect consumers—such as tariffs, network expansion, and quality of services—will respond differently to privatization than to liberalization. Local tariffs, for example, will likely rise and long-distance ones drop in a liberalized regime; this is not necessarily so if changes in the sector are due to privatization. Private monopolies enjoying a secured high rate of return will tend to invest in network expansion in a way in which companies functioning in a liberalized market generally would not.

In sum, dominant reforms in the telecom sector worldwide have been driven mainly by the privatization of SOTEs, the liberalization of domestic markets, and the deregulation (or reregulation) of the sector. While different in various aspects, these three phenomena are also interrelated, and governments around the world are learning that if they introduce changes in one of these policy areas they will likely face transformations in the others. Three industrialized countries, the United States, Britain, and Japan were the first to initiate reform in the sector. The next section briefly depicts recent transformations in those countries, their origins, and the role of political institutions in the process.

Roots and Outcomes of Reform in Selected MDCs

Reforms in MDCs were driven by forces within the telecommunications sector itself. Growth of an increasingly interdependent and information-intensive global economy created a need among large corporate users for diversified and customized telecom services. While technological innovations and the merger of telecom and computers provided the technological infrastructure needed to satisfy those customized demands, traditional regulatory and ownership arrangements in the telecom sector made it difficult—if not impossible—for large users to benefit from new information technologies. From the late 1950s on, large corporate users have pressed governments of the industrialized world for reforms in telecom services.

It was in the United States that many of the current worldwide reforms began.[18] The roots of these transformations can be traced back to the authorization of private networks in the late 1950s. As American corporations became increasingly dependent on telecommunications systems, a strong coalition of large corporate users started pressing the Federal Communications Commission (FCC) to reduce long-distance prices and dismantle cross-subsidization.[19] Responding to corporate demands, the FCC issued a report in August 1959 authorizing the construction of private microwave systems in the band above 890 megacycles (Mc).[20]

In the early 1960s the "managers" of an infant company—Microwave Communications Inc. (MCI)—filed an application with the FCC requesting permission to install a point-to-point private line communication system between Chicago and St. Louis.[21] After several years of hearings and studies the FCC approved MCI's petition. Shortly afterwards a variety of new companies filed applications to offer similar lucrative services.[22] In the early 1970s MCI pushed the boundaries of the monopoly, requesting permission from the FCC to interconnect its customers through the public network. Five years later MCI was allowed to operate as a full common carrier by using the public network to connect customers in two of its isolated private networks.

Throughout the 1970s and early 1980s large telecom users increased the pressure for market liberalization and the reform of the traditional arrangement for service provision.[23] The transformation of the American telecommunications system reached its peak with the decision on the antitrust suit filed by the Justice Department in 1974. The suit was settled in January 1982, when representatives of the United States government and AT&T signed what came to be known as the "modified final judgment" (MFJ). In general terms the settlement established that AT&T had to spin off seven regional Bell operating companies (RBOCs), which would operate in a protected monopolistic market. AT&T would face competition in its long-distance service market, but the restrictions established by the 1956 consent decree were lifted and AT&T was allowed to enter noncommunications service and equipment markets.[24]

By the 1990s telecommunications and information services were provided by private companies under competitive and monopoly conditions. Long-distance and value-added network services (VANS) were offered by various firms in an open market, while local services were still a monopoly under the operation of the RBOCs.

In Britain, telecom reform began in 1981 with the separation of the British Post Office from the national telecom company, British Telecom (BT). Four years later, under the 1984 Telecommunications Act, the British government sold 50.2 percent of BT's shares to private investors.[25] The government nevertheless remained the major shareholder in the firm. Parallel to the privatization of BT, Britain opened its the market for long-distance services, granting a second carrier—Mercury—a license to compete with BT. Mercury's license requires that a parallel network linking the major cities of the country be built, but this company was not required to provide universal services—an obligation that BT still has to fulfill. Mercury's network is based on fiber-optic technology, which will allow the company to target the business market where demand for digital broadband services is high.

The liberalization of telecom services in Britain was spurred by the Value-added Network Service Licensing Act of 1982. The regulatory reform provided the sufficient conditions for an explosion of value-added network services. By 1986 more than two hundred VANS companies were operating in the country. The tariff and services opportunities offered by this flourishing information market lured a number of large multinational corporations (MNCs) operating in continental Europe, thus putting considerable pressure on European governments to match British reform initiatives.[26]

As in the case of the United States, British telecom reform was largely instigated by large corporate users. Large telecom users with shared interests joined their lobbying capacity and created the Telecommunications Managers Association (TMA) in the late 1950s. By the mid-1980s the Association's membership included the largest 400 corporations operating in Britain (Duch 1991, 236). This group played a central role in the reform of the British telecom sector.

Japan is the third industrialized nation that carried out considerable reforms in its telecom sector. Since 1952 telecom services in the country were provided by the Nippon Telegraph and Telephone Public Corporation (NTTPC). In 1985 the company was incorporated, giving birth to Nippon Telegraph and Telephone Corporation (NTT). The government—which originally owned 100 percent of the firm—floated up to 49 percent of the firm's shares in the stock market (Takano 1992). The government will progressively reduce its participation, but it will retain one-third of NTT's shares.

In 1985, concurrent with the privatization of NTTPC, legislation was passed to introduce an overall reform of the Japanese telecom market. The NTT Corporate Law and the Telecommunications Business Law established two types of service providers: Class 1 and Class 2. The former comprises basic service providers, while the latter—which was divided in two subcategories, general and special—covers enhanced service companies (Crandall and Flamm 1989). The Telecommunications Business Law established the regulatory framework required to introduce widespread competition in most segments of the telecom market.

In the case of Japan, the initial pressure for reform in the telecom sector also came from outside the state apparatus. But unlike the U.S. and British cases, the forces that pushed for change came from outside the country. U.S. firms, with the strong support of the American government, pressed Japanese administrations to liberalize and later privatize their domestic market. The pressure of U.S. government and American firms began in the early 1970s and unleashed domestic tensions in favor of reform. Large Japanese corporate users, in conjunction with the Ministry of International Trade and Industry (MITI) and other local agencies interested in liberalizing the domestic market, achieved a radical transformation of the traditional telecom arrangements of Japan by the mid-1980s.

In sum, in MDCs the pressure of large corporate users and actors outside the state apparatus played a key role in bringing about the initial push for telecom reform. This is an important difference with LDCs, where the reform emerged at the core of the state itself, and will help later to explain how similar political structures in each region of the world provided different opportunities and obstacles to reform.

Reform Patterns and Trends in LDCs

Differing from events in MDCs, in the developing world the drive for reform was not instigated by large corporate users in search of better and cheaper services, but by the executive branch of each government pursuing a solution to fiscal economic constraints. The fact that telecom reform in LDCs was promoted mainly by the state, and not by actors in civil society as it was in MDCs, has affected the nature of reform (privatization has predominated in LDCs, while liberalization is the dominant pattern in MDCs), its pace (LDCs have moved faster than MDCs in their reform programs), and the degree of politicization of the process, since privatization is the prevalent mode of reform, opposition has been higher in LDCs than in MDCs.

The search for solutions to some of these fiscal and economic problems pointed to the privatization of state-owned telecom companies and the liberalization of the local telecom market. Yet not all of the countries were successful in achieving their initial goals. Some privatized their SOTEs, but others failed to do so. Some were able to largely liberalize their markets; others did not (Fig. 1.1 and 1.2).

Privatization efforts have produced different outcomes depending on the country under consideration. Argentina, for example, initiated its reform attempts in early 1980s. Since then, both a military regime (1976–1983) and a democratic government (1983–1989) attempted and failed to privatize the national common carrier—Empresa Nacional de Telecomunicaciones (ENTel). In 1989, a new democratic government was able to overcome political opposition; in December 1990, it engineered the sale of 60 percent of the company to a group of private investors. A year later the remaining shares were transferred to private shareholders through a public offering in the stock market.

Thailand replicated the first privatization experiences of Argentina, but achieved a different outcome regarding liberalization. Public-sector reform plans began in the mid-1980s. By 1988 the Thai government officially launched a state-reform plan proposing the privatization of several SOEs. Telecommunications was among the three most important sectors to be sold to private entrepreneurs. However, strong resistance from state unions, working in alliance with certain groups in the army and with opposition politicians, killed the project in March 1990, when the government, buckling to the pressure, signed an agreement canceling the privatization program. Similar patterns of

Figure 1.1

**Successful Privatizations of
State-owned Telecommunication Enterprises in LDCs**

Date	Country	N° of Lines (millions)
1987-1990	Chile	625,466
	Jamaica	85,179
	Malaysia	1,247,687
1990	Argentina	3,519,664
	Mexico	5,189,802
1991	Venezuela	1,494,776

Figure 1.2

**Failed Privatizations of
State-owned Telecommunication Enterprises in LDCs**

Date	Country	N° of Lines (millions)
1981-89	Argentina	2,664,518
	Thailand	1,324,552
1991	Colombia	2,414,726
	South Africa	3,254,246
1992	Uruguay	415,403
1993	Greece	3,948,654

Source: Yearbook of Common Carrier Telecommunications Statistics 1994

failed privatization can be found in Colombia, South Africa, and Uruguay where
governments had to cancel privatization programs due to domestic opposition.

Differing from the previous cases are Mexico, Malaysia, Chile, Jamaica,
and Venezuela. These countries achieved their initial privatization goals. The
Mexican government, for example, announced in 1989 its intention to sell the
national telephone company—Teléfonos de México (TELMEX)—and liberalize
its telecom market. In December 1990, the government sold the controlling
shares of TELMEX to a private consortium, and a year later the remaining
shares were sold in the stock market.

In Malaysia telecom reform started in 1985 with the official proposal for the corporatization of the national common carrier, Jabatan Telekom Malaysia.[27] In 1987 the company was restructured into a private company—Syarikat Telekom Malaysia (STM)—with the state still holding 100 percent of the company's shares. Two years later the government sold almost 20 percent of STM shares in the Kuala Lumpur Stock Exchange. The governments of Chile, Jamaica, and Venezuela are also among those nations that succeeded in their privatization efforts. Chile and Jamaica sold their state-owned carriers between 1987 and 1990, and Venezuela followed with the sale of Compañía Anónima Nacional de Teléfonos de Venezuela (CANTV) in December 1991.

Similar cross-country variations can be seen in the outcome of liberalization attempts. The governments of Mexico and Malaysia, for example, were able to achieve a considerable degree of competition in their domestic telecom markets. Most services are either open to competition or the government retains the right to open them when it considers appropriate to do so. Others, such as Thailand, despite failing to privatize their SOTEs, have been able to introduce competition into various segments of the telecom market. On the other hand, Argentina, despite its successful privatization, was unable to liberalize its telecom market. The privatization of the national carrier was accompanied by the official concession of monopoly over most telecom services for a period of up to ten years. Similarly, the Jamaican government has been able to privatize its SOTE, but it has granted private investors a closed market for twenty-five years.

In sum, while most countries started their reform journey with a state-owned telecom firm operating in a closed market, and most intended to move to private ownership and competition, not all were able to achieve their initial goals. The question that drives this study and for which the next chapter attempts to provide a theoretical framework is, Why countries with shared telecom reform goals and similar patterns of development achieve different outcomes in their restructuring attempts?

NOTES

1. The United States and some countries once dominated by European colonial powers are among the few in the world in which telecom services were provided by private firms.

2. In African and Asian colonies telecom services were provided by the dominant carriers of the imperial power.

3. The value of a telecommunication network is based on the expansion of its subscriber base. The larger the number of users connected to the network, the higher the utility and value of the network.

4. Building up a system that held unique technical standards was also a strategy to lock in customers and raise barriers to the entry of competing firms.

5. Mueller, on the contrary, contends that the notion of universal service was not an explicitly social policy, but emerged out of the pricing inertia that reined in the PTTs. Originally the price of providing local services was quite low, while long distance services were an extremely expensive operation. From the 1950s major technological innovations reduced long-distance costs approximately 90 percent;

however, the pricing structure remained unchanged. Mueller argues that the decision was purely political and responded to electoral strategies (Mueller 1993). For studies on universal services, see Institute for Information Studies 1991, and OECD 1991.

6. The assumption was that business and long-distance users were high-income customers with inelastic demand curves that would be able to subsidize the provision of services for low-income customers.

7. PTTs not only had a tight control of the sector at the domestic level, but they also established, through the International Telecommunication Union, a global cartel that until recently had discretionary control over international provision of services. On the origins and transformation of the international telecommunication regime, see Drake 1993a.

8. The adoption of ISI in LDCs has been portrayed as a purely domestic initiative, often occurring against the interests of MDCs. However, recent studies have convincingly shown that the policy was adopted in several developing countries not only with the consent, but also with the support of, the United States. See Maxfield and Nolt 1990.

9. For arguments on why LDCs privatize, see also Luis 1991, and Ramamurti 1992.

10. In the external sector, international loans and foreign investments retreated, debt interests jumped draining scarce resources, the value of primary commodities declined in international markets, and the export ratio of most countries dropped below their historical levels, which lowered the relative share of most LDCs in world trade. For some Latin American countries the economic crisis was accompanied by a process of progressive deindustrialization that started in the late 1970s. See, for example, Katz and Kosacoff 1989, and Fajnzylber 1990.

11. Others, such as the UN Economic Commission for Latin America (ECLAC), argue that factors most responsible for the region's macroeconomic imbalance are related to the external debt service and its consequences for public sector finances. See ECLAC 1990; Fanelli, Frenkel, and Rozenwurcel 1990; and Williamson 1990.

12. The complexities inherent to ISI set the conditions for higher levels of protection and antitrade bias. The large volume of capital required, the cost of technological innovation, and the small size of domestic markets did not allow for significant economies of scale. To protect "infant" domestic industries from deadly competition with foreign firms, governments raised barriers to entry in local markets. This policy sparked the development of "lazy" monopolies that, in the face of "easy profits" in protected markets, ignored technological innovation, competitiveness, and incentives for export production.

13. We might be able to separate countries in three different categories. Those in which fiscal crisis drove the reform (Argentina), those in which telecommunications issues are at the basis of reform initiatives (Singapore), and those in which a mixture of both factors stimulated change (Mexico and Malaysia).

14. The seven hundred firms that were members of the International Communications Association, for example, had in 1992 an average telecommunications expenditure of US$21.5 million (Steinfield 1993, 6). For large financial institutions, like Citicorp, telecommunications had become by the mid-1980s the third largest expense (after salaries and real estate).

15. In LDCs it is not clear if the reduction of sunk investments is significant enough to justify more than one provider (Sinha 1991, 76).

16. See, for example, Mueller 1992, Noam 1987, and Saunders et al. 1994. For early studies on the monopoly vs. competition debate, see Bergendorff, Larsson, and Naslund 1983, and Langdale 1982.

17. The different forms and extent of privatization adopted by each country is also a question to be explored. However, this is not the task of this work, and, therefore, variation in privatization patterns is set aside to concentrate on the success or failure of transforming the firm into a private operation.

18. For studies on recent transformation of the telecom sector in the United States, see Horwitz 1989; Stone 1989; Temin and Galambois 1987; and Henck and Strassburg 1988.

19. This alliance of private users and suppliers included, for example, the Automobile Manufacturers Association, the National Retail and Dry Goods Association, the American Newspaper Publishers Association, the National Association of Manufacturers, and the Central Committee on Radio Facilities of the American Petroleum Institute (Horwitz 1989, 225). Corporate demands did not remain solely at the lobbying level; some of them—such as Central Freight Lines and Minute Maid Corp.—filed in the courts for judicial permission to set up their own private systems, arguing that AT&T was incapable of meeting their telecom needs (Henck and Strassburg 1988, 84).

20. This band was above the radiospecturm range used by the public network. Further, in the view of FCC officials, established carriers would not be technically or economically affected in any relevant way because microwave systems were too expensive to build. Therefore, the ability and incentives for large corporate users to exit the public network were very limited.

21. The 1960s was a period when challenges to the monopoly diversified. With the emergence of computers and information services new problems of boundaries and interconnection raised new conflicts between providers of data services, the dominant carrier, and the regulatory agency. The conflict was sparked by a small service corporation—Bunker-Ramo—who invaded with the provision of information services what it was understood as the traditional domain of common carriers. Bunker-Ramo provided stockbrokers instant stock information from a database that the customers could access by dialing one of the computer-coded numbers of the company. Western Union disconnected the company from the public network with the argument that the firm was violating carriers rights by developing a private parallel communication system by using the public switched network to interconnect its customers. The case was settled in 1966 when Western Union agreed to reconnect the service company with the condition that it would introduce modification to its data operations to accommodate some of the carriers concerns (Stone 1989, 205).

22. Applicants for new licenses included Data Transmission Company (DATRAM), South Pacific Communications Corporation, seventeen companies affiliated with MCI, and several miscellaneous common carriers (Stone 1989, 170).

23. On the role of large users in the transformation of North American telecommunications system, see, among others, Schiller 1982b; Teske 1990b; and Steinfield 1993.

24. The RBOCs could not enter other competitive markets, such as long-distance toll, information services, or terminal equipment. The new regional companies had also the obligation to connect to the local loops, on equal price and quality, any long-distance service company. The RBOCs lost the manufacturing capabilities of Western Electric and the R&D provided by the Bell Labs., but at the same time the gained the freedom of purchasing their hardware from any domestic

or international provider. AT&T lost its RBOCs and the provision of basic telephone services, but keep for itself the profitable intercity long-distance service, Western Electric, and Bell Labs. The company also agreed not to buy the stock of any spun-off RBOC.

25. On the reform of the British telecom system, see Hills 1986; Newman 1986; and Duch 1991.

26. For studies on European telecommunications, see, for example, Noam 1992; Elixmann and Neumann 1990; Foreman-Peck, Haid, and Muller 1988; and Snow 1986.

27. Corporatization is the process by which a state-owned company is removed from state control and operates as does any other private firm, with the only difference being that the state retains the ownership of the company's shares.

2

Explaining Divergent Policy Outcomes

This study does not attempt to explain why telecom reform policies emerged and why were they adopted by some countries and not by others. The work instead starts at the point in the late 1980s at which many governments—for whatever reason—decided to privatize their state-owned telecommunications enterprises (SOTEs) and liberalize important segments of their telecom markets. The question that drives the study is why certain countries have been more successful than others in implementing reform in their national telecommunications sector.[1] What are the political and economic conditions that enhance or diminish the viability of privatization and liberalization of telecommunications services in less developed countries (LDCs)?

This chapter begins by offering a theoretical framework for the understanding of cross-country variations in telecom privatization attempts. It moves later to the question of liberalization, examining conceptual tools for explaining divergent outcomes resulting from liberalization attempts. The next section reviews events in the light of a variety of social science approaches to the analysis of the policy-making process.[2] Virtues and flaws of the most common theories are discussed in regard to their applicability to the cases explored here. Argentina, Mexico, Malaysia, and Thailand illustrate these theoretical issues.

The chapter closes by comparing the seemingly contradictory conclusions arrived at by this study with a similar study carried out in Europe.

EXPLAINING TELECOMMUNICATIONS REFORM

Telecommunications in LDCs has long operated as a highly subsidized public service that benefited individuals and organizations involved in the provision of services as well as consumers. Reversal of this arrangement encounters considerable resistance from telephone workers, equipment providers, politicians, certain customers, and citizens with political preferences for welfare state policies. Opposition from these fairly powerful political actors has often hindered and dismantled reform initiatives. Pressures from civil society, therefore, played a major role in privatization efforts. But resistance is not limited to societal actors. Since privatization implies the dismantling of state agencies and enterprises, there is also a strong resistance within the state itself. In most cases government officials, state managers, and civil servants have resorted to institutional instruments to delay or block the implementation of privatization projects (Aharoni 1991, 78, and Cowan 1990, 12).

Given resistance in civil society and from certain actors within the state apparatus, this study concentrates on two variables crucial to the explanation of the state's effectiveness in implementing telecom privatization policies: the relative autonomy of the state vis-à-vis interest group coalitions, and the degree of power concentration within the state (more precisely in the head of the executive branch, be it a president or a prime minister).[3]

But, although political factors—such as state autonomy and power concentration—played a crucial role in the privatization of SOTEs, they were less important in the liberalization of the telecom market, and they failed to explain why certain countries were able to liberalize while others failed to do so. Economic variables, instead, offer a more accurate explanation of liberalization success. This study argues that at the moment of privatization current and predicted attractiveness of the domestic economy—and in particular of the telecom market—is a key element in determining a country's ability to enforce partial market liberalization while simultaneously selling its SOTE.

For these methodological and theoretical reasons, whenever possible this study disaggregate the analysis of privatization and liberalization as two different and distinct phenomena. The following two sections explore and present the conditions under which states are likely to succeed in the privatization of SOTEs and in the liberalization of local telecom markets.

PRIVATIZATION AND THE STATE

In Western industrialized democracies, social science theories that emphasize the role of societal actors have dominated the study of politics and policy-making in recent decades. State-centered theories have largely taken a back seat in political studies.[4] Contrary to the statelessness of the Anglo-

American theorizing, the developing world—and particularly Latin America—has created approaches in which the state plays a central role in the study of politics and society.[5] In these countries erosion of the intellectual credibility of society-centered modernization models coincides with the exhaustion of import-substitution industrialization development strategies and the deterioration of the political regimes that were associated with it (Cardoso and Faletto 1979). And, despite a renewed attention to societal actors, which occurred in the early 1980s due to the return of democratic regimes, by the late1980s the fiscal crisis and the dismantling of the entrepreneurial and welfare public sector brought the state back to the center of political and economic studies of developing societies.[6] In this study, since we are concerned with the privatization of state-owned enterprises and the liberalization of monopolic markets controlled by the state, a state-centered analysis is even more justified than it might be in the examination of other political processes.[7]

Because in most LDC telecom privatizations were strongly affected by resistance in civil society and within the state the study explores under what conditions states achieve greater levels of political insulation, internal cohesion, and effective governance.

State Autonomy

As Skocpol argues, state autonomy "is not a fixed structural feature of any governmental system." There are social, political, and economic factors that enhance or diminish state autonomy at different points in time (Skocpol 1985, 14). However, despite its contextual nature, state insularity often results from factors that have consolidated over time in such a way that they operate as if they were structural patterns of the state.[8] Autonomy that has characterized the Mexican state since the 1920s, for example, is much less contingent than the temporary insularity gained by the Menem administration in Argentina in the late 1980s. To be able to identify those quasi-structural and contextual elements would help us recognize which countries, at what historical moments, are most likely to achieve state autonomy, and subsequently, better conditions for implementation of politically controversial policies.

Recent state theory, dominated by neo-Marxist approaches, has generally defined autonomy as the capability of a state to operate against the will and interests of dominant groups (Hamilton 1982, and Trimberger 1978).[9] However, historical evidence points to the fact that state autonomy often depends on the task in which the state is involved, and from whom the state must win autonomy.[10] States are ultimately concerned with two basic economic functions: capital accumulation and redistribution.[11] Which function is dominant often determines state autonomy. In other words, if state policies are aimed at achieving redistribution of resources among lower income populations, pressures against such policies will often come—as the neo-Marxists argue—from interest groups concerned with capital accumulation, such as large business (Hamilton 1982).[12] However, if the state seeks policies that are aimed at capital accumulation and the expansion of entrepreneurial class—such as privatization—

then government officials must gain autonomy from other politically powerful actors, such as workers, consumers, protected and subsidized small entrepreneurs, and others who may have benefited from the redistributive functions of the welfare state.

Beside the nature of state tasks—redistribution or accumulation—there are historical factors that affect the extent of insulation that governing elites gain from civil society. A factor to consider in this regard is the historical genesis of state organization. In this regard there seems to be an important difference between those states that arise following major social dislocations—such as revolutions, independence movements, wars, etc.—and those that slowly emerged out of progressive transformation of the political and social system.[13] In the former instance states tend to gain and maintain high degrees of insulation from societal demands, while in the latter, states are generally more vulnerable and permeable to social pressures (Neher 1991). Of the four countries considered in detail in this study, the current political system of two emerged out of an upheaval—a revolution in Mexico in 1917 and an independence movement in Malaysia in 1958. In both countries the state is significantly insulated from the demands and pressures of civil society. In Argentina and Thailand, however, the current political system evolved slowly, and both states have been permeable to social demands. Emergence of new political systems through radical transformation provides the required political conditions for development of highly insulated and "strong" states.[14]

Existence of weak and fragmented opposition parties also contributes to the reinforcement of state autonomy. In Mexico and Malaysia, opposition parties are small and did not, until recently, present a significant threat to the hegemony of the governing party. In Argentina and Thailand no one party has dominated politics for several decades. In those two countries the distribution of power among parties is significant, rendering them enough leverage to permeate the state apparatus and block government initiatives.

These historical and structural conditions underlie the constitution and consolidation of certain patterns of state-society relations, but there are other less permanent factors that may also provide adequate conditions for the enhancement of state autonomy. Economic crisis, for example, offers unique conditions to reverse a country's entrenched political dynamics. In cases of long-standing, authoritarian, autonomous states, stringent economic conditions have eroded the state's insulation and destroyed preexisting regimes, as it was seen in Latin America and Eastern Europe during the mid- and late 1980s. In countries where political backlash and the balkanization of the state occurred, economic crisis has often disrupted preexisting power structure, offering state officials a limited period of insulation from domestic pressures, such as occurred in Argentina at the end of the 1980s (Gourevitch 1990, and Torre 1992).

Finally, state autonomy and the insulation of state officials from the policy-making process often depends on the issue-area under consideration. There are certain policy areas in which states achieve greater autonomy.[15] But insularity or openness are not fixed patterns of issue-areas. The vulnerability of certain areas to social pressures varies according to the kind of policies the government intends to implement and the actors involved. Telecommunications, for example, was traditionally a highly technical, depoliticized area in which policy making was the business of bureaucrats and regulators. However, the mere consideration of privatization—something that affects welfare and subsidization policies—moved telecom policy making to the forefront of public concern.

In sum, in both Mexico and Malaysia, elites isolate themselves from societal demands and pressures while at the same time they legitimize this *modus operandi* by incorporating most social constituents through a limited number of well-controlled corporatist organizations—such as the large Mexican unions that incorporated industrial workers, peasants, and other social groups into the national political systems. In Argentina and Thailand the state slowly emerged in the midst of fragmented political competition among a variety of equally powerful social actors, remaining therefore vulnerable to challenges and opposition from civil society.

Concentration of Power within the State

The second variable crucial to understanding the outcome of telecom policy reform is the concentration of power at the state level—specifically, the degree to which that power is centralized in the head of the executive branch.

Political scientists and economists have highlighted the fact that treating the state as a homogeneous institutional actor conceals a variety of conflicting and contradictory interests constituted by the pubic sector (Allison 1971).[16] Mindful of the existence of conflictual forces within the state, social scientists have argued that cohesiveness of policymakers is crucial to effective state intervention (Haggard 1990, 43). It is one of the basic conditions for the articulation of a persuasive discursive front for shaping or changing preferences of reticent social groups. The cohesiveness of state officials is also central to the deployment of state resources to fragment, neutralize, and counter societal opposition. In short, states are more effective in introducing and implementing reform policies when bureaucrats and government officials share goals and means than when administrations are divided internally.

Cohesion is, however, threatened when the issue around which state constituents converge is the reduction of their political and economic power through privatization. When cohesion of policymakers does not emerge naturally, the dominance of the top leader or leaders in the executive branch over other competing groups becomes crucial to the effectiveness of state actions and policy implementation. In privatization attempts, an important reduction of the bureaucratic control over the economy is implied, which leads to disagreement and resistance among state constituents that, in turn, tends to be an important factor in the program's success or failure.

In Mexico and Malaysia, for example, strong power concentration in the executive branch and cohesion among governing elites has been a dominant feature of the political system.[17] The state bureaucracy is a tightly integrated group of politicians and technocrats drawn from groups long in power (Smith 1979, Ronfeldt 1989, and Puthucheary 1987). In Argentina and Thailand, on the other hand, the processes of political opening at the societal level have affected the patterns of power distribution in the state (Yoon 1990, and Waisman 1992). In the last twenty years both countries have had a diffuse state power structure. Weak presidents and prime ministers and permanent conflicts among relatively strong interest groups in the governing elite have often resulted in the blocking of policy (Hewison 1989, and Oszlak 1990). In Argentina, nevertheless, these features were reversed during the Menem administration. Most state reform was carried out through presidential decrees from the executive branch, a process that excluded the standard mechanisms of checks and balances set by presidential systems. This unusual concentration of power in the president's hands undermined the input of other institutions such as ministries, technical secretariats, Congress, and provincial or state-level governments.

If we apply these features of the political system to the particular historical transformation of the telecom sector in the countries explored in detail here, the correlation between state autonomy, power concentration in the executive, and policy outcomes is present in all cases. Events show that the Thai government postponed indefinitely its initial privatization plans due to domestic political opposition (mainly labor, the army, and political parties). When the government was overthrown by a military coup, a continuous and unresolved struggle regarding telecom privatization ensued. Argentina's government was able to privatize only when opposition coalitions were weakened and Congress gave the president special legislative power to reform the sector. In Mexico and Malaysia, traditional state autonomy and concentration of power in the executive branch granted both governments the political muscle necessary to overcome opposition. In these cases, the state, in control of a vertically integrated and highly disciplined political machine, was able to reach far into civil society, breaking alliances and disrupting the resistance to telecom privatization.

LIBERALIZATION AND THE ECONOMY

Besides privatization of their SOTEs, most LDCs that embarked on telecom reform tried to achieve what is becoming a global pattern in the sector: liberalization of telecom services.[18] However, not all countries achieved that goal. Why, then, have some countries—like Mexico, Malaysia, Chile, and Thailand—considerably liberalized the telecom markets, while others—like Argentina and Jamaica—failed to do so?

As argued earlier, privatization and liberalization are regulatory reforms that have affected the telecom sector of LDCs at a similar historical moment, but are, nevertheless, different phenomena. Liberalization in most LDCs is a much less politicized process than is SOTE privatization. If the success or failure of privatization was largely tied to the structure of the political system of each country, the likelihood of liberalization is much more dependent on the condition and prospects of the country's domestic economy.

Besides the economic profile of the country, timing of SOTE privatization affects liberalization. In cases where governments attempted competition before privatization (if privatization was considered at all) opposition was generally weak, coming mainly from managers and employees of the national carrier.[19] In such cases, since the government remains the sole owner of the company, the success of liberalization is tied to the political strength of the administration and its ability to overcome resistance within the state in order to enforce the policy. In certain ways, liberalization dynamics resemble closely those of SOTE privatization, and a political explanation thus seems appropriate.

A different picture arises when a country attempts liberalization simultaneously with privatization. In such cases, an extension of political variables is not an adequate approach. If political factors were the appropriate explanatory factors we should expect that countries that privatized would also be able to liberalize, and those that failed to sell their SOTEs would also fail to open the market. What we find instead, is that some governments privatized their SOTEs, yet failed to liberalize their telecom markets, while others that failed to privatize were nevertheless successful in introducing competition. Thus, political variables poorly explain telecom liberalization.

In cases in which liberalization and privatization appear together on the policy agenda, there are two possible options: (1) domestic opposition to reform is co-opted, dismantled, or shielded at an early stage, or (2) the opposition succeeds in blocking and canceling reform initiatives. When the government controls its opposition, and the process moves into the sale and liberalization stage, new players—namely private investors—take prominence. The presence of private investors jeopardizes liberalization and its likelihood becomes tied to the bargaining power of governments and investors: governments strive for competition, and investors for monopoly.[20] A variety of economic variables determine the bargaining strength of each of the players.[21]

In most LDCs, the capital-intensive nature of telecom ventures and the scarcity of domestic capital makes privatization of SOTEs dependent on foreign investments.[22] The benefits and disadvantages of foreign capital in LDCs has been hotly debated for decades. Controversy split between a pro-foreign-investment school[23] and a *dependencia* approach.[24] Recently two new approaches to foreign investment studies have developed. Known as the structural and "bargaining" schools, these lines of analysis have concentrated more on individual investment negotiations, discriminating by industry, country, and the particular conditions of the project.[25] Special attention has been paid to the strength of each of the bargaining parties (government and investors), and how the balance of power between them affects and shapes the evolution of the investment project. From this perspective a variety of structural and contextual factors will enhance or diminish government and investor's bargaining power.

Structural industry-based factors are similar in most countries and, therefore, play a less important role in explaining cross-country variation in liberalization attempts.[26] What does appear crucial are factors that vary across countries, such as the degree of the government's centralized control over reform negotiations and the number of firms competing for investment. This latter factor deeply affected the bargaining strength of local administrations during telecom reform.

Participation of private investors in the bidding process for would-be-privatized SOTEs fluctuates according to the trade-off between perceived risks and prospective rewards. A country with high economic and political stability, low inflation, predictable currency devaluation and interest-rate fluctuations would generally gain investor confidence.[27] In short, industry-specific variables such as high growth potential of the local market, low or banned competition, the potential for development of other high-margin services, the possibility of greater profits than in home-country or other business ventures, adequate taxation policy, propitious regulation of the sector—including low risk of expropriation[28]—and clear and transparent rules of the game tend to attract investors' participation.[29]

Attracting investment for privatization was a top priority for most LDC administrations. Degree of market liberalization, therefore, was the outcome of a complex dynamic between investor pressure to retain a closed market and government resistance tempered by the need to successfully sell the SOTE. Because political conditions were not strikingly different in privatizing countries, the evolution of the domestic economy, and economic indicators in the telecom sector became crucial to the investors' decision making.

Liberalization experiences of Argentina and Mexico illustrate the importance of an attractive local market when liberalization is carried out simultaneously with privatization. In Argentina a shaky economy and a gloomy investment outlook at the time of ENTel's privatization diminished investors' interest in the sale. A chaotic and disorderly privatization process and the existence of other more attractive possibilities in a booming privatization market left the Argentine government with only one possible purchaser for each region. In an effort to keep investors interested in ENTel, the government granted a monopoly for a period of ten years over all profitable services that had not yet been open to competition. In Mexico, however, the bright future of the recovering economy attracted major investors. The government was not only able to sell TELMEX for a high price, but it kept the market open in all telecom services, except basic telephony. Despite the intention of both the Argentine and Mexican administrations to liberalize their telecom sector, the attractiveness of their domestic markets affected the government bargaining position, enabling Mexico to achieve both privatization and liberalization while shattering Argentina's hope for liberalization of its telecom market.

ALTERNATIVE THEORETICAL PERSPECTIVES

Social scientists have attempted to explain how and why policy changes are developed and implemented. Studies from a political perspective have stressed various levels of analysis, such as ideas and ideology, international factors, domestic interest groups and coalitions, political systems (political parties, presidential and parliamentary systems, regime type, electoral and representational mechanisms, etc.), and the state.

Ideas and Ideology

Students of politics have often emphasized the role of ideology and ideas in policy making. According to this approach, policy options and outcomes are deeply shaped by the ideological framework of political parties in power and by the economic and political ideas available to them. Some studies have stressed the role of ideas and ideology at a national level (Adler 1987, and Goldstein 1989), while others emphasized the workings of new ideas in the emergence of changing international political and economic agendas (Hall 1989, and Drake and Nicolaidis 1992).[30]

Take for example the case of the recent regulatory reform in the U.S. telecommunications sector. Derthick and Quirk argued that ideas played a central role in the deregulation process (Derthick and Quirk 1985). A similar approach can be found in a study of the breakup of AT&T by Temin and Galambois (Temin with Galambois 1987). Others believe that the dominant ideology of governing elites concerning the role of telecom in economic development explains well recent telecom reform in certain LDCs. In his study of Southeast Asian countries, Ure argues that the presence of a national development ideology led some countries to introduce reform in the telecom sector. Where reform did not emerge, governments lacked a coherent and clear vision of development (Ure 1993).

An approach that emphasized ideas is suited to exploring the origins of a particular policy option, but it fails to account for the transformations and changes suffered by policy during adoption and implementation. At this second stage the dynamics of pragmatic political bargaining, and struggles among various interest groups and the state, have more relevance than do the ideas that nurtured the initiative.

In the case of telecom reform, revived and updated neoliberal ideas clearly contributed to setting the agenda and the general policy framework under which privatization and liberalization were carried out. But there is little evidence that neoliberal ideas affected the different ways in which each country articulated its own reform. Further, since most countries studied here shared similar ideas of what should be reformed and how, despite their different policy outcomes, one must look beyond ideas for better explanations of what most influenced the evolution of the policy-making process.

In Argentina and Mexico, an ideology and/or idea approach would also fail to explain the origins of telecom reform policies. Although party ideology was a strong explanatory factor for telecom reform in England under Thatcher, in the United States under Reagan, and in Chile under Pinochet, it is far less relevant in Argentina, Mexico, and New Zealand, where reforms were carried out by political parties with a long tradition of welfare and state-interventionist ideologies.[31]

International Actors and Coalitions

In developing countries scholars have often paid special attention to the influence of international political actors in shaping LDC domestic policies. Throughout the 1970s this analytical approach flourished, using general conceptual tools offered by dependency theory, world-systems theory, and a variety of neo-Marxist theories.[32] Although the popularity of this approach receded during the 1980s, this does not mean that the role of international forces in LDC policy making faded away. On the contrary, fiscal and economic crises have made LDCs more permeable to international pressures.

In the case of LDC telecom reform, international actors and structures played an important role throughout the process. Key players, such as lending institutions—mainly the International Monetary Fund and the World Bank—pressed governments to reform, providing at the same time financial support for the task.[33] With their technical expertise, international consultants shaped the design of the reform, and, in more advanced stages of the process, international investors influenced the sector's final regulatory framework and determined the openness of local markets.

Although the presence of these actors is common in most telecom reforms in LDCs, their impact is strongly correlated with domestic political and economic conditions. Where reform was rushed under pressure of unstable local politics and the need to overcome deep fiscal crisis, the government fully opened the policy process to international actors, and as was true in Argentina, this made the state vulnerable to the demands of international investors. Mexico's political stability, on the other hand, enabled it to control the reform process, and, although international actors had some influence, it was less significant than in Argentina.

Even though international actors clearly had a major role in shaping telecom reform, it is difficult to assess the magnitude of their influence on the success or failure of privatization and liberalization. Both investors and international lending institutions supported privatization but worked to promote it through local governments. Whether the emergence and survival of a particular official policy is the result of a genuine local initiative or if it was introduced and promoted (or dismantled) by international institutions is uncertain. The role of international actors becomes clear only in the few cases where they clashed with governments over preferences and interests in the reform process—such as the price and liberalization struggle in Argentina. Finally, since most of their actions and demands were directed to, "filtered" through, and transformed by the peculiar institutional arrangements of the state apparatus of each country, this study looks at the influence of international factors from the perspective of the host state.

Domestic Actors and Coalitions

Interest group theory, which flourished in the United States during the late 1950s and 1960s, has dominated North American political science academic circles ever since. Empirical-democratic, or pluralist theory, is probably the most salient of the various ramifications of interest-group theory (Dahl 1961). From the viewpoint of empirical-democratic or pluralist theorists, domestic politics evolves out of a plurality of interest-group coalitions that struggle over policy making in order to influence policy formation and outcomes on their own behalf. Interest-group theory still remains a key element in the explanation of political processes in industrialized countries.[34] The predominance of this approach in the United States is based on the fact that in American institutions, interest-group coalitions—and not the state—are the central actors in policy formation. The state is an arena where societal actors clash and work out their interest preferences.

In most LDCs, where the state plays a central role in the management of politics and economics, scholars have paid less attention to the role of interest-group coalitions and have focused instead on the state.[35] An interest-group approach applied to developing countries can also present methodological problems. In the settled political environment of most industrialized democracies, coalitions and their impact in the policy process are easily identifiable. LDCs experience a continual reconfiguration and transformation of the political scene, which makes the task of detecting interest groups difficult. The fleshing out of causal correlation between coalition preferences and policy outcomes is even harder.

Although an interest-group approach in the study of politics in LDCs presents problems, I argue that the magnitude of difficulty varies according to the scope of the issues explored and length of the period under inquiry.[36] In studies like this one, which focuses on a limited regulatory reform that extended over a short period, the identification of interest groups and their influence on policy reform is more feasible.

Furthermore, the controversial nature of the event—the privatization of an important public utility—and the short time in which the reforms were carried out forced interest groups to oppose or defend the initiative publicly, which made visible positions and interests vis-à-vis the proposed changes.[37] This visibility of domestic interest groups revealed the central role that some of them—such as labor, state officials, and the like—played in shaping the reform process. However, as in the case of international actors, the influence of domestic coalitions was more or less effective and relevant according to the particular institutional features of each state. As in previous cases, the study examines the role of domestic interest groups in the telecom reform process from a state perspective.

Political Institutions

Approaches that stress the characteristics of the formal political system have emphasized the role of different national institutions as the key independent variables in the policy-making process. Some highlighted the role of political parties and the electoral process, others stressed the presidentialism-parliamentarism dichotomy or regime type (authoritarian or democratic), and some have brought the influence of Congress and the judiciary to the forefront of policy analysis. In the telecommunications sector, as Cowhey argues, "the structure of political incentives and political institutions in each country powerfully shapes how the country will reallocate the property rights and reorganize the regulation of the communications system" (Cowhey 1991, 3).

Electoral Mechanisms and Political Parties

For American scholars—along with interest group theories—electoral mechanisms have been a dominant way of understanding the emergence and implementation of new policies, and it has been used to explain policy making in LDCs (Shugart and Carey 1992). The approach has often been used to explain regulatory reform in the telecommunications sector. Roger Noll, for example, argues that narrow economic-interest coalitions—such as those pressing for the liberalization of the telecommunications market—are more likely to succeed in political systems with single-member districts elected by plurality vote and a fairly autonomous legislature than in countries with nationwide proportional representation.[38]

Noll's correlation between electoral mechanisms and the policy-making processes is a convincing one. However, as Cowhey warns, one of the crucial distinctions in this regard is between true electoral systems and those that are not (Cowhey 1991). In LDCs, even during periods of democratic governance, the relation between electoral politics and the policy process has been tenuous (Haggard 1990, 34).

In the cases studied here, the absence of a transparent electoral process, or weak links between electoral programs and the policy agenda in the aftermath of elections, calls into question the validity of this approach as an explanatory variable of divergent policy outcomes among reformer countries. In Malaysia and Mexico, for example, the existence of a long-standing party in power, with a tight control over domestic politics, turns formal elections into a quasi-meaningless political exercise. In Argentina and Thailand the gap between electoral-campaign discourses and postelectoral government actions are so contradictory that the theoretical causal correlation established between modes of electoral systems and policy outcomes becomes unclear.[39] Hence, lack of transparent elections in some cases, and the disconnection between electoral politics and effective government in others, weakens the explanatory power of electoral politics theory.

Political parties have also been considered a key element in the formation and transformation of national policies. The socioeconomic patterns of their constituents and party ideology have generally affected policy formation when parties become governments (Sartori 1976, and Rose 1980). Based on the British experience, Rose, for example, reviewed evidence proving that political parties do make a difference in policy making.

Although political history in LDCs tends to confirm this assertion, and a party approach generally offers important clues for our understanding of policy making and politics, in the particular case of recent state reforms political parties in power have generally "betrayed" their constituents and their ideological roots.

By dismantling the state and its welfare functions, the Peronists in Argentina and the Partido Revolucionario Institucional (PRI) in Mexico not only acted against their basic political philosophy, but, more importantly, hindered economically most of their party constituents while benefiting a few local and foreign business interests. Thus, attempting to explain telecom policy reform in Argentina and Mexico from a political-party perspective may not be the most fruitful approach.

Presidentialism, Parliamentarism, and Regime Type

In Western democracies there are two dominant modes of political organization: presidentialism and parliamentarism. It has often been argued that these two governing arrangements have affected differently the survival rate of policy initiatives and the effectiveness of governance. Similar arguments have been developed for LDCs, and, in particular for cases in Latin America (Nohlen and Fernández 1991, and Shugart and Carey 1992).

Although this approach contributed significantly to the study of policy making in LDCs, it does not seem to provide much explanatory leverage in the cases considered here. When we look at country outcomes, we find success and failure under both presidential and parliamentary governing arrangements. If we take, for example, the cases of Argentina, Mexico, Malaysia, and Thailand, we find no correlation between parliamentarism or presidentialism and privatization or liberalization success. Malaysia and Thailand, organized under a parliamentary system, share no common outcome in their reform policies. Similarly, reform outcomes in Mexico and Argentina, which are organized under a presidentialist system, are also considerably different. Clearly the particular organization of governments in presidential or parliamentary systems is not the key variable that separates countries that failed in their reform efforts from those that succeeded.

Whether countries are under a democratic or authoritarian regime also fails to provide an explanation of reform outcomes. Due to recent—and in some cases current—authoritarian governments in certain LDCs, there has been a tendency to explore political and economic transformations on the basis of the political regime of the country (O'Donnell, Schmitter, and Whitehead 1986). However, a new wave of recent research shows that democracy or authoritarianism are not relevant to government effectiveness in implementing economic policies (Remmer 1990, and Haggard and Kaufman 1993).

Looking at the cases explored here, we find that nondemocratic South Africa followed the same path to failure that democratic Uruguay did. The authoritarian regime of Pinochet in Chile implemented reforms in the same way as did democratic Venezuela. The same conclusion is reached when we look at one country as it passed through different regime types. Argentina's 1976–1982 authoritarian regime failed to reform in the same way that the democratic government that took power in 1983 did. However, the 1989 democratic administration was able to achieve what the previous governments failed to accomplish.

Congress and the Judiciary

Interactions between the executive and Congress and between the executive and the judiciary are central elements in the policy process of democratic administrations. This is particularly true when policy making unfolds in a context of politics-as-usual. The situation is quite different when the executive operates in a political environment in which Congress does not play a crucial role in blocking or reshaping presidential initiatives—as in the case of Mexico—or when that power has been delegated to the executive due to economic or political emergency—as in Argentina in 1989 (Shugart and Carey 1992, 143). When presidents bypass Congress through regulatory decrees or gain special legislative powers granted by Congress itself, the role of the legislature in shaping regulatory reform moves to the background of the political scene and the executive takes center stage.

Furthermore, when dealing with economic and socially sensitive issues such as the privatization of large public utilities, normal legislative relations between the executive and congress are overshadowed by the active input of new external actors from various and often opposing interest camps. The juxtaposition of labor and foreign investors is a good example. The presence of these extralegislative actors in the shaping of new regulations for the telecom sector calls for a theoretical framework that extends beyond the institutional boundaries of policy making during periods of politics-as-usual.

The judiciary is another important element in the check-and-balance mechanism of a country's political system. In the telecommunications sector several studies have stressed the role of the judiciary in the reshaping of the sector. Stone, for example, looked at the judiciary to explore the break up of AT&T (Stone 1989). The World Bank has recently carried out studies that emphasize the role of domestic institutions—in particular that of the judiciary system of the country—as an important institutional element in telecom reforms in LDCs (Spiller and Sampson 1992, and Hill and Abdala 1994).[40]

In the cases under consideration in this study, there is no concrete evidence that the features of the judiciary system of each country played a major role in the sale of telecom systems. But the existence of an independent judiciary (able to interpret and enforce privatization legislation) might have played an important role in regard to the level of investor confidence. Failure of the judiciary to act as a backup legal system to government's discretionary actions can reduce the number of bidders competing for the company, and, in turn, affect a government's ability to impose tougher conditions on the remaining potential buyers.

INSTITUTIONS AND THE SOURCE OF REFORM

The claim that a closed, centralized political system is more suited to carrying out reform in the telecom sector than is an open, decentralized one, directly contradicts a study carried out by Raymond Duch on the telecom sectors of England, France, and Germany. Duch asks—in the same way this study does—"How do we account for cross-national variation in the implementation of liberalization and privatization policies?" For Duch—as it does for this study—the answer lies in the domestic political and institutional arrangements of each country. In other words, both studies share the research question and the relevance attributed to the domestic political system as a key variable in explaining variations in telecom policy outcomes.

But the studies differ radically in what it is identified as the most conducive political arrangement for telecom reform. In exploring the European cases, Duch argues that open, pluralist political systems are more prone to liberalization and privatization than are closed, corporatist institutions, which provide the least promising environment for interests demanding reform (Duch 1991, 7). He finds support for his argument in the fact that open, pluralist Britain has carried out far larger telecom reforms than closed, corporatist Germany. These arguments stand in obvious opposition to the explanations offered here, which conclude that a closed policy process with a high concentration of power in the state[41] is more likely to succeed in introducing reforms in the telecom sector than open, decentralized ones.[42]

One tends to assume immediately that one of the two arguments must be completely wrong. I argue, however, that both explanations are on the right track despite their opposite conclusions. The clue to these contradictory explanations of similar outcomes lies in the particular political dynamics of the cases selected for study.

In most developed economies pressures for telecom reform were usually endogenous to the sector, induced by technological innovations, and carried out by large corporate users. In LDCs initiatives for reform were exogenous to the sector, deeply rooted in the economic and fiscal crisis, and governments—more specifically the executive branch—were primarily responsible for pushing reform onto the political agenda. If we take the state apparatus as the loci of policy making, then, in the former cases, initiatives and pressures for reform came from outside the state, while in the latter reform was promoted from within the state. This would lead similar political arrangements to respond differently to similar issues.

In MDCs, where pressures for reform come from outside the public sector, an open, pluralist political system—such as Britain—with multiple points of entry to the policy process would be more receptive or vulnerable to new demands. In closed, corporatist systems—such as Germany—where entry barriers to outsiders' interests and demands are higher, the likelihood of new initiatives penetrating the policy process is lower. On the other hand, since LDC reform initiatives come from the executive branch of the government and confront strong resistance from societal actors with vested interests in the sector, a closed polity with high concentration of power in the head of state would enhance the government's ability to overcome opposition and enforce reforms in the sector.

This exercise comparing MDCs and LDCs highlights the fact that similar institutional arrangements may affect policy processes in very different ways. Outcome depends on the source of the reform initiative and, subsequently, on what direction the arrow of causality points (i.e., whether it is from the state towards society or vice versa).

CONCLUSION

In the late 1980s many LDCs attempted a broad reform of their national telecommunications systems. Countries shared the goal of privatizing national carriers and liberalizing telecom services. However, despite this dual aim, countries have followed different paths and arrived at different outcomes in their journey to a privatized and liberalized telecom sector. While some, like Mexico, Malaysia, Chile, Jamaica, Venezuela, and Argentina (during its 1989–1995 administration), were able to sell their national telecom enterprises, others like Thailand, Colombia, South Africa, Uruguay, and Argentina (during the 1976–1989 administrations), failed to do so.

Privatization and liberalization are sociopolitical and economic events undertaken by the state, which affects not only civil society but also state agents. This study has therefore placed the state at the center of the analysis. The impact of other factors, such as ideas, domestic coalitions, international actors, and various features of the political system are also studied from a state perspective.

Based on the theoretical tools offered by a statist approach, the conceptual contributions of other lines of inquiry, and the evidence presented here, this study suggests that the likelihood of privatization depends strongly on the degree of insulation of the policy-making process and degree of concentration of power in the head of the executive branch. More specifically, the study argues that governments with high levels of both are better prepared to carry out controversial regulatory reforms in the public sector than are those in which these features are low or absent.

Besides privatization, LDCs have often attempted to follow worldwide trends by liberalizing most telecom services; however, not all of them succeeded in their goals. The cases explored in this study point to an important distinction of timing, specifically, whether liberalization is attempted simultaneously with privatization, or if it is pursued prior to the sale of the SOTE. In the latter case the government must battle domestic coalitions with entrenched interests in the sector. However, in these cases, since the opening generally targets nonbasic services—something most national carriers in LDCs are not able to provide in the short run—the opposition to liberalization has been low. Furthermore, since the company is still under the control of the government there are a variety of political and economic mechanisms that the administration can use to achieve its target.

When liberalization is pursued simultaneously to the sale of the SOTE, the bargaining process often affects the prospects for liberalization. The ability of the administration to achieve the opening of the local telecom market will depend on the attractiveness of the domestic economy, the number of bidders left at the end of the privatization process, the government's urgency to sell the company and attract private investments, etc. According to the evidence collected, countries with reasonable economic prospects should have a better chance to achieve liberalization. In the cases of Mexico, Malaysia, and Thailand, which had attractive domestic markets, liberalization was successful. Argentina, facing an economic crisis and a dire need of new capital, sacrificed liberalization for a successful privatization.

In summary, states with insulated governments and a high concentration of power in the executive are more prone to achieve privatization of their SOTEs than are exposed and permeable administrations with executives who lack a monopoly of power within the state. Similarly, countries with an attractive economic profile are more likely to simultaneously achieve both privatization and liberalization than are those with poor economic prospects. In the following chapters, a variety of cases offer evidence in support of these premises.

NOTES

1. Other important patterns of reform include why certain countries carried out total privatization of their SOTEs, while others privatized only partially, why some did it through direct sale, while others reformed through share floatation, and so forth. However, these are not the main issues of this study and, therefore, they are explored only briefly in Chapter 1.

2. Policy making is an extremely complex and ambiguous process, with fuzzy boundaries, and elements that intermingle and overlap each other. The categorization of theoretical approaches to policy making that follow are human constructs, product of efforts to introduce some order and clarity in an otherwise disorderly and messy reality. It is only after we narrow complexity with pseudoboundaries that we can describe what happened and attempt to interpret it. In this process of charting social process onto constructed conceptual categories, we gain simplicity and clarity, but we lose diversity and complexity. In other words, we lose reality. But to live between reality and fiction, and attempt to explain one from the other is the destiny in which the social sciences—or I should say all science—is condemned to live.

3. The insulation of governing elites from societal pressures and the cohesion of policymakers has been emphasized in policy studies of LDCs as an important element in the effectiveness of state intervention. See, for example, Evans and Rueschemeyer 1985, and Haggard and Kaufman 1993.

4. Based on comparative historical analysis, Nettl argues that this "statelessness" of social theory in developed nations comes from the predominance of the North American social sciences in the post-World War II period, and the historical and empirical factors that made the United States a country centered in civil society. "The relative 'statelessness' of American social science coincides with the relative statelessness of the United States, with the long period during which the egalitarian and pluralistic society ... was becoming institutionalized over a vast continent" (Nettl 1968, 54).

5. The seminal work of Guillermo O'Donnell (1972) on bureaucratic-authoritarian regimes and the prolific academic debates generated around this topic highlight the relevance that the notion of the state as an actor has generated in Third World studies.

6. The roots of state theory can be found in the work of Karl Marx and Max Weber. Although Marx's writings on the role of the state in society have been interpreted in various different ways, the dominant reading depicts the state as an

instrument of the ruling class to coordinate and divide society on behalf of their narrow personal interests. The national state is, therefore, an organizational product of capitalist societies. Its function is to serve the macroadministrative needs of the capitalist mode of production. Max Weber, instead, understood the rise of the state and the spread of centralized administration as an inevitable outcome to manage the growing complexity of social life—an inescapable fate of human development. Despite this emphasis on the administrative and bureaucratic origins of the state, Weber emphasized the fact that the state's uniqueness comes from its monopoly of physical coercion at a national level, an element that makes it a key political actor in society.

7. In this work I limit the notion of the state to include only the executive branch (president or prime minister and cabinet) and national bureaucracy. Confining the definition of the state to the head of the executive, the cabinet, and the federal bureaucracy makes it a more coherent and cohesive entity for analytical purposes. In this way the state is reduced to all constituents that respond to the authority of the executive, and all other institutions that constitute separate powers in themselves, responding to different principles, values, and goals are left aside. Defining the state as only those political powers that respond to the head of the executive branch highlights two important aspects of the local political environment. First, it reveals the level of cohesion and integration within the state—which ultimately reflects the discipline and accountability to the president's authority. Second, it clarifies the extent to which the president (or prime minister) has control over Congress or the judiciary.

8. It has been argued that state autonomy does not imply state capacity or effectiveness to govern. From this perspective a state can be autonomous, yet too weak to enforce policy initiatives. I would argue that in such cases we are in the presence not of an autonomous state, but of a politically marginalized state that performs only as a subsidiary formality to the real politics that unfolds in civil society. State autonomy, in my understanding, presupposes the monopoly of means of coercion and the ability to enforce policy initiatives.

9. Instrumentalist neo-Marxists argue that state autonomy is achieved when the state gains insularity from the dominant classes. This perspective is based in the fact that they see the state as an instrument of the dominant economic class. Miliband, for example, argues that there is an important distinction between governing—making day-to-day decisions—and ruling—exercising ultimate control. While state officials govern, the dominant economic groups rule. In support of his arguments, he brings evidence of the close interpersonal links that exist between the bureaucracy and the most powerful economic groups in society. He argues, however, that to be politically effective and ensure the long-term stability of the capitalist system, the state must be able to act independently from the dominant classes, and occasionally implement initiatives against the short-term interests of these powerful groups (Miliband 1969).

10. Diverging from instrumental Marxist approaches—such as Miliband's—structuralist neo-Marxists authors have argued that the state protects and nourishes the development of capitalist modes of accumulation, not because of alliances with particular classes also interested in accumulation, nor because state officials bend to pressures from powerful economic groups, but because the state has a self-interest in the expansion of capitalist accumulation. Institutional separation between state and economy means that the state is dependent—through taxation and financing from capital markets—upon the continuity and expansion of profitable production. Since this vast pool of resources is beyond its direct control

and management, the state has an institutional self-interest in the vitality of the capitalist economy. However, in its aim to protect capitalist accumulation, the state might face charges of not being an impartial arbiter of class interests. This has led modern states in capitalist societies to face the often contradictory tasks of accumulation and legitimation, to which redistribution becomes central. The state, in this view, is in a permanent process of reaccommodation in its effort to overcome the capitalist contradictions in which it is enmeshed. See, for example, Block 1977, and Offe 1984.

11. Issues on state autonomy and state functions have also been tackled by non-Marxist authors, such as Eric Nordlinger, who articulate a theory of state autonomy in democratic societies. For him the state constitutes one more actor in the policy-making arena to whom one should not attribute any specific function and purpose, such as the protection of the status quo or the reproduction of capitalism (Nordlinger 1981).

12. The events related to the nationalization of oil in Mexico are a good example.

13. For some authors, such as Evans and Rueschemeyer, ethnicity is also an important factor that may enhance or diminish state autonomy. They argue that "when ethnic cleavages are hierarchically ordered and when a single ethnic group manages to gain continuous control over the state apparatus, ethnic cleavages may enhance state autonomy (Evans and Rusechmeyer 1985, 65). When applied to the cases of this study the hypothesis seems to hold certain validity for the case of Malaysia and South Africa where ethnic strife is a dominant pattern of local politics and has provided a rationale for state intervention and insulation.

14. The dismantling of the preexisting order generally becomes the main political function of the new state and, therefore, justifies higher-than-usual levels of concentration of the means of coercion in state officials. Often this initial pattern of power distribution continues for an extended period of time.

15. For studies that concentrate on the relevance of issue areas, see, for example, Evangelista 1989.

16. For a similar approach in the field of economics, see King 1991.

17. In the late 1980s both governments confronted serious challenges to this vertically integrated political system. In both cases, the most important threat came from within the coalition itself, and the governing coalitions responded by restructuring their political alliances and strengthening presidential power through legal and administrative reforms.

18. Whenever I refer to liberalization it should be understood that it is partial. There is no case—with the exception of New Zealand—in which all telecom services were opened to competition.

19. The weak opposition has often been rooted in the fact that liberalization—which has been aimed at value-added services—affected only the margins of the local market, without eroding the large profits earned from basic services.

20. When some services have already been liberalized, investors have only two options: (1) they participate in the bidding for the SOTE, accepting competition in the liberalized segments of the market and trying to keep remaining services closed, or (2) they do not participate in privatization at all. For an illustration of this situation, see Telefónica's attitude in the attempted privatization of ENTel during the Alfonsín administration.

21. This is not to say that political factors—such as political stability—are completely irrelevant in the process. But, since most of the cases considered

portray fairly stable political systems, the economic variable becomes the principal consideration for investors.

22. In Argentina, for example, foreign capital accounted for 78 percent of the purchasing capital of ENTel. In Mexico, the participation of foreign capital in TELMEX after the privatization accounted for 54.3 percent of the company. The participation of large domestic economic conglomerates in bidding consortiums is significant. However, considering the transnational nature of their operations and the increasing irrelevance of corporate nationality, I will treat all private investors— whether foreigners or locals—as unitary actors with shared interests. For thought-provoking analysis of the diminishing relevance of corporate nationality in the current globalized economy, see Reich 1992, 136, and Ohmae 1991, 137.

23. Advocates of foreign investment argue that, because overseas investments are a productive form of channeling capital resources into developing economies, foreign companies can contribute to the host economy with resources that are generally scarce in LDCs. Businesses from abroad, for example, generally carry their own financing, relieving local governments of the burden of supporting credit lines for the sector—in the current international context, multinational corporations have better prospects for accessing credits than LDC governments. The presence of foreign investment could also provide an upgrade of technological capability in the recipient country, as well as managerial experience in operating in international markets. If guided by adequate trade policies, the presence of multinational corporations should also help to reverse the prevailing LDC productive system from inward-led-growth economies to an export-oriented ones. Large transnational corporations control worldwide commercial networks that would facilitate access to markets abroad. Pro-foreign-investment arguments can be found in Freeman 1981, McCormack 1980, and Todaro 1981.

24. The *dependencia* school, instead, views the presence of foreign capital detrimental to the host country. Presumably multinational companies tended to soak up local capital for their projects, bringing in few of their own resources, implement inappropriate technology disrupting the local labor capital ratio, and through various predatory mechanisms drive most domestic producers out of the market. The consequence of overseas investments for LDCs was foreign domination of key sectors of the domestic economy, exacerbation of unemployment, and "decapitalization" of the domestic economy through the transfer of large profits abroad. A *dependencia* approach and critiques of foreign investments can be found in Cardoso and Faletto 1979, Hymer 1979, Lichtensztejn 1990, and Moran 1985.

25. Studies that take a bargaining or structural approach are, for example, Grieco 1984, Encarnation and Wells 1985, Kobrin 1987, Evans 1979, Gereffi 1986, and Newfarmer 1985.

26. Bargaining power of host governments increases when the investment is actively sought by competing firms and requires small amounts of capital, or if it is large and once in place is not easily liquidated or moved, when it is targeted at serving the domestic market, and requires low technology and factors of production not easily substitutable across countries. The negotiation of the investment by a centralized government agency and the involvement of the government as a financier, consumer, distributor, supplier, or regulator would strengthen even further the bargaining power of local administrations (Encarnation and Wells 1985, 51). In LDCs' telecom reform programs, investors' bargaining capabilities were enhanced because telecom services require large investments, high technological capability, and are based on factors of production easily sub-

stitutable across countries, and do not rely on governments for financing, consumption, or supply of inputs. Governments' bargaining power increased due to their role as regulators of outputs, which are provided mostly to the local market.

27. Investors' concerns are reflected in the words of ITU Secretary General, Pekka Tarjanne, who warned Latin American government officials that "only with political and economic stability private investors will be willing to channel their capital [to the telecom sector]." Tarjanne's statements were reinforced by Organization of the American States (OAS) officials, who recommended clear rules and confidence measures to attract private investments to the sector. According to Alvaro López Cayzedo, OAS Telecommunications project coordinator, confidence factors include stable exchange rates, adequate fiscal policies, the possibility of capital repatriation, and the authorization to create new companies and engage in transnational business. *La Jornada*, 9 April 1992, 39.

28. Expropriation can be outright—as in the case of nationalization—or partial and progressive through regulatory reforms—such as by increasing service requirements and lowering tariffs. See Levy and Spiller 1991, and Hill and Abdala 1994.

29. For more detailed investment criteria in the telecom sector, see Sonnenschein and Yokopenic 1995; and Salomon Brothers, Inc. 1991.

30. See also Goldstein and Keohane 1991, and Jervis 1976.

31. Curiously, former socialized political systems such as New Zealand and Mexico are today among the most liberalized telecom markets in the world.

32. Some selected works in this line of theorizing are Cardoso and Faletto 1979, Evans 1979, Frank 1978, and Gereffi 1986.

33. The World Bank, for example, provided loans for attractive early retirement packages for SOE workers in order to gain their support for the reform.

34. See, for example, Olson 1965, Gourevitch 1986, and Katzenstein 1978.

35. The influence of international factors in the formation and transformation of local politics is another factor that dominated Third World studies during the last twenty years.

36. In studies that explore policy variation of macroeconomic policies over an extended period of time, the intermittent reconfiguration of coalitions and alliances would certainly pose a challenge to the researcher.

37. In times of politics-as-usual when political stakes are less significant and visible, interest groups and coalitions would tend to influence policy making in a more subtle and veiled fashion, making it more difficult for the observer to detect their presence in the policy process.

38. Noll defines each system by stating that under nationwide proportional representation "the share of the party's representation is determined by its share of the total vote, and candidates on the party list are declared elected to the point at which the party's legislative seats are exhausted." In a single-member geographic district "each party nominates a candidate to fill a legislative seat representing a specific constituency. The ultimate winner can be either the candidate with a plurality of the vote in the first election or the eventual majority winner after a sequence of runoffs." Legislators in the former case represent a specific constituency, and, therefore, specific interests (in this case telecom reform) are more likely to reach the legislative agenda than in cases of broad-based interest representation (Noll 1986).

39. Although it might be argued that the gap between electoral campaign and later government action is present in most political systems, the shift in the case of

some LDCs is so striking that it blurs any attempt to link electoral politics with policy implementation and outcomes.

40. Most of these studies emphasize the role of the judiciary and other regulatory and administrative institutions in consolidating (or harming) investors' commitment to the sector following privatization.

41. Such as Argentina (1989), Mexico, Malaysia, Chile, Jamaica, etc.

42. Such as Argentina (1976–1988), Colombia, Thailand, South Africa, Uruguay, etc.

3

Argentina 1980–1989: The Rocky Road to Reform

Chapters three and four explore attempts during the 1980s to reform Argentina's telecommunications sector. Three administrations tried to privatize the national common carrier, Empresa Nacional de Telecomunicaciones (ENTel). The first two failed, but the last succeeded in transferring ENTel to private investors. These chapters will look at each administration and its efforts to reform the sector as a case in itself. This approach offers the possibility of a diachronic comparative analysis, in which similar events at different stages in time can be compared in one industry within one country.

The first telecommunications services were provided in Argentina in the late 1870s at the initiative of local entrepreneurs; however, large foreign companies rapidly took control. From the end of the nineteenth century until the mid-1940s, telecommunications service was private, foreign-owned, and operated in a competitive and unregulated market. In 1946, the first Perón administration nationalized the sector. And, despite managerial and financial problems, it grew at a reasonable pace. By 1989, ENTel boasted a telephone density of ten instruments per hundred people (Sindicatura General de Empresas Públicas 1990).

In the late 1970s and early 1980s the governing military regime attempted for the first time to undertake a restructuring of the telecommunication sector, which included a plan to privatize ENTel. The project foundered when conflicts arose among various groups within the military and between them and the team of civilians that led the initiative in the Ministry of Economy. When the military left power in 1983, it had failed to privatize the company.

The democratically elected Radical party government that then took power attempted again to introduce private management and ownership in ENTel. In 1985 the administration of Raúl Alfonsín announced its intention to privatize the telecom sector, and it launched a specific initiative to accomplish this in 1987. However, the growth and consolidation of opposition forces after 1987, and the lack of state autonomy from interest groups opposed to privatization, created obstacles that the government could not overcome. Conflicts and disagreements among top state officials and the lack of presidential involvement in the issue further weakened the government's chances of implementing privatization policies. In 1989, when the new administration of the Peronist Carlos Menem came to power, ENTel still remained under state ownership and control.

Failed efforts of the military regime and the Alfonsín administration point to the importance of cohesion within the governing elite. Alfonsín's failure, in particular, highlights the importance of state autonomy. In both cases, the lack of an integrated and cohesive government or, in its absence, a high concentration of power in the executive led to recurrent struggles and clashes. In the case of the military, it paralyzed the project; in the case of the radicals, it weakened the government vis-à-vis opposition forces. Finally, the lack of state autonomy during the Alfonsín years was a major obstacle to the success of ENTel's privatization.

This chapter provides a historical overview of privatization and liberalization attempts in Argentina since the early 1980s. Since privatization is not a mechanical or automatic transfer of ownership carried out in a political vacuum, but a politically loaded socioeconomic event, it is necessary to understand privatization in light of the country's political system as well as in terms of its evolving economic situation.

THE POLITICAL ENVIRONMENT OF REFORM

Like Mexico and other Western presidential democracies, Argentina's political system has a president, a national Congress (constituted by the chamber of deputies and the senate), and a judiciary system. Since the system corresponds to a federalist state, provinces have their own power structure that, with some minor variations, replicates the national political system.

Since the 1930s, however, this constitutional political arrangement has been honored more in word than deed. Cyclical military coups and democratic governments dominated the political scene until the early 1980s, when the harshest and most violent authoritarian government in Argentine history stepped down from power. Even in periods of constitutional rule, politics have been dominated by conflict, rather than by cooperation and coordination. From the demise of Perón's government in 1955 until 1983, political violence and antagonism expanded with each new cycle of military and civilian administrations (Cavarozzi 1986). From the 1930s to 1989 the country was led by twenty-five different presidents, some of whom lasted only a few days or weeks in power (Rock 1985, and Lewis 1990). This shocking record of government instability is indicative of an extremely volatile political system. Unlike the more stable Mexico, Argentina has been submerged in political chaos for more than sixty years.

It has been argued that Argentine political instability is due to the absence of a dominant coalition that could provide a strong centralized power leadership for the nation.[1] This explanation reflects the general theoretical proposition offered by Olson, who argues that the proliferation of distributional coalitions in a society inhibits economic growth and the ability of a society to efficiently adapt to economic and political changes (Olson 1965, 75). Since no political group has been able to dominate the political scene for an extended period, the creation of a state-corporatist system has failed despite recurrent attempts by successive governments. Countries with state-corporatist systems generally display a system of interest representation in which

> the constituent units are organized into a limited number of singular, compulsory, noncompetitive, hierarchically ordered, and functionally differentiated categories, recognized or licensed (if not created) by the state and granted a deliberate representational monopoly within their respective categories in exchange for observing certain controls on their selection of leaders and articulation of demands and supports (Schmitter and Luhmbruch 1979, 13).

In this regard, Argentine politics lacks the clear and orderly hierarchical relations that characterize vertically integrated societies like Mexico or Malaysia.

Argentina also has not permanently consolidated some form of competitive pluralism. In such a system interest groups and the state enter a bargaining process in which policy making is the outcome of mutual accommodation and concessions. Civil society must accept the final decision of the state, and the state, in turn, must keep the policy process open enough to allow multiple points of entry to a wide variety of societal actors (Wynia 1978, 246). This, of course, has not been the case in Argentina. Widespread distrust among interest groups and state officials, the unwillingness to accept any state decision that might imply a concession of one's own interests, and the pendular selective exclusion of interest groups, has turned Argentina into an unmanageable, conflict-ridden society.

In constitutional terms the Argentine president had very weak legislative power (Shugart and Carey 1992, 156). Historically the presidency had to face a confrontational Congress that made everyday government an extremely difficult task. Due the state's vulnerability and the high level of conflict that surrounded policy making, presidents tried to avoid widespread participation from fear that their ability to govern would deteriorate further. However, by rejecting private interest participation, the executive only reinforced people's distrust, which fired up public opposition and resistance to public policies. This is reflected in continuous questioning of presidential authority by antagonistic unions, uncooperative entrepreneurs, powerful governors, and an adversarial Congress.

Permanent conflict and unstable politics also undermined the development of a stable and highly professionalized state bureaucracy. The political "fundamentalism" that underlies attitudes and perceptions led each group that took power to sweep clean the state by removing most agents appointed by the previous regime. Each new government replaced most officials, bureaucrats, and even low-ranking civil servants. Consequently most Argentine political actors view the state as a distributive tool up for grabs.[2]

Despite this picture of an unstable political system, scholars have argued that Argentina's ongoing political instability has been a surface phenomenon that "concealed a quite stable power system, whose dynamics followed consistent patterns" (Waisman 1992). In this view, two coalitions based in civil society alternated control of the government. One consisted of agrarian exporters, big foreign and domestic industrialists, and large financiers. The other comprised the domestic industrial bourgeoisie, particularly small- and medium-sized firms, and the labor movement. Yet, these interest group coalitions lacked self-definition and never achieved any significant level of internal cohesion and political discipline, nor did they share a political project other than that of advancing their own particularistic interests to the detriment of the other bloc. Struggles and clashes within subgroups dominated and characterized the political life of each group.

After the mid-1970s changes in both the Argentine and the global economy led to a structural shift in the distribution of power. By the early 1980s the underlying power structure was seriously weakened, opening the door to the emergence of new political forces and forcing the realignment of old ones.

In conflict-ridden societies like Argentina, the lack of a minimally institutionalized and cooperative polity is a major impediment to policy formulation and implementation. In these cases local politics may run into permanent stalemate and subsequent policy-making paralysis. To overcome these deficiencies and assure a basic level of social governance, there are two major strategies: raw state coercion (Chile under Pinochet) or social and political consensus (Bolivia 1985, and Mexico 1987).

Although necessary to control social conflict, these strategies are insufficient when the issue at stake is the reform of the state apparatus. In this more specific case, besides achieving control of or cooperation from diverse societal interests, governments require considerable internal coherence among officials, or, in the absence of that, a concentration of power in the head of state.

The military regime and democratic government, both of which attempted to privatize state-owned enterprieses (SOEs), failed due to the absence of one or both of these conditions. The military implemented policy through coercion and insulation of the decision-making process, but they failed to reform the state due to the lack of cohesion among governing elites and power centralization in the head of the executive. Historical factors prohibited the democratic government from achieving either social discipline (through accommodation or coercion) or bureaucratic cohesion for support of state reform.

The initiatives and dynamics of ENTel privatization attempts are better understood when placed in historical perspective. The following section provides the context in which the efforts to sell the company during the 1980s unfolded.

THE ARGENTINE TELECOM SECTOR

As in many other less developed countries (LDCs), Argentine telecommunications was initially provided by branches of foreign telephone companies. The roots of the telecom service industry thus were both foreign and private. This scenario was radically transformed in the late 1940s when the dominant carrier was nationalized. Since then, and for more than forty years ENTel was the primary provider of telecom services in the country, enjoying a quasi-monopoly in the service sector and a monopsony in equipment procurement. During the 1980s three different governments attempted to privatize the firm and opened some segments of the market to competition. Only in 1990 did a new administration succeed in selling the state-owned telecommunications enterprise (SOTE), but competition in basic services remained banned until the year 2000.

The birth of the telecommunications sector in Argentina dates as far back as February 12, 1878, when the first telephone connection was made in Buenos Aires. As in Mexico, this first initiative was purely local. Carlos Cayol and Fernando Newman, two local engineers, were responsible for these seeds of the domestic telecommunications industry. But, as in Mexico, it did not take long before foreign telephone companies took over. After three years of local operations, various foreign companies were allowed into the Argentine market to develop a national network.

After six years of harsh, unregulated competition the number of companies in the market was reduced to three foreign and one local. The three foreign companies were the Société du Pantéléphone L. de Loch et Cie. from Belgium, the Gower-Bell Telephone Company from England, and the River Plate Telephone Company from the United States. The Cayol & Newman Society was the only local company at that time. To avoid the harming effects of a market in which there were no rules of the game the three foreign companies joined forces in 1886, marginalizing and pushing the local company out of business.[3] This merger gave birth to the United Telephone Company of the River Plate, Limited. (more commonly know as Unión Telefónica—UT), a private dominant carrier that will remain in the Argentine market for an extended period of time (Figure 3.1).

A year later, in 1887, large users facing rising prices and deteriorating services formed a cooperative—Sociedad Cooperativa Telefónica (SCT)—to offer an alternative competing with UT. SCT was fairly successful in its ventures, quickly attracting a large number of customers.[4] Despite its considerable growth, by the late 1920s SCT was facing serious financial

Figure 3.1

Corporate History of ENTel

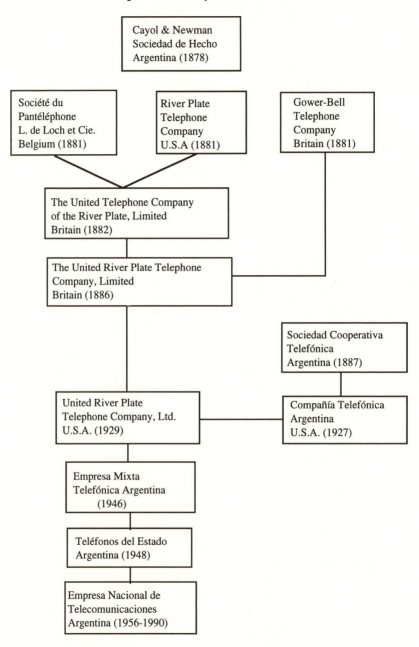

Source: Tesler 1990

problems. By that time, too, a rapidly growing American company, the International Telephone and Telegraph Corporation (ITT), had entered the Argentine market and was searching for a way to consolidate its position.[5] The financially troubled SCT offered ITT an excellent opportunity to gain control of an existing well-developed network, and in 1927 the American company absorbed the Argentine firm.

ITT came into Argentina with all the financial and technical support necessary to take a significant share of the market in a short time. With strong financial backing from Morgan Guaranty Trust Corporation and National City Bank of New York and technology and know-how recently acquired from AT&T, the new entrant was with able to provide improved services at much lower cost. By the end of 1929, keeping up with its expansionist policy, ITT bought UT. Once again, most of the telecommunications services of Argentina were brought under the control of one private firm.

The only part of the market that was not controlled by UT was the interior of the country, where two small private firms and a number of local cooperatives provided services. Typically, scarce and disperse populations with limited economic resources did not constitute an attractive market for large foreign operators. Hence, services in the interior of the country were mostly provided by local public cooperatives. Rising throughout the interior of Argentina from the early 1920s, these companies operated local networks which were initially closed and limited to their original town and later connected to other neighboring networks to give rise to closed regional networks. By the early 1940s public cooperatives provided services to more than 4 percent of the Argentine telecom market.

In the mid-1920s two small private firms—branches of a large foreign telecom corporation—sprang up in the interior of the country. Ericsson, the Swedish manufacturer, was granted a license to operate in the province of Entre Rios under the commercial name of Compañia Entreriana de Teléfonos (CET). Later, in 1927, Ericsson extended its operations to Mendoza where it started Compañía Argentina de Teléfonos (CAT). Shortly afterwards the two companies merged under the name of the latter. CAT remained the only private provider of services in the country until the privatization process in 1990. By then, the company had expanded its operations and was serving six provinces.[6]

During the 1920s and 1930s teledensity grew and the network expanded geographically throughout the country. While in 1930 there were 210,000 telephone subscribers, by 1941 the number had doubled reaching 460,587 subscribers. As the number of subscribers grew so did the number of firms operating in the market. By the early 1940s there were forty-three telephone companies offering services in the country. Despite this large number of suppliers, the services remained largely under the control of UT, which supplied 89.42 percent of the market, while CAT and local cooperatives served 6.29 percent and 4.29 percent of the customers, respectively.

Private foreign firms, the main actors in the early development of the Argentine telecom sector, operated free of state intervention and control for several decades. Argentina was infused then by a strong belief in economic liberalism, an ideology in which private unregulated entrepreneurship was conceived as the engine of growth. However, in the early 1940s, the country's political climate began to change. By 1945, the rise to power of Juan D. Perón set the beginning of four decades of state expansion and intervention in key sectors of the economy.

The Rise of State Ownership

Telecommunications became progressively conceived as a key asset not only to boost economic growth but mostly to effectively achieve national integration and defense. Telephone and telegraph services constituted, in the words of Perón, "the nervous system of the nation." For him, foreign control of the system was an anachronism "incompatible with sentiments of national sovereignty and the level of domestic development" (Donikian et al. 1990). Motivated by these and other related arguments Perón's administration bought the assets and controlling shares of UT in September 1946 (Law 12864).

The nationalization of the telephone company was viable due to, among other factors, the overwhelming popular support that Perón enjoyed in his nationalist policies. This extensive backing of the Argentine population for Perón's initiatives rested largely on his ability to build up coalitions with representatives of the most powerful social groups in the country. In the case of telecom nationalization he brought the Argentine state together with key representatives from the labor sector and the national industry. The new company, Empresa Mixta Telefónica Argentina (Telefónica Argentina), had—as its name proclaims—a mixed ownership shared by the Argentine state, public sector employees, and private investors. However, shortly after Telefónica Argentina began its operations, the government initiated a campaign against private investors in the firm arguing that they were only interested in the political control of the business and not in the needs of the public. In a few months the state took over the firm and changed its name to Teléfonos del Estado.

The appeal for state interventionism under the Perón regime grew rapidly. To achieve a more active and significant presence in the telecommunications sector the government created in 1949 the Ministry of Communications and the Secretary of State Telephones. Teléfonos del Estado began to expand its operations nationally and in doing so absorbed a large number of cooperatives in the interior of the country.[7] The consequences of this early state expansionism is that by the early 1970s the Argentine state controlled 92 percent of the telecommunications market in the country, while CAT served 7 percent and local cooperatives provided services to 1 percent of the subscribers.

In 1955 a military coup overthrew Perón and installed a new government that quickly began replacing many of the statist policies of the Peronist administration. However, due to its strategic importance, telecommunications services remained under state control. In January 13, 1956 Teléfonos del Estado was transformed into Empresa Nacional de Telecomunicaciones (ENTel). This company would remain the key player of the Argentine telecommunications sector for the next thirty-four years—until its privatization in 1990.

State ownership brought mixed results to the telecommunications sector in Argentina. In early years due to a strong state commitment to the development of telecommunications, the system grew rapidly. Later, network growth went through cycles of rapid expansion and stagnation. During the 1960s penetration slowed; in the late 1970s it picked up again, reaching in 1979 more than 10 percent growth over the previous year. In the early 1980s network growth dropped again to an average of 2.5 percent a year, and in the mid-1980s another expansion wave (linked to a special program called Megatel) brought yearly growth to approximately 11 percent.

These cycles in network evolution had a direct negative effect on the equipment industry (Herrera 1989). The eradication of private ownership and competition provided the required conditions for the emergence of a monopsony in the equipment market. The state relied on a few foreign equipment providers.[8] Erratic development of the network and high politization in the procurement process brought considerable instability to the industry. Public procurement was linked to the perpetual political instability of the country, which implied that each new administration generally canceled preexisting contracts with suppliers and negotiated new ones with different providers. Political instability and monopsony also provided high incentives for corruption. It was not unusual that ENTel would pay two or three times the international price of a product.[9]

Politization of the procurement process was just one aspect of the much larger process that politics played in the provision of services. State ownership of the telecom business brought about an important shift in the philosophy that had been guiding the sector for several decades. As the notion that telecommunications was an important tool to achieve social, security, and industrial goals grew, the perception of its commercial value diminished. A state monopoly constituted an excellent mechanism to achieve most of the social and political goals perceived at that time as crucial—but at the same time it removed efficiency and productivity incentives.

One area in which this process became fairly clear was in the pricing policies of the company. In its aim to increase demand and provide telephone services accessible to the low-income population, Argentina, as many other countries around the world, implemented a financial mechanism by which the revenues for expensive long-distance services were used to cross-subsidize the provision of low-priced local telephone services. Besides this general pricing policy, the state regularly implemented specific strategies aimed at supporting welfare programs, subsidizing industrial development, aligning tariffs with anti-inflationary plans, and, more often than not, at creating political clientelism for electoral purposes. Since the 1970s inflationary pressure led to even sharper deterioration of tariffs in real terms. By 1989 tariffs had reached their lowest historical level, dropping 830 percent from the same month in the previous year (Figure 3.2).

The erosion of tariffs had an important effect on the economic performance of the company. In the early 1980s, for the first time since the state took over, ENTel showed a deficit, which grew steadily in the following years (Figure 3.3). But, it was not low tariffs alone that affected the profitability of

Figure 3.2

ENTel's Evolution of Tariffs (Jan. 1988–Nov. 1990)

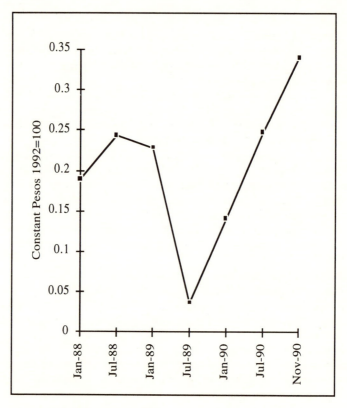

Source: ENTel and SIGEP

ENTel. Exchange rate fluctuations led to a rapid increase in the debt of the company, while at the same time taxes over telephone services grew steeply (Garutti 1990).

In recent years shrinking revenues affected, among other things, annual investments in network expansion. In earlier times the problem of poor network development was not based so much on low profits as on government's decisions over the allocation of ENTel's revenues. Since the income of the company was controlled by the Ministry of Economy, it often found its way into subsidizing other sectors under state control rather than being channeled back into the company for investment. The financial situation of the company was also affected during the 1980s by the foreign debt crisis, which led to a sharp drop in foreign loans to Argentina, harming in this way an important source of financing for the company.

Figure 3.3

ENTel Performance Indicators (1976–1990)

Year	Lines inst. (mill.)	Annual average growth	Teleph. density	pending requests (% total)	Compl. loc. call (%)[1]	Compl. LD call (%)[2]	Net profit after tax[3]
1976	1,808	3.67	6.8	37	na	na	2.36
1980	2,205	4.90	7.8	50	na	na	31.90
1984	2,601	2.00	8.6	50	47	25	-591.18
1985	2,699	3.76	8.8	22	44	22	-221.81
1986	2,843	5.33	9.2	20	45	18	-113.77
1987	2,917	4.39	9.3	12	46	na	-138.08
1988	3,264	11.89	10.3	11	47	23	-10.24
1989	3,437	5.30	10.7	9	49	29	-292.57
1990	3,500	1.83	10.8	12	49	30	na

Source: ENTel and SIGEP

1. The standard for local calls is 95 percent success of all attempted calls.
2. The standard for long distance calls is 85 percent success of all attempted calls.
3. Constant pesos 1992=100.

A poor and random investment plan led to progressive deterioration in the company's response to demand for new service and affected network upgrade and quality of services. Waiting lists for new services grew rapidly during the first years after nationalization and remained thereafter at a steady 40 percent of the population with telephone services.[10] The waiting period for a new telephone connection in some regions of the country was between twelve and fourteen years. The situation improved in the mid-1980s due to a massive expansion program called Megatel.[11] The plan was quite successful and brought, for the first time in many years, the level of unmet connection requests to 24 percent of all lines in service.

The politization of the business affected also the profile and performance of management and labor. On the management side, since ENTel was controlled by the state—that is, the essence of politics in a nation—politics routinely spilled over from both the executive and congress to the administration of the company.[12] Top management of ENTel was appointed by the Argentine president. It was inevitable that their policies, strategies, and fate were closely tied to those of the government. As governments came and went in a period of high political instability, so did the top management of the company and the plans and programs initiated by each administration. In the thirty years previous to the privatization of ENTel, twenty-eight different executive directors headed ENTel.[13]

Close dependency on the government not only destabilized ENTel's top management but also affected the decision-making process in the business. Due to the peculiar organization of the Argentine state apparatus, ENTel's management was highly constrained in its ability to shape operations in the company. Key decisions were made by a scattered group of top government officials that had little to do with the business of providing telecommunications services. The Ministry of Economy, for example, decided ENTel's budget but often also had a say on telephone tariffs, the Secretary of Industry decided the procurement of the company; the Ministry of Labor established salaries; and the Secretary of Communication designed general telecommunications policies, which were often in conflict with general public service policies decided by the Ministry of Services and Public Works.

Labor policies of the company were also bound to national politics. The size of the firm's workforce and the hiring and firing strategies were not based on criteria of efficiency or productivity but on larger national political and social issues such as the unemployment rate of the country and the search for political support by the party in government. The interest of politicians was reinforced by the presence of a strong national labor movement, in which ENTel's union played a very important role. During the 1980s ENTel's workforce oscillated around 47,000 employees, most of which were members of one of the four unions of the company.[14] The loose, politicized labor policies of ENTel were reflected in the fact that the company had by 1980 a ratio of fifty-one installed lines-per-employee and ENTel employees worked only thirty-five hours a week. This ratio placed ENTel below other similar companies in the region.

In the mid 1980s two factors converged to improve ENTel's labor productivity. On the one hand the company implemented the Megatel Plan, which drastically increased the number of lines per employee in a very short time. On the other hand, the government froze the hiring of public employees, a policy which also affected SOEs such as ENTel. By 1989 the employee per line ratio had—at least in statistical terms—improved, reaching a ratio of seventy-five lines per employee (Figure 3.4). In reality, this improvement in the numbers grossly distorted the underlying reality. While the number of employees in the company remained stable, the number of extra hours worked by each employee increased dramatically, representing, by 1989, an increase of working hours equivalent to a growth of 24 percent of ENTel's workforce.

In the year prior to privatization the performance of the national network deteriorated rapidly. In 1989, for example, network failure reached 46.6 percent per hundred access lines. This lead to the sour fact that only one out of two local calls nationwide went through, while only 20 to 30 percent of national long distance calls reached their final destination.[15] The number of customers out of service increased by 65 percent, and overcoming network faults took an average of fourteen days (Figure 3.3). The number of new lines installed in 1989 was 450 percent lower than the number installed in the previous year, while projects for new connection suffered delays that largely exceeded the historical averages.[16] On the financial side the debt of the company increased during 1990

Figure 3.4

Comparative Labor Productivity
in Selected Telecommunications Firms (1989)

Company	Access Lines (Mill.)	Employees	Lines per Employee
NTT (Japan)	54.30	261,600	207
France Telecom	26.98	156,451	173
TELMEX (Mex.)	5.27	49,518	105
British Telecom	25.01	245,700	102
Hongkong Telec.	2.02	19,850	101
CTC (Chile)	0.68	7,500	91
ENTel (Arg.)	3.44	46,040	75
STM (Malaysia)	1.59	28,041	56

Source: *Yearbook of Common Carrier Telecommunications Statistics and Baring Securities* 1991.

from US$1.29 billion (December 1989) to US$2.14 billion at the moment of privatization (December 1990).[17]

Despite all these deficiencies in the development and operation of the system, the number of lines in service reached 3.1 million by 1989, giving Argentina an average of ten lines per hundred inhabitants. Compared to other developing countries in the region, Argentina had a reasonable teledensity.[18] However, it was not so much the extension of the domestic network (i.e., teledensity) which ultimately led to the decision to privatize ENTel and liberalize the market during the last three governments. In the first attempt under the military regime that governed the country from 1976 to 1983, much of the initiative was grounded in a very strong ideology that favored private entrepreneurship and a free market economy. In the following democratic administrations—from 1983 to 1990—the drive for privatization and liberalization was based on sharp fiscal crisis and the perception that a private liberalized market will bring better, cheaper, and more diverse services enhancing economic performance and luring private capital into the domestic economy.

It was under these assumptions that the attempts to privatize ENTel were carried forward in the early, mid-, and late 1980s. While the two first initiatives (in the early and mid-1980s) failed, in 1990 the Menem administration was able to transfer the company to private owners. The following sections lay out the first two privatization experiences under the military regime of the 1970s and the democratic government of Alfonsín in the 1980s.

PRIVATIZATION UNDER AUTHORITARIANISM

Initial attempts to reduce the role of the state in the economy began with the neoliberal economic team in charge of the Ministry of Economy during the military regime governing Argentina from 1976 to 1983.

In the early 1970s the growing presence of leftist guerrillas and the subsequent social and political chaos began to threaten the stability and continuity of Argentine capitalist system. The military took power with an appealing anticommunist security discourse that unified the army in the defense of the nation. But the new regime lacked an economic and political vision of civil society that would complement its "national security" philosophy.

Army leaders invited a group of neoliberal economists and businessmen to join the regime to develop the new government's economic program.[19] While the military fought on the guerrilla front, a group of civilians initiated a neoliberal program of deep structural changes in the Argentine economy. One of the main goals was to dismantle traditional state interventionism, and strengthen the market as the main mechanism for the allocation of resources. State reform and privatization of SOEs were at the core of the program, and one of the key SOEs to be transferred to private owners was ENTel.

Aware that Argentine society was accustomed to the overwhelming presence of a welfare state, and fearing resistance to the privatization initiative, government officials implemented a massive and persuasive political campaign run under the slogan "shrink the state to enlarge the nation." But the campaign was misguided. Reformers did not realize that the resistance lay within the administration.

While the 1976 Argentine military regime has been generally characterized as closed vis-à-vis domestic pressures, the military administration suffered all the same from a lack of unity within the army and in the government that grew out of it. Despite the public image of a monolithic, insulated, hierarchically integrated administration, the Argentine military regime suffered from serious clashes and conflicts among various branches of the army. In contrast to the highly integrated and disciplined one-man Chilean regime—in which General Augusto Pinochet controlled almost every aspect of the government—every issue of political relevance the Argentine authoritarian government suffered from the lack of centralization of power and decision making in the head of the executive.

From the regime's inception all activities related to the control of the central government and the provinces were divided among the three military branches: air force, navy, and army. This feudal division of power assured future intergroup conflicts on issues of national interest. The reform of the state was probably the one in which pro-and-con struggles became most evident. Widespread conflicts among the various military groups, and between them and the civilian economic officials, blocked privatization efforts.[20]

In March 1980, in an effort to overcome widespread bureaucratic conflict, Law 22177 was approved. This law granted the executive the authority to proceed with partial or total privatization of SOEs. Under this legal framework the executive was empowered to issue decrees to sell the firms. A special article ruled that no legal procedure could suspend or interrupt privatization initiatives, and this is clear evidence of the difficulties that implementation of privatization posed for the government.

In response to the existing division of power, the executive left the implementation of privatization to the discretion of the ministries to which the SOEs were attached. In other words, each ministry had the power—based on the general framework provided by the executive—to set the basis for and conditions of a particular sale. Lack of centralized control at all stages of the process led to escalating bureaucratic infighting, resulting first in a slow down and then in a complete halt of most privatization projects.

Failing to Privatize ENTel

ENTel's privatization was no exception to this pattern. The initiative was subject to a long and controversial process with "stop-and-go" cycles that ended with the final collapse of the project. Reform of the telecom sector started in the late 1970s with the contracting out of some of ENTel's activities, such as line installation,[21] which occurred when ENTel's management—unwilling to hire new employees— argued that the volume of installation work to be carried out in the near future was too large to be handled by the existing ENTel work force.[22] A few month later, ENTel's chief was forced to publicly deny the existence of plans to privatize. In August 1981 telephone workers, disbelieving the official announcement, began to organize opposition to possible sale of the company. Rumors flew that the sale would imply a considerable dismissal of employees. In November the Under Secretary of Communication once more denied the existence of a plan to privatize the state-owned telephone company. Then, in February 1982, the often-denied plans were officially announced.

The announcement revealed that the telecom sector would be largely restructured and the company partially divested from government ownership. ENTel would remain in control of international services and interurban switches, while local and long-distance services would be divested into five regional operating companies (ROCs). ENTel would remain as the head of a holding company integrated by the five new private firms. The new companies would be integrated by local equipment providers, users, and other private investors.[23] Under the new scheme tariffs would be set freely by the new owners with a minimum of control by the government to avoid price abuses. The potential future owners of ENTel supported the project, but at the same time requested a protected market and a guaranteed rate of return.

Powerful nationalist groups within the army impeded the implementation. Some military groups feared that the proposed neoliberal program would dismantle the industrial capability of the nation, especially in strategic sectors that could jeopardize national security. The sale of ENTel was an extremely sensitive issue because the military had a strong presence and control of the telecommunications sector since the 1940s. Security issues, national industrial policy, and the fact that the military had ruled the nation for most of the time since the 1930s progressively "militarized" the national telecommunications system. This was reflected in the fact that the five administrative regions into which ENTel was divided was nothing else than the partitioning of the company's control among the five military regions in which the country was divided for security reasons.

At the time of the announcement, every political and economic event in the country was viewed in light of the antiguerrilla war to which the military was highly committed. In this regard, some military leaders believed that the sale of SOEs would weaken the traditional right-wing union leadership, thus fostering the resurgence of communism among the working class (Canitrot 1988). These leaders were gravely concerned with the possibility of massive layoffs, and the potential resurgence of social disorder and politicization.[24] Anything that would weaken traditional conservative powers or generate social unrest was viewed as an undesirable political move. In their view, privatization of major public utilities and industrial SOEs was an "irresponsible" project.

Furthermore, the common argument that Argentina's state had overextended was, in comparative terms, unrealistic. The Argentine public sector is smaller and more restricted in its functions than those in many other industrialized and developing nations.[25] Second, inconsistencies of the regime in regard to the state's role in the economy were obvious and public. While some government officials advocated shrinking the state's economic role, others were working to expand its presence by turning the public sector into the recipient of the largest foreign loans that Argentina had ever received.[26]

These contextual elements, the opposition's charismatic leadership among the lower strata of the army, and interference from private economic groups exacerbated the already existing conflicts among various government coalitions. Ultimately these factors led to a paralysis of privatization.

During 1982 the severe economic crisis and revival of social unrest pushed the regime to search for political alternatives to keep the population under control. The invasion of the Malvinas islands (Falklands for Anglo-Saxon countries) was, from a military perspective, the best strategy to regain popular support and block opposition. The initially successful maneuver lasted only three months. At the end of June 1982, the defeat of the Argentine army exposed the irreversible decay of the military regime. To avoid social unrest, the government announced immediately after the surrender that it would legalize political activities and call for elections in the near future.[27]

In August 1982, only two months after the end of the war a new general took over ENTel and announced that all plans for its privatization were canceled. He supported a policy that ENTel must play a central role in the generation of new jobs, in the consolidation of national industry, and in the economic and social integration of the nation. "Important decisions that would affect the structure of the company would have to be studied more in detail, at the right time," he concluded.[28] When a new democratic government came into power at the end of 1983, the state was not only virtually intact, but it had further expanded its role in the economy and in Argentine society overall (Boneo 1985).

PRIVATIZATION UNDER DEMOCRACY

On December 10, 1983, a democratic government—headed the Radical party leader Raúl R. Alfonsín—began a new period of constitutional rule. In its effort to differentiate itself from the previous, antipopulist government, the new ruling party started to play a two-sided policy game. On the one hand, following its electoral campaign discourse, preexisting neoliberal policies were swept away, giving rise to a new set of state-interventionist welfare policies. On the other hand, overwhelming external debt, fiscal crisis, and spiraling inflation forced the government into progressive "rationalization" and constriction of the state expansion.

The Argentine public sector faced serious account imbalances at the outset of the 1980s. An increase in the number of pensioners,[29] a reduction prices with a subsequent reduction of agricultural rents, massive tax evasion (and serious loopholes in the tax system), growing inflation, and overwhelming foreign debt were all factors in the public sector financial crisis (Machinea 1990, 95) In this deteriorating fiscal context, government officials started to search for structural reforms that would enable permanent reduction of public expenditures and an expansion of revenues.

But the fact that the popular vote brought a Radical administration to power made it necessary to reject authoritarian rule and support an open, democratic, participatory polity. Alfonsín was outspoken on this and placed strong constraints on any future unilateral, antipopulist government action. As a democratic-transition government, the Alfonsín administration was charged with the task of achieving political stability and taming friction among powerful and highly politicized interest groups.

In the wake of retreating authoritarian regimes, the shape of the new democratic political order is often undetermined (Torre 1992, 10). In this undefined political environment, interest group coalitions battle to reshape the patterns of the political system and their position within it. The fluid and unstable evolution of political relations during this early pluralist and participatory period is in blatant contradiction with the vertically integrated and controlled policy processes required to implement harsh economic reforms. Such reforms are usually achieved through coercion or the emergence of social and political agreement among key political actors. However, Alfonsín was unable to achieve or implement either. The dynamics of transitional politics affected the ability of the government to introduce any significant reform in the state apparatus, and, in particular, to privatize core SOEs such as ENTel.

Besides the political constraints posed by the historical mandate of maintaining an open, participatory polity, the Radical government suffered—as the military had—from the lack of internal unity and coherence. Ideological opposition to state dismantling was rooted in Keynesian economics, import-substitution industrialization strategy, and welfare politics. For the Radicals—with their political philosophy inspired by European social democracy—the notion of shrinking the state's role in the economy was something that threatened the very roots of the party. This, in turn, affected the commitment of the government to the reform initiatives. It was not until late 1987 that the economic team realized the seriousness of the fiscal crisis and the need for profound public sector reforms. And, even then, the initiative lacked the strong presidential support that was required to overcome opposition to the project.

Moreover, because Alfonsín won the election with dissident Peronist and independent votes and not with the sole support of the Radical voters,[30] there was considerable fear that he would lose popular support if the electoral campaign platform that advocated interventionist welfare policies were to be abandoned.

The irony of the Alfonsín administration is that the Radicals lost support nevertheless. This occurred not because they implemented state reform but, instead, because they did not enforce public sector restructuring that would help to overcome Argentina's economic crisis. By late 1987, when the government decided to move forward with state restructuring, its time had past. National elections for governors and deputies showed a significant loss of popular support for the party. Henceforth their policies would be challenged and resisted.

Early State Reform

In early 1984, shortly after coming into power, Alfonsín created Commission 414, an ad hoc government body charged with pursuing the privatization of selected SOEs. The commission formally comprised of representatives from various ministries. However, on an everyday basis it functioned with only eight people and responded directly to the president. Compared to later privatization attempts during the Alfonsín administration, the commission was fairly successful in its mission and sold three SOEs.[31]

Several factors, absent later in the administration, seem to explain this success. First, the privatized firms were fairly small compared to large firms such as ENTel. Second, all were initially private businesses that the government had taken over due to bankruptcies mostly during the military regime. Third, none were public utilities involving services affecting the population at large. Fourth, possible opposition forces were too involved in sensitive political issues related to the military regime—such as human rights—to pay any attention to the privatization of small business. Finally, and specifically related to the central arguments of this chapter, the commission was an executive body, consisting of a few select members, who operated directly under the control of the president. Although the commission was modestly successful in its early stages, it soon faced trouble as it moved to sell larger and politically more controversial SOEs.

In search of a broad social coalition to support his reform goals, and with the aim of blocking opposition groups within his party and the government, Alfonsín created, in July 1985, the Ministry of Growth Promotion, under the leadership of Manuel Tanoira—a businessman not affiliated with the Radical party.[32] Tanoira called for an expansion of private participation in traditional public utilities, such as communication, transportation and general infrastructure.[33] Lacking power and autonomy to carry out his projects, Tanoira resigned after a year-and-a-half without having privatized a single SOE. He complained that intragovernment conflicts and the lack of support from SOEs managers made any changes in the public sector impossible.[34]

While struggling to discipline civil servants and government officials,[35] Alfonsín created the Secretary for the Control of Public Enterprises in December 1985.[36] A year later, with poor results in hand, he replaced it with another agency—the Department of Public Works (Directorio de Empresas Públicas— DEP), operating under the jurisdiction of the Ministry of Public Works and Services. The new agency performed as poorly as its predecessor.

By 1986 the economic team had begun to realize that Argentina's fiscal problems were deeper and more structural in nature than they had originally thought. Up until then, the deficit was managed and reduced through steep cuts in public investments.[37] But this produced a deterioration in the social and economic infrastructure that could not continue.[38] Therefore, state reform plans shifted from the reprivatization of small business to target major public utilities and industrial SOEs. Due to the magnitude and political relevance of this new stage in state reform efforts, conflict moved from the inner circles of the governing elite to the public realm, attracting the involvement of different political forces and interest-group coalitions.

Failing Once More to Privatize ENTel

The first official announcement about the possible privatization of ENTel reached the press in mid-1985.[39] The government argued that the public sector was in no condition to respond to the communications needs of a modernized society; the private sector must provide the capital and the expertise needed. The initiative met the immediate opposition of the telephone workers union, who based their position on issues of national sovereignty. The elaborate project had as its first step the privatization of activities related to the installation of new lines—a task that had been partially subcontracted since 1979. The privatized services would be controlled by a consortium comprising construction companies, equipment suppliers, and private banks. In this way planning contracts, construction, and financing of network expansion would be under the management of one economic conglomerate. The goal was to double the number of lines in a nonspecified period of time. The total privatization of ENTel would follow (Tanoira 1988, 48).

However, intragovernment conflicts led to the collapse of the project before it ever got underway. The Secretary of Communication, an advocate of state control and provision of telecom services, managed to get the president's approval for an alternative project—Megatel—and that displaced the privatization initiative.

In mid-1987 the idea of privatizing the company revived.[40] Ministerial reshuffling in October brought renewed energy to plans for the sale of the ENTel. Rodolfo Terragno was appointed minister of Public Works and Services. He proposed the partial privatization of ENTel as a solution to its chronic deficiencies. The new company would be a joint venture with the Spanish telephone company, Telefónica de España. The Argentine state would keep 60 percent of the shares, while Telefónica would control the other 40 percent and manage operations. The arrangement would spawn a new company, a private firm, operating under the commercial name of Telefónica de Argentina. Telefónica would pay approximately US$750 million for its share in ENTel,[41] and in exchange it required that all telecommunication services in Argentina—with the exception of unprofitable services such as telegraphy and those in remote rural areas—remain a monopoly under the control of the new Telefónica Argentina.

But the Radical's initiative came at a bad time politically. Deterioration of salaries, shrinking employment opportunities, and the interminable economic crisis, which expanded during the first four years the Alfonsín administration, ignited social discontent. In 1987 the population punished the government's inability to cope with economic decay by voting for governors and deputies from outside the Radical party.

When ENTel's privatization was officially announced, the Peronist party, the unions, ENTel managers, and telecom equipment suppliers formed an opposition front that successfully blocked the upcoming sale. The effectiveness of this coalition of interest groups—which usually found themselves in conflict—highlights the relevance of domestic coalitions to the policy-making process, even in LDCs where states tend to overwhelm the political initiatives of civil society. However, as privatization during the Menem administration ultimately showed, the impact of interest groups in policy making is tied to the political and economic conditions of the country at the moment the policy is being developed. During the Alfonsín administration the circumstances surrounding democratic transition opened the state to entry of multiple political actors, leading to disruption and the blocking policy initiatives. This was clearly evident in the government's efforts to transfer ENTel to the private sector.

Unions in Argentina are well known for their political power and the extensive role they play in the nation's political life. During the Alfonsín years, the activism of unions deepened due to their conflictive relationship with the Radical government.[42] Beginning in 1984 the Confederación General del Trabajo (CGT) organized thirteen national strikes, and supported thousands of minor strikes and protests by affiliated unions.

Privatization announcements were met with massive opposition from public sector employees, who accounted for almost 30 percent of Argentina's employed population. Out of almost four million unionized workers, 45 percent were public sector employees (Palomino 1988). Resistance was possible due to this high level of political organization of state employees.

Telephone workers—organized under the Federación de Obreros y Empleados Telefónicos de la República Argentina (FOETRA) with CGT support—began an active public campaign to disrupt the privatization project. The campaign followed well-known patterns of union opposition in Argentina. It started with fliers and street protests, was followed by recurrent two-hour work suspensions during several days, reached momentum with a one-day national strike, and ended in physical aggression against Minister Rodolfo Terragno, the official responsible for the project.

But the union was not alone in its campaign against ENTel's privatization. National equipment manufactures and the Peronist party worked together to kill the official initiative. There were two different groups of equipment suppliers, each of them with a slightly different stake in the project, but both ultimately opposed to the sale of the SOTE. One comprised the dominant European and Japanese multinationals. Despite enough commercial and industrial strength to survive in a privatized telecom market, these companies refused to lose their secured, monopsonic market in which ENTel generally paid much higher prices than would have been possible in a competitive market. The other group consisted of a variety of small local firms that had forcefully gained and consolidated a small share of the Argentine market and who feared their demise in the face of widespread competition.

Along with equipment suppliers, the Peronist party opposed the project for both explicit and implicit reasons. The explicit reasons were based on the official position of the party; the implicit ones were those underlying political strategies in a preelectoral period. In particular the Peronists rejected the project because the government had excluded Congress, had arbitrarily picked a partner for ENTel without opening the process to public bidding, and had discretionarily arranged the conditions of the sale.

Under the leadership of Senator Eduardo Menem (brother of the future president, Carlos Menem), the Peronists rejected as a matter of principle any project that implied a reduction of the role of the state in Argentine society. Senator Menem opposed ENTel's privatization arguing that, "if every time that a public enterprise is in decline, instead of trying to make it work right, we give it away or sell it, we will soon remain with almost no enterprises owned by the state and the country" (Arango de Maglio 1990, 48).

This rhetoric veiled the implicit reasons the Peronists were unwilling to support the privatization of the national telephone company. With elections upcoming, the Peronists, who had rejected automatically any government initiative throughout the period, deepened their oppositional stance to detach themselves from the deteriorating image of the Radicals and to simultaneously avoid any possible improvement of the government's image in the months prior to the election.[43] Moreover, dismantling public-sector enterprises would also imply a weakening of unions, a traditional pillar of the Peronist party. A smaller work force—due to state restructuring—would mean fewer workers to organize, and the Peronists were unwilling to upset union loyalty on the threshold of a national election (Baur 1991, 18).

Finally, Peronist leaders were increasingly aware that privatization was gaining wide popular support. With a possible successful presidential election only a few months away, it would have been a foolish political mistake to hand the opposition a political victory of the magnitude that the privatization of ENTel would entail.

ENTel's privatization bill was sent to Congress for its approval in January 1988. But the Peronists had won the majority of seats in both the Chamber of Deputies and the Senate in the elections of October 1987. With the Peronists controlling Congress, the bill was set aside and never considered by the legislative body.[44]

Besides the direct opposition of labor, equipment suppliers, and the Peronist party, the project also failed due to deficiencies within the government. The lack of a strong presidential commitment, for example, weakened the support of some sectors of domestic capital, and enhanced the strength of opposition forces. The meager strength of the administration was finally undermined by the resistance of some cadres of the Radical party and ENTel administrators who refused to give up years of benefits and privileges granted by the state.

The Radicals, nevertheless, were able to implement a reform that slightly transformed the periphery of the Argentine telecom market. In November 1987, the president signed a decree calling for public bids to install and operate cellular telephone services in Buenos Aires proper. Four consortiums made up of banks and foreign telephone companies bid for the concession.[45] In July of 1988 it was granted to Compañia de Radiocomunicaciones Moviles S.A. (Movicom).[46]

Why did the government succeed in this partial opening of some segments of the Argentine telecom market while failing to completely privatize ENTel? There are several factors that contributed to this seemingly contradictory outcome.

First, liberalizing cellular telephony did not require that Congress pass a law, and, therefore, Peronist party opposition was avoided with the issuance of a presidential decree.[47] Furthermore, internal Radical party politics had clearly tilted by 1988 in favor of those sectors pushing for a retreat of the state in the area of provision of emerging new services (such as cellular telephony and data communication). Clear signals from top economic officials in favor of deeper state restructuring reinforced the ascendance of reformers within the governing party.

Second, ENTel employees and managers did not oppose the more modest project in the way they resisted ENTel's sale. The concession of band frequency to provide cellular telephony was not as relevant and politically meaningful as the overall privatization of the national common carrier. ENTel workers had concentrated all their human and political efforts to stop the possible sale of the company, but cellular telephony was viewed as a sophisticated service for wealthy users, having only a marginal effect on ENTel's market. Moreover, ENTel had no solid arguments to oppose the project since the company was unable to provide such services in the near future.

Finally, the only serious opposition to this liberalization project would have come from Telefónica de España, which demanded a closed market for all services in exchange for their participation in the would-be-privatized ENTel.[48] However, the Spanish firm reached the scene of the deal too late. By the time Telefónica started negotiations with the Ministry of Public Works and Services, Alfonsín had already signed a decree calling for bids to win the cellular telephony concession. Inability to reverse this was acknowledged by Telefónica, since it participated in the bidding process along with the other three groups seeking the concession.[49]

CONCLUSION

Telecommunications services in Argentina emerged in the late 1870s as a consequence of local private initiatives. In the initial competitive and unregulated environment, it soon came under the control of large foreign telecom firms. Despite the lack of data for that period, there are historical events—such as the creation of a users' cooperative due to bad services and high prices—that indicates that private ownership during those early days did not perform much better than its successor, the state-owned ENTel.

In 1946 the state took over Argentina's telecom operations and there began a period characterized not so much by the slow growth of services but rather by its poor quality. ENTel's mediocre performance during the 1960s and 1970s turned even worse during the 1980s. The debt-ridden fiscal and economic crisis of that decade in convergence with bad managerial practices, high inflation, lack of investments, and low labor productivity further eroded the performance of the company. After decades of profitable business the company started to show loses, its debt grew, and the overall quality of services dropped. The length of time for repair of equipment and line failure increased, the number of successful calls dropped, and the time for new service installation remained at its historically high levels.

During the 1980s three different administrations tried to transfer the company to the private sector. The first attempt—carried out in the early 1980s by the military regime that governed the country from 1976 to 1983—failed to achieve its goal. The second attempt by the Alfonsín administration in 1987 met the same fate. The lessons learned from the state-reform initiatives of the military and the Alfonsín administrations relate in important ways to the theoretical issues discussed in this study.

First, they highlight the limits and possibilities offered by an approach that relies on ideas as a key independent variable. During the military regime neoliberal ideology that guided economic policy played a central role in bringing state reform onto the policy agenda. It is also true that Keynesianism and national security considerations emerged as the counteracting notions to the reform ideology. Although this war of ideas was at the center of state-reform dynamics informed and gave coherence to the position of different groups, in the end it was the inability of those in favor of reform to overcome intragovernment opposition that led to the failure of the program. During the Alfonsín administration, ideas also played an important role. Party and state officials who espoused state expansion and interventionism in the economy were crucial in blocking early reform efforts.

Second, they point to the importance of cohesion among governing elites, or, in the absence of the former, the concentration of power in the head of the executive. During the military administration, lack of cohesion among top state officials, and the absence of centralized power in the hands of the president turned bureaucratic politics into a major impediment to the implementation of state reform. A similar situation existed during the Alfonsín government, when the president suffered from a decentralized power structure and a nonresponsive bureaucracy. Both administrations stand in sharp contrast with Menem's tight control over ministries and lower-level agencies.

Third, in the case of the Alfonsín government, privatization failure shows that, in transitional democracies, domestic interest group coalitions and electoral politics tend to play a crucial role in the policy process. In this case, opposition from the unions, SOE managers, the local telecom industry, and congressional opposition together were able to block ENTel's privatization project in congress until the election of the new administration. Furthermore, the inability of the government to overcome congressional opposition emphasizes the importance for the governing party of controlling a majority of seats in both the Chamber of Deputies and the Senate. The deadly attacks on the project by the unions, equipment suppliers, Peronists, and Congress indicated that privatization in Argentina would have to be carried out in a rush and by avoiding most standard legislative mechanisms. The Menem administration was able to achieve that due to the economic and political conditions that the new government faced during its first year in power.

NOTES

1. As Di Tella (1970, 108) stated "each group has just enough power to veto the projects originated by the others, but none can muster the strength to run the country as it would like." Other scholars have emphasized the fact that the political divisions and conflicts that permeate Argentine society are largely the reflection of rivalries and interpersonal conflicts among the elite rather than disagreements at the base of the society (Smith 1974).

2. As the French scholar, Alain Touraine, has argued, "Argentina never had a state. It had a 'distributist' system and a highly developed political system. But the professionalism of the public administration is very poor. Argentina and Colombia are the two countries in Latin America that have no idea of what the state is." *Clarin*, 22 April 1990, 12, cited in Arango de Maglio 1990, 53.

3. Société du Pantéléphone and the River Plate Telephone Company had previously formed a joint venture in 1882.

4. By the mid 1920s SCT controlled almost 35 percent of the market.

5. Founded in 1920 by the Behn brothers, the new company quickly expanded throughout Latin America (and the world) merging and acquiring telephone companies in Argentina, Mexico, Brazil, Chile, and Uruguay. By 1929 the North American firm controlled two-thirds of the telephones and half of the cables in Latin America. See Headrick 1991, Sobel 1982, and Rosenberg 1982.

6. San Juan, Mendoza, Salta, Tucumán, Santiago del Estero, and Entre Ríos.

7. When the government was overthrown in 1955, Perón was about to overtake CAT, the only remaining private company.

8. At certain periods the state attempted with no success to develop a local telecommunications equipment industry.

9. This became evident after privatization when the same equipment suppliers offered the same products to the new owners for half the price that ENTel used to pay.

10. While in 1941 there were 8,500 unmet requests (2.2 percent of all connected lines), in 1946 requests pending connection climbed to 135,800 (29

percent of all connected lines). It is estimated that by 1981 the number of pending connections had reached to 901,600 (45.3 percent of all connected lines). It is hard to tell if the sharp rise of unmet requests after the mid-1940s was due to the fact that the company was inefficient in responding to the demand (which in some ways is accurate regardless of other variables), or if demand boomed compared to previous periods—due to low costs based on state subsidies—pressing the state for a level of response it was not prepared to take. For data on waiting lists, see Garutti 1990, 3.

11. The new plan was based on a saving mechanism by which future customers contributed to the expansion of the network by paying in advance monthly allocations of the connection fee.

12. On management of state-owned enterprises see, for example, Aharoni 1986.

13. Twelve different presidents headed the the country during that period.

14. ENTel's labor was organized in four different unions: FOETRA (Federación de Obreros y Empleados de la República Argentina), FOPSTA (Federación de Organización de Personal de Supervisión Telefónicos Argentinos), UPJ (Unión de Personal Jerárquico), and CPU (Centro de Profesionales Universitarios). These unions held considerable power over the management of the company. For example, they had a say on procurement decision making of the company, they bargained salaries for all employees, and they interfered in the allocation and distribution of employees within the firm.

15. The international standard for acceptable local service is 95 percent success for all attempted calls, while the standard for long-distance calls is 85 percent. Other Latin American countries had a much better performance rate. Chile had a completion rate of 97 percent for local calls and 93 percent long-distance calls, while Mexico had 92 percent for local calls and 90 percent for long-distance calls.

16. The deterioration of the network and its performance, resulted, partially, from the lack of financial resources and poor management of the business. But it also was a consequence of the shrinking ratio of mantainance workers vis-à-vis administrative staff. While the labor force for maintenance was reduced by more than 40 percent throughout the 1980s, the number of administrative and executive positions increased by 35 percent.

17. SIGEP 1990. It has been argued that the company's deteriorating performance resulted from a conscious decision of the government, which tried to prove to the public that ENTel needed a radical change—like privatization. Others argued that because ENTel's managers were focused on privatization negotiations, little or no attention was given to everyday operations. The performance of the company may also have declined because most workers and second-level managers opposed privatization and therefore did not cooperate with the newly appointed management.

18. It almost doubled the average for Latin America, which in 1990 was 6.7 lines per hundred inhabitants.

19. The group, led by Martinez de Hoz was composed of professionals from the upper class who hled strong ideological biases in favor of free market policies and private-sector involvement in the economy.

20. For privatization during the military period, see Fontana 1985. For political risks created by bureaucratic infighting, see Cowan 1990.

21. This process came to be known as "peripheral privatization." See "La Privatización de Obras Telefónicas," *Clarin*, 2 June 1980, 2.

22. These companies were C.S.C. S.A., Soinco S.A., Iecsa S.A., Sideco S.A., J. Sueiro y Cia., Teyma SAICFA, Natelco-Aion, CSEAT Retsa, and Gardebled Hnos.

23. The potential new owners were mainly equipment providers of ENTel: Siemens, NEC, Perez Companc, Ericsson, and the ITT-Bridas group.

24. This concern was reflected in the fact that privatization legislation required compensation for affected employees. If the privatized SOE or the new owners could not provide the necessary funds, the state would supply a special compensation (Vuylsteke 1988).

25. The number of public employees in Argentina represents 5.88 percent of the total population of the country, a figure that is significantly lower than the 10.97 percent registered in Australia, the 8.07 percent of the United States, and the 7.80 percent in the Canadian public sector. Compared to the total working population of the country, the Argentine public sector has a similar percentage of employees in state-run entities (22.72 percent) as do developed countries (23.42 percent), but it is well below the average of other developing countries (55.92 percent). See Oszlak 1990, 7.

26. The Argentine state, along with Mexico, Brazil, and Venezuela, borrowed more than 46.4 percent of all international commercial bank credits worldwide between January 1976 and December 1979. Eighty to ninety percent of those loans were to the public sector, in particular public enterprises, while the rest were guaranteed by the state. There is an large literature on the debt in Latin America. See, for example, Frieden 1981, Kuczynski 1988, and Stallings and Kaufman 1989.

27. Democratic elections were called for October 1983.

28. "Quedaría en Suspenso la Privatización de ENTel," *Clarin*, 6 August 1982.

29. The number of pensioners grew at an annual rate of 7.4 percent between 1950 and 1987.

30. It has been estimated that the votes from affiliates and supporters of the party amounted to approximately 26 percent of the electorate (Machinea 1990, 127).

31. The privatized companies were SIAM, Opalinas Urlingam, and Sol Jet.

32. Decree 1356, 24 July 1985.

33. One of the main tasks of the new Ministry of Growth Promotion was the elaboration of a privatization law to replace Law 22177, established during the military regime.

34. Whenever Tanoira proposed the privatization of a state business, the initiative was coopted and incorporated to the plans of the Secretariat that would be affected by the measure. Such was the case of Megatel and Privatel-Finantel in the telecommunications sector. For more details on this period, see Arango de Maglio 1990 and González Fraga 1991.

35. Efforts to block state reform were so intense that the Ministry of Economy had to intervene to reverse decisions taken by SOEs' managers, which disrupted not only reform plans but also jeopardized national economic plans.

36. Decree 2452, 26 December 1985.

37. During the Radical administration, public investments were 33 percent lower than their level during the second half of the 1970s.

38. Statement by government economist José Luis Machinea (1990, 96).

39. "Privatización de ENTel?" *Clarin*, 28 June 1985.

40. "Proponen que se Privatize la Mayor Parte de ENTel," *Clarin*, 13 June 1987, 16.

41. The Spanish common carrier planned to form a consortium with Citibank and Chase Manhattan Bank, which together would provide the capital for the venture.

42. Even before coming to power, Alfonsín had damaged his relationship with the unions by denouncing an alliance between the military and union leaders to control the political life of the country. Once in power, one of his first initiatives was a bill to restructure and "democratize" union organizations. Its central aim was to reduce the power of union leaders. It was defeated in the Senate by an alliance of the Peronist majority and small provincial parties.

43. Innumerable examples of this open hostility of the Peronists to government initiatives can be seen in issues ranging from the democratization of the unions, the debt negotiations, the peace treaty with Chile, government-military relations, and, of course, state reform and structural adjustment programs.

44. Success of Congress in defeating the project was enhanced by Minister Terragno's naiveté in believing he could carry out the privatization of a major public utility like ENTel in a "cautious and gradual" fashion and still get Congressional approval for the project. See Terragno 1989.

45. Compañia de Radiocomunicaciones Moviles S.A. was composed of Bell South who provided the most capital and the managerial expertise, Motorola who provided the hardware, Citicorp, BGH, and Socmalecsa who participated in various ways in the group. The other consortiums that applied for the concession were Sade-US West S.A., Movitel Argentina, and Telefonía Celular.

46. Movicom was, until 1993, the only cellular operator in the country.

47. Decree 1757/87.

48. This is an interesting precedent of the investors-government bargaining dynamic that would hinder the intended liberalization of the local telecom market during the Menem administration.

49. Movitel S.A., one of the bidding consortiums was composed of Telefónica de España and Ericcson.

4

Argentina 1989–1991: Full Privatization, Limited Liberalization

The first part of this chapter examines ENTel's privatization during the Menem administration. It pays special attention to political and economic conditions during the transition from Alfonsín to Menem and to the means by which these historical factors affected privatization politics. The government's renewed attempt to sell Empresa Nacional de Telecomunicaciones (ENTel) and restructure the Argentine telecom sector is placed in context by examining the support and resistance to the project as well as the economic and political factors that limited and enhanced the power of each group. The impact of the variables highlighted in this work—state autonomy and centralization of power in the state apparatus—are tested throughout the historical account of the process.

The second part of the chapter lays out the politics of telecom liberalization in Argentina. This section critiques the generalizability of a political approach to the whole reform process, and it highlights the fact that liberalization of the telecom market is better explained by economic factors. I argue that liberalization, when attempted with privatization, is affected more by the attractiveness of the domestic telecom market to private investors than by political factors such as the autonomy of the state and the cohesiveness of the government. Lucrative telecom markets give governments leverage to impose liberalization goals, while weak and risky markets push governments to relinquish liberalization in order to lure the capital required to achieve privatization of the state-owned telecommunications enterprise (SOTE). Argentina falls into this second category.

The chapter concludes by comparing differences and similarities in ENTel's privatization and the liberalization of the Argentine telecom sector during the Menem administration to the two previous reform attempts.

THE ECONOMIC AND POLITICAL CONTEXT

The military regime and the Alfonsín administration's failures to privatize highlight the political difficulty of selling ENTel. Prerequisites for the project's success were the insulation of high-level state officials and the weakening of opposition forces. Both these goals were achieved in the early phases of the Menem administration.

Menem's success in achieving autonomy from opposition groups and consolidating his power was greatly enhanced by Argentina's political and economic situation. The economic and fiscal crisis of the 1980s had halted the emergence of strong and competing social demands. Economic constraints dismantled traditional political coalitions, discouraged political participation, and led to a progressive demobilization of social forces. Throughout the Alfonsín years political participation disintegrated from the massive, well-organized rallies of early 1982—which protested the military regime, the foreign debt, military rebellions, and the state policies—to inarticulate attacks by a starving population on supermarkets in 1989.

By the end of the decade the deepening economic crisis further damaged the legitimacy of the already discredited welfare-state policies, shifting popular opinion in favor of reform initiatives. Furthermore, Menem's solid commitment to an overarching privatization and liberalization program gained the support of large sectors of the local and international business community.

The Argentine economic collapse of the 1980s reached its peak in 1989, only months before Menem came to power. Throughout the 1980s the percentage of gross national income per capita fell by 15.9 percent, resulting in a growth in poverty of 68.6 percent. Then, in 1989, the country was confronted with its worst-ever hyperinflation, deepening fiscal crisis, negative economic growth, and prospects of social disruption (North-South Center 1993, 2). Prices rose by 76 percent in May, 175 percent in June, and reached an unprecedented 197 percent in July—the month in which Menem came to power—bringing the total inflation of that year to 4,923 percent (Figure 4.1). Real wages for industrial workers dropped as much as 43 percent compared to the same period in the previous year. In the second quarter of 1989, the gross domestic product (GDP) fell by 9.5 percent, while the public sector—with 305 SOEs on its payroll—was running a deficit of an estimated 10 percent of GDP. In May the economic situation set off riots. The populace violently attacked supermarkets to steal food. By June Argentina's political situation was so unmanageable that it led to an exceptional political event in Argentine history: the resignation of Alfonsín five months before the completion of his presidential term. The last days of the Alfonsín administration disrupted "politics-as-usual" and its legacy granted the incoming administration special economic and political space to carry out a "crisis-driven" reform (Grindle and Thomas 1991).

Figure 4.1

Argentine Annual Inflation 1989

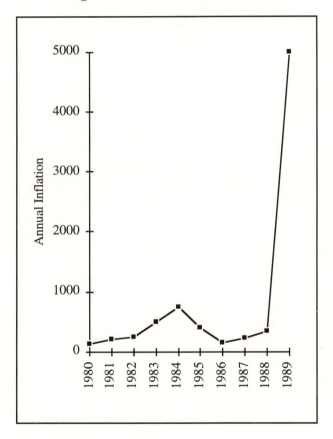

As noted, economic hardship calls for a realignment of traditional political and economic arrangements, making the system of political relations and compromises more fluid (Haggard 1990, 44, and Gourevitch 1990, 22). In the period in which old loyalties crumble while new ones are not yet consolidated, governments generally gain relative autonomy from domestic interest groups, thus achieving a considerable degree of political insulation for the articulation and implementation of new economic and political programs. In the case of Argentina, the unprecedented economic crisis of 1989 dismantled sectors traditionally involved in backlash politics, insulated the government's policy making, and concentrated the political process in the hands of the president.

How do countries find adequate political balance to govern such a crisis and overcome impending social chaos? Torre argues that countries that suffered hyperinflation and successfully implemented economic reforms avoiding at the same time the chance of social chaos, did so "by means of a strong and unilateral presidential initiative" (Torre 1992, 11). As Menem forcefully argued two years into his administration, "there was the need for strong political leadership."[1]

Although the crisis gave Menem the political leverage to overcome domestic opposition, it also eroded confidence of private investors in Argentina's future. As literature on investment strategies highlights, economic and political stability of the host nation is a critical variable for attracting private investments. Since Argentina did not fulfill either requirement in 1989, the incoming administration had to give up some of its initiatives in order to attract private capital for its massive privatization program.

ENTEL'S PRIVATIZATION: THE THIRD ATTEMPT

In his bid for the presidency in 1989, Menem campaigned along the lines of traditional Peronist political philosophy, which placed the state at the center of the social, political, and economic life of the nation.[2] Following such rationale, Menem argued that "the state has to be put in order, moralized, and made efficient, but—he warned—beware of those who say that the state is monstrous and pretend to shrink it, to give away the nation." To dispel any doubts about his commitment to Peronist values he asserted that, "we [the Peronists] will not privatize the main state enterprises, we will make them efficient."[3]

But Argentina in those days was undergoing one of the most severe economic crises in its recent history, and the fiscal crisis was at the heart of the matter. Despite all electoral rhetoric, the new president who took power in July 1989, immediately and drastically recanted his pre-electoral promises and began to implement a sweeping privatization program that would turn Argentina in the following two years into the country with the largest number of privatized companies in the world.[4] This plan was mostly grounded in long-standing arguments that the inefficiency of the state was based on its large size.[5]

However, implementing with Peronist political appointees a policy that in many ways ran opposite to the Peronist social and political philosophy did not seem feasible. Besides, the new administration had to avoid the friction with the dominant economic groups that had created so many problems for the previous administration. The most practical solution to this rather complicated policy shift was the one that Menem followed: insulate key players from his own party and appoint powerful local economic players to key political positions. In this way, a top executive of the country's largest multinational corporation was appointed as Minister of Economy—the most crucial political position after the presidency—while other members of the national business community were assigned to other key positions in the cabinet.

Following a similar strategy, María Julia Alsogaray, a proactive member of the Unión de Centro Democrático party (UCD)—a party of free marketers, traditionally opposed to welfare Peronist policies—was appointed as *interventora* of ENTel.[6]   A group of politician and local professionals, supported by international consultants, were appointed to carry on the privatization of ENTel.[7] There was some initial bureaucratic struggle to get control of the process with the Minister of Services and Public Works leading the opposing faction.[8] But soon the scramble was over and the small privatization team headed by ENTel's *interventora* became the main actors in the sales process.[9]

This ad hoc privatization team rapidly assembled a plan for the sale of ENTel that emphasized the need to demonopolize, liberalize, and deregulate the sector to make it more efficient. To achieve the demonopolization goal ENTel would have to be divided into several regional operating companies.[10] Controlling stock in the companies (60 percent) would be sold to foreign and local private investors and telephone operators, while the remaining 40 percent would be divided among ENTel workers (10 percent), local telephone cooperatives (5 percent), and the national and international stock market (25 percent). Liberalization would be reached through opening the market on both value-added and basic services.[11] Under the initial scheme basic services were to be licenses in exclusivity for the first five years, but open to competition thereafter.

According to official assessments privatization goals could not be achieved relying only on domestic financial and technical resources. It soon became evident to the Menem administration that, as in the previous privatization initiative, capital and expertise to be involved in the new company would have to have a high foreign involvement. But the likelihood of attracting private capital and expertise was closely linked to the political and economic stability of the country. Although bringing key figures of the local business community to the government tamed economic instability and boosted Argentina's image among international investors circles, the risk of political unrest still haunted the administration. The success of ENTel's privatization program relied largely on the ability of the government to overcome domestic resistance to the project. ENTel, the first of the large public utilities to be privatized, was presented by the government as the showcase of the official commitment to a private, free market economy. For this reason, there was a clear sense that the failure to privatize ENTel would jeopardize Menem's entire economic program.

The experience of the Alfonsín administration taught the fact that if the government hoped to implement its neoliberal program, it would have to block the participation of labor, opposition parties, and the national Congress in the design of ENTel's sale. Menem perceived that his window of opportunity was small. Reforms had to be quickly launched before resistance could mount again. The privatization team received a presidential mandate to sell the company within fourteen months of the public privatization announcement.[12] With only a couple of months of delay from the original schedule, ENTel was sold to a joint venture of foreign banks and telephone companies in November 1990.

How do we explain Menem's "success" in privatizing ENTel when previous governments failed to achieve that same goal? At the core of the answer are a favorable political environment, the skillful management of the political and bureaucratic opposition, and the ever-declining performance of ENTel. During his first months in power, Menem dismantled party and labor opposition, co-opted powerful segments of the domestic private sector, and gained the support of international capital.

The Political Struggle for Reform

While the profound effects of the economic crisis of the 1980s gave a legitimacy to government's shock policies, the sweeping 1989 electoral victory granted Menem the popular support he needed for implementation of draconian economic reforms. However, the efficacy of the reform depended on the sudden modification of social expectations, which is generally attained via quick unilateral decisions and actions (Torre 1992, 12).

Since the 1987 elections the Peronists controlled the majority of the provinces. Given the outcome of the 1989 election, Menem's party was able to extend Peronist control to the Congress, where the party achieved a majority in the Senate and was short by only two votes in the Chamber of Deputies.[13] Yet, this did not present a problem since the third largest party, the Unión de Centro Democrático (UCD), was the traditional advocate of the neoliberal policies that Menem was about to implement.[14] This almost absolute control of the Peronist coalition over the legislative process granted the new president the required leverage to pass two pieces of legislation that became crucial to reform the state and carry forward the privatization of a wide range of public utilities. These new and temporary laws—the Economic Emergency Law and the Public Sector Reform Law—concentrated much of the policy-making process in the hand of the president, leapfrogging, in this way, the intervention or participation of Congress in the crafting of reform regulations and decrees.[15] The latter, in particular, concentrated power in the executive branch.[16] This legislation enabled the executive to carry on the privatization of ENTel almost entirely through presidential decrees.[17]

The autonomy gained by the executive was so great that Menem ruled by "need and urgency" decrees more than 100 times in the space of two years; in the previous 136 years presidents had used this exceptional power only on twenty-three occasions (Ferreira Rubio and Goretti 1992). Menem's confidence in his ability to rule outside regular constitutional mechanisms became evident in September 1992 when he sent Congress a bill for the privatization of the national oil company, Yacimientos Petroliferos Fiscales (YPF). The freedoms granted to the executive by the State Reform Law of 1989 had expired, so Menem threatened to circumvent a procrastinating Congress with a return to *decretazos*—a government by decree.[18]

In spite of these public displays of power vis-à-vis Congress, the main challenges to Menem's privatization program emerged not from the legislative body but from the Argentine labor movement. After announcement of the forthcoming ENTel's sale, labor mounted a resistance campaign that included a wide range of public displays of power with its most significant manifestations in several national strikes aiming at paralyzing the country's communication capabilities. In the recent past similar actions of the unions—with the support of the Peronist party and certain segments of the local telecommunications industry—were crucial to the dismantling of the Radical party's privatization efforts. However, this time the social and political scenario was different, and the workers' resistance was progressively subdued and pushed to the background of the privatization process. Three factors were crucial to the Menem's success in overcoming labor opposition.

First, Menem showed a strong determination to marginalize labor interference from the sales process. This is a significant difference from the Alfonsín administration which, due to a shaky political situation, took a much softer approach to handling workers' opposition. Probably the event that depicts most clearly the commitment of Menem to achieve his reform goals was the official response to a general strike of the telephone workers in August 1990.[19] In 1989 the government had warned unions that it would declare illegal all strikes that were aimed at blocking the progress of the state reform program. Hence, when the telephone workers disconnected Argentina's telecom system from the world, Menem responded by calling out the army to operate the system and by firing more than 400 workers.

The second key factor in labor's defeat in the privatization struggle is the fact that unions in Latin America, and particularly those in Argentina, had by then lost much of their political strength. During the late 1970s and early 1980s, under the military regime, Argentine unions witnessed a major decline in the number of workers in their ranks, and this downward trend continued during the Alfonsín administration.[20]

The third factor that affected the ability of workers to oppose the sale is basically a deepening of this structural weakness—in this case induced by government action. For the last five decades the Argentine labor union has been a fairly monolithic vertical movement that achieved most its political victories due to these factors and to its many affiliates. However, by the late 1980s, while economic crisis considerably reduced the number of unionized workers, the government managed to break the unity of the movement, weakening it even further. By appointing the head of the telephone workers union—a long time member of the Peronist party—as the Secretary of Communication, Menem created controversy and clashes among different groups within the union. While some sectors supported the appointment, other groups strongly opposed what they saw as a co-optation of their leadership. The incorporation of the worker's leader into government ranks created a major schism in the telephone workers' movement, eroding, in this way, the very essence of labor power.

In contrast to active and outspoken position of unions, the main political parties—the Radicals and the Peronists—find themselves paralyzed for various reasons. The Radical party, for example, has been politically shut off from the process for two main reasons. First, the Radicals were the original authors of the privatization strategy. It would have been illogical to promote the privatization of ENTel a few months before and to oppose it now. Second, Alfonsín, the previous Radical president, did not finish his constitutional term in power, having resigned a few months before due to widespread economic and political crises. With this recent precedent, party representatives in Congress were publicly delegitimized and could not have any significant participation in the state reform process.

Within the Peronist party Menem's policies were not easily accepted. Decades of a strong statist philosophy had rendered orthodox cadres of the party strong advocates of political strategies that were directly opposed to those that Menem intended to implement. However, the president's ability to overcome these opposition groups was enhanced by his position as the head of the Peronist party. Menem's control over the political and financial power of the party gave him significant power over the actions of rebellious groups and enough leverage to derail intraparty opposition.[21] Interference from more traditional, welfare state-oriented sectors of his own party was blocked by appointing outsiders of the party or party members loyal to the new policies. Those who showed any resistance to Menem's unconventional program were not invited to government positions and left with no voice in the political game.

In contrast to unions and certain sectors of the political parties which clearly opposed Menem's program, consumers were initially passive spectators of the impending sale of ENTel. In fact in the early stages ENTel's incredibly poor performance led to widespread public support for privatization.[22] A survey at the time of the privatization announcement showed that 70 percent of the population favored ENTel's sale to the private sector.[23] However, as the process evolved and "preparing ENTel for sale" translated into surging tariffs, users evidenced doubts about the value of privatization. In March 1990, when the government announced the third tariff increase in three months (in this case a hike of 433 percent) popular protest erupted in the streets, making the administration suspend the change.[24] Nevertheless, consumers as a bloc are a disparate group, with a low per capita stake in their interest and, therefore, had to organize. Unclear coercive mechanisms and lack of a permanent institutional presence in the national political system weakens their ability to influence the political process. Hence, their role in the process was quite different from the unions and had little impact—besides this particular moment of resistance to a tariff increase.[25]

The local and foreign business community was not a major obstacle to the project. Although there was some friction with the government, problems were related not to the spirit or general guidelines of the reform project but to implementation details that would benefit certain players while hindering the interests of others. Support to the official initiative ranged from public statements in favor of the reform to the supply of resources required to overcome opposition to the project. In gaining this strong support from the local and international business community the appointment of business leaders to key government positions was crucial.

Finally, to avoid any reversal of the project, the new administration introduced a variety of organizational reforms in the judiciary system, mainly in the Supreme Court. By expanding from five to nine the number of seats in the Supreme Court and by asking for the resignation of some members, Menem introduced enough loyal followers to give him control of the country's highest judiciary body. But the project could still be challenged, and indeed was, at lower strata of the judiciary system, so changes of similar nature were introduced in some of the fiscal and administrative institutions of the state—such as the Control Secretariat of the Treasury, the General Fiscal Secretariat of Public Enterprises, the General Inspection of Justice, the Commission of Political Trial (Verbitsky 1991).

The clearest and most publicized example of the threat that the judiciary system could pose to state reform came from the outspoken opposition of the Inspector General of Justice, Alberto R. González Arzac, who criticized the handling of ENTel's privatization by the central administration.[26] The inspector's complaint instigated a suit in the federal courts filed by members of Congress. As a result, president Menem requested González Arzac's resignation and replaced him with a loyal appointee (González Arzac 1990). These changes gave Menem considerable control of Argentina's main federal judicial institutions.

During the first year of his administration, the new president built solid support from powerful national and international actors and dismantled the equally powerful domestic opposition. With opposition under control, Menem put in motion the process that ultimately transferred ENTel to the private sector.

Although the government overcame opposition to ENTel's sale, the pace and dynamics of the company's privatization were affected by latent objections to the official agenda. Menem sought to control the coalescence of potential interest-group coalitions and to maximize the window of opportunity granted by the manipulation of Congress and the restructuring of the judiciary. Consequently, the time required for the sale and the restructuring of the sector, for example, was only fourteen months from the day of the official announcement. This short time frame limited the ability of the government to prepare the company for sale and hindered the administration's bargaining leverage with private investors. These two factors had an impact on the attractiveness of the offering, the price paid for ENTel, and the overall profile of the telecom sector— such as the closeness of the market to competition. Thus although domestic interest groups, Congress, and the judiciary did not have a direct role in shaping ENTel's sale, they nevertheless affected the process in an indirect and "passive" fashion.

Financial and Institutional Reform

Overcoming domestic resistance was crucial to the survival of the privatization program but much more than that had to be done before the company could be transferred to the private sector. Financial and institutional restructuring was as crucial as taming opposition. In the year prior to the sale, while the president and his collaborators struggled with the political adversities of reform, the privatization team worked in crafting a new commercial and regulatory profile for the company and the sector.

Financial Reform

It has become widely accepted that the privatization of a SOTE should be preceded by a considerable restructuring of the firm's and the sector's financial and commercial patterns and practices. Such was the case in the Mexican and Malaysian reforms.[27] In the case of ENTel, instead, time constraints put a limit on the ability of the government to carry on extensive financial reform. The most significant of these few changes was related to pricing policies. The government sharply raised the level of tariffs and modified the criteria for tariff increases thereafter. The other important financial change in the company's profile was the striking increase of its debt and the announcement that the Argentine state would absorb the existing debt at the moment of the sale.

The most problematic and controversial financial reform for the government was the raise of telephone tariffs. At the time of ENTel's privatization announcement, tariffs were at the lowest level in the last decade, a fact that worked against the government's desire to attract private investment. To guarantee prospective buyers a reasonable rate of return on their investment, tariff increase prospects were included in the privatization legislation.[28] Reflecting this official commitment, telephone tariffs jumped 112 percent on February 7, 1990. A few weeks later, another increase of 300 percent was announced. In the middle of March, ENTel's head tried to implement a 400 percent increase. But, by that time, the public was coming to grips with the economic consequences of privatization. The announcement ignited a national uproar that resulted in consumer protests, a plan by the telephone union for a national strike, and a coordinated opposition of Radicals and Peronists in Congress and elsewhere. Facing a national political storm of such magnitude, the government chose to retreat and postpone the increase. Yet, by September, ENTel's administration had managed to raise tariffs by 42 percent once more.[29] These tariff increases brought ENTel's tariffs into line with those of the most profitable companies in the world. In the government's view, the tariff problem was a settled issue.

However, prior to signing contracts, the Bell Atlantic/Manufacturers Hanover consortium—winner of the northern region bid—dropped out of the process leaving the government with only two remaining bidders—Telefónica de España and the STET/France Cable et Radio consortium. The government, straining to meet the privatization schedule, rejected a petition to postpone the deadline to sign the contracts. The rejection further weakened Menem's bargaining capabilities vis-à-vis the remaining consortium. The increasingly vulnerable position of the government became more evident when representatives of Telefónica and STET threatened to withdraw from the process because telephone rates were "insufficient to ensure a profitable operation." After a strident and widely publicized struggle, the government, bound by its commitment to privatize on schedule, gave in and granted an increase of 96.57 percent over the previous telephone charges—approximately US$0.24 per minute—turning the tariffs of privatized ENTel into one of the highest in the world (Figure 4.2).

Figure 4.2

International Comparison of Local Call Charges (1989)
(Weekdays, Daytime, Three-Minute Rates)

Country	Local call charge p/ minute
Japan	.08
United States	.10
Mexico	.10
France	.11
Germany	.14
Britain	.24
Argentina	.72*

Source: Takano 1992, and Ramamurti 1993.

* For long distance the rate per minute (US$2.4) has to be multiplied by an index based on distance. The maximum charge is based on a distance of 840 kilometers--minimum charge is three minutes--and it adds up to US$2.55. For an international call from Buenos Aires to New York the tariff is an average of US$2.95 per minute, while the same called reversed adds up to an average of US$0.87 per minute.

One other important pricing issue negotiated prior to the transfer of ENTel was the mechanism to raise tariff. The government's initial approach was to guarantee 16 percent rate of return over a base rate of US$3.2 billion—which a gross estimate of ENTel's operating assets. The guarantee of profits to the new private owners was a politically sensitive issue, which led to a reconsideration and change of the pricing policy a few weeks before the transfer. The original rate of return formula was replaced by the now widely implemented RPI-X model (Littlechild 1983),[30] with supplementary adjustments to compensate for unexpected changes in the levels of exchange rates and domestic consumer prices.[31]

In this financial restructuring two other changes brought considerable benefits for new owners at the expense of potential profits for the Argentine state. First, to improve the chances of luring private investors the government announced that it would take over all pending debt of the company prior to its transfer. Although in political terms the announcement was not a popular decision, it was taken as an "inevitable" sacrifice to sell the SOTE.[32] At the moment the decision was taken, the debt of ENTel stood at US$916 million.[33] The problem, however, grew more sensitive as the head of ENTel, Ms. Alsogaray, in an effort to sweeten the privatization deal (for both prospective owners and established local equipment suppliers) signed procurement contracts for new equipment; in effect, this instantly doubled the historic debt of ENTel.[34]

Telephone taxes met a similar fate. Before ENTel came up for privatization, the Argentine state applied a tax on telephone services equivalent to 31.58 percent of the tariff, which was used to finance the national pension fund. As part of the privatization package the taxes were erased from the tariff and transferred to the new owners as a tariff increase. Although this process was not manifest to consumers, it undoubtedly affected their welfare since the government transformed what was one a public revenue into a private one.

Institutional Reform

Besides tariff, debt, and tax changes, the government carried out some significant transformations at the institutional level. On the one hand, ENTel was divided into several companies operating in various segments of the market and in two different regions of the country. On the other hand, the policy and regulatory functions were separated giving birth to an autonomous regulatory entity.

Dividing ENTel into two regional operating companies (ROCs) reflected the efforts of the government to demonopolize the provision of services.[35] In the view of the administration the creation of separate carriers would set the stage for competition in the near future.[36] The final creation of two companies to operate in the north and south of the country also reflects the view of international consultants and prospective investors. While the government originally intended to divide the company into five ROCs—and later into three—the international investment community showed no interest in such arrangements.[37] Finally, the country was divided in two regions. The north includes thirteen provinces and the northern part of Buenos Aires, and the south includes nine provinces and the rest of Buenos Aires.[38]

The division of ENTel into two ROCs led to the creation of five different companies. Two of them—Telco Sur and Telco Norte—provided basic domestic services in each region of the country, the third—Proveedora de Servicios de Valor Agregado or Startel—held jointly by Telco Sur and Telco Norte provided value-added services, the forth—Servicios Internacionales or Telintar—also jointly owned by the two firms provide national long-distance and international services, and, the fifth one—ENTel Residual—held the remaining 40 percent of shares and existed until the shares were sold or transfered to the private investors in public offerings (Figure 4.3).[39]

Aside from breaking ENTel into several regional businesses, the government decided to modernize its regulatory institutions by creating a relatively autonomous regulatory body: the Comisión Nacional de Telecomunicaciones (CNT). The creation of the new regulatory agency mirrored trends worldwide. In most industrialized countries the increasing complexity of telecommunication markets has lead to the rise of relatively autonomous regulatory bodies, with considerable normative power, and staffed with experienced and expert personnel.

Figure 4.3

ENTel's Divestiture Scheme

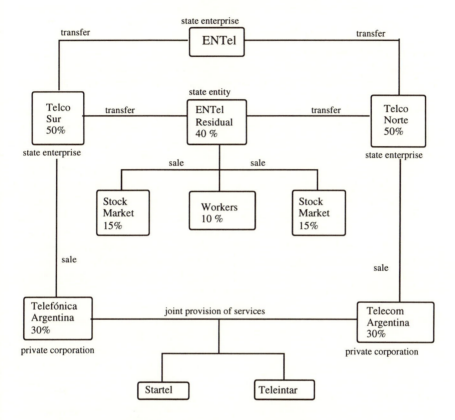

In the case of Argentina, CNT has according to the new legislation considerable independence. In practice, however, this autonomy is often undermined by bureaucratic struggles at higher levels of the executive branch. The agency is governed by a five-member executive board, appointed by Argentina's president. Its main function is to "apply, interpret, and enforce laws, decrees, and other norms in the telecommunications sector."[40] One of the main functions of CNT is to monitor the achievement of established goals by the new carriers, the resolution of conflicts among companies and between them and consumers, and the approval of equipment standards.[41] Financially CNT is supported by 0.5 percent of net profits of the private companies. Unlike other countries such as the United States, Argentina has had almost no experience with the regulation of private utilities, and it is not clear up to what point CNT will be able to cope with the complexities and rapid changes of modern telecommunications markets.

Argentine Telecom Company for Sale

Parallel to the regulatory and market restructuring of the telecommunications sector as a whole, the government had to move forward with the sale of ENTel. In this regard one of the main initial concerns was to attract foreign carriers to supply technical expertise and technology and large foreign investors to gain a strong financial basis of the rapid development of the sector. With those two goals in mind the government tailored the requirements to bid for ENTel in such way that only American telephone companies and large international banks could participate in the process.

In the selection of companies the initial aim of ENTel's privatization team was to indirectly exclude European PTTs from the bidding process.[42] The government argued that the exclusion of European firms was related to issues of sovereignty, national integrity, and the risk of falling back again into the hands of the state—in this case a foreign one.[43]

In spite of this initial attempt to be selective about the nature and origin of prospective owners, it did not take long for the government to realize that the sale of ENTel should not be taken for granted and that reducing the pool of potential purchasers also shrank both the chances of success in privatization and the government's bargaining power throughout the process. A few months after the announcement that European SOTEs would be excluded from the process, the administration reversed its decision and allowed European PTTs to participate in the sale of ENTel as prospective buyers.[44]

Besides attracting qualified foreign carriers, the other major challenge to the privatization team was to lure large foreign commercial banks creditors of the country's large foreign debt. This was a consequence of the mechanisms adopted to pay for ENTel. The initial approach announced by the government was that to purchase ENTel, prospective owners would have to pay cash. In the view of some high government officials this was an excellent opportunity to raise greatly needed financial resources for the cash-starved public sector. However, it did not take long for officials in the Ministry of Economy to oppose the strategy and suggest instead that a debt-equity swap approach would, in the long run, be more beneficial to the country. In their view a debt-equity swap in the first stages of privatization would be "a good international signal for the process as a whole."[45]

Those that emphasized the cash method were at a considerable disadvantage because there were widespread doubts that there would be many telecommunications companies with the financial resources and entrepreneurial spirit to take over ENTel. On the contrary, there were a large number of international banks eager to rescue their poorly rated debts in exchange for potentially profitable assets in the country.[46] Furthermore, those advocating the debt-equity swap method had in their favor an important international commitment. The previous administrations in their attempts to renew international loans, offered state-owned firms in mortgage to foreign commercial banks. Since then, foreign creditors had the right to ban financial operations affecting the ownership of SOEs. Based on this international engagement, the government argued that Argentina's creditors would not allow the sale of ENTel if a debt-equity swap mechanism was not adopted.

Despite the involvement of Congress—where both Radicals and Peronists were against a debt-equity swap transaction[47]—who struggled to change the sale regulation to ban a swap sale, the Ministry of Economy finally imposed its criteria and ENTel was sold in what constituted at that moment, "Latin America's largest debt-equity swap transaction."[48]

Once the mode of payment was settled, the conditions to purchase ENTel were established in the following way: maximum of US$214 million in cash, US$380 million in Argentine foreign debt payable over a three-year period, plus the maximum amount of debt papers that each consortium could offer, with a floor of US$3.5 billion. The ceiling of US$214 million cash was established by the government to induce bidders to compete on the debt side of the deal by offering the largest possible amount of debt.

The technical and financial requirements led to the formation of consortiums integrated—in most cases—by a foreign telecommunications operator, an international bank, and a local economic group. Although at the early stages of the process several American, European, and Japanese companies showed interest in the privatization of ENTel, it did not take long for several of them to withdraw from the process.[49] A messy regulatory framework, shaky domestic economic and political conditions, and lack of clear and fixed rules of the game in the sale of the Argentine SOTE drove away a large number of potential bidders. By the closing of the application period only three companies were left: Telefónica (Spain), STET-France Cable et Radio (Italy and France), and Bell Atlantic (USA).[50]

Despite the low number of final bidders the Menem administration was able to announce in June 1990 the successful privatization of ENTel. The southern region of the country was won by the Telefónica consortium, while the northern region was granted to the Bell Atlantic consortium. However, the complicated chapter of ENTel's privatization was not closed for the northern region. Shortly after being awarded the license Bell Atlantic announced that its financial partner, Manufacturers Hanover, could not take up the contract because it was unable to acquire in secondary debt markets the amount of debt papers required for the swap, and hence requested a delay in signing of the contracts. The government, however, remained fixed in the belief that failure to comply with the privatization schedule would erode its domestic and international image. It therefore rejected the proposal and, very much contrary to its preferences, granted the nothern region to the STET-France Cable et Radio consortium.[51]

Due to this unexpected event, telecommunications services in the country are now provided by the Telefónica de Argentina in the south and Telecom Argentina in the north. Telefónica de Argentina was constituted at the time of the purchase by Citibank (57 percent), Telefónica de España (30 percent), and Techint (10 percent).[52] While Telecom Argentina was constituted by France Cable et Radio (30 percent), STET (30 percent), Compañía Naviera Perez Companc (30 percent), and J. P. Morgan Bank (10 percent).[53]

For the sale, the Argentine state received US$214 million in cash (US$114 million for the south, and US$100 million for the northern region) and US$5,029 billion in debt and interest at face value (Telefónica paid US$2,720 billion and Telecom US$2,309 billion).[54] When placed in perspective, this means that Argentina received the lowest price per main line of all the companies privatized in developing countries at that moment.[55]

After the sale ENTel shares were distributed in the following way. The Telefónica consortium controlled 30 percent, the STET/France Telecom controled 30 percent, ENTel workers had 10 percent, while the remaining 40 percent float in the national and international stock market. In sum, after the privatization of ENTel, telecommunications services in Argentina are owned largely by foreign governments, international creditors of the country, and powerful local economic groups, and, to a much smaller extent, by telephone workers and small private investors.

FAILING TO LIBERALIZE

Parallel to the privatization of ENTel the Menem government initially planned a sweeping liberalization of the Argentine telecommunications market. Under the early official plan value-added, domestic long-distance and international services would be immediately opened to competition, while basic local services would operate under a regime of exclusivity for five years after the privatization of ENTel; after this period they would follow the fate of other public services, and competitors would be allowed and encouraged into the market.[56]

Despite the government's intentions to liberalize the Argentine market, the economic and political situation of the country would not allow it to achieve both of these—often contradictory—goals. In attempting to attract private investment for ENTel's sale, the conflicting dynamics of privatization and liberalization became even more apparent. Investors would consider purchasing ENTel only under conditions of a market protected for an extended period of time.

From a foreign investor's perspective, a "good deal" is one in which benefits of high-growth opportunity and profit potential greater than in home-country markets compensates the overall investment risks. Given this context, investors tend to assess country-specific factors, such as the political climate, prospects for economic growth, inflation, currency devaluation, exchange-rate trends, and other economic and political factors that ultimately determine the level of country risk.

Private investors particularly examined Argentina's economic and political instability. A confidential report of the Manufacturers Hanover Trust Corporation, one of the initial investors interested in the Argentine offering highlighted the fact that "The proposed offering involves substantial risks. Investment in the proposed transaction requires the financial ability and willingness to accept the high risks inherent in the investments of the type describe herein, including the possible loss of the full amount of such investment" (Baur 1991, 29).[57] Investment consulting firms warned that "firms must be cautious. Corporate strategic analysts will have to devote considerable attention to Argentine economic and political forecasts, more than with most of their other foreign investments."[58]

Doubts were rooted, mainly, in the country's chronic high inflation—a phenomenon that afflicted every aspect of Argentina's economic activities. As pointed out, one of the main consequences of high inflation is the reduction in time available for economic decisions. Inflationary waves and the subsequent sharp price fluctuations increase uncertainty of key economic variables, obscuring the accuracy of prices and, therefore, the accuracy of investment forecast. Historically, years of currency overvaluation and high interest rates have been followed by years of extremely undervalued exchange rates and low interest. Unstable interest and exchange rates reduce most economic activity to short-term cycles, and this makes long-term decisions and investment commitment extremely difficult. Most economic activity moves away from productive investments into short-term speculative ventures (González Fraga 1991, 89).

At the time of ENTel's privatization the international business community appraise Argentina's market as risky. International perception was reflected in the estimated price for ENTel, which on the altar of international risk judgment was slashed by 20 percent.[59] At the end of 1989, following a few months of declining inflation, the monthly inflation rate rose again to 40 percent, reinforcing investors' perception of Argentina as a risky and unstable business environment (Figure 4.4). A top manager of Telefónica summarized the outlook when he argued that "the executive board of the company considers Argentina a high risk country, and it is not worth it to bid for ENTel."[60]

More specifically, investors in the telecom sector tend to consider the following variables when determining the worthiness of a company: revenue and operating costs per access line; access lines per employee; total revenue per employee; elasticity of demand and customers' ability to pay higher rates; potential for development of other services with high rate of return; quality of plant, network, and technology (or the ability to improve versus replace installed base); and the regulatory and competitive environment. In most aspects ENTel performed poorly compared to other companies for sale in the international telecom market (Salomon Brothers Inc. 1991).

Despite this negative assessment of Argentina's investment environment and ENTel's poor profile, the government felt confident that it would achieve its targeted goals. Within a few months after the privatization announcement, fourteen companies had shown interest in acquiring rights for the provision of basic services and four were potential bidders for international services. The nature of the investment and the way the bidding process unfolded, however, diminished the Argentine government's power to defend its liberalization initiative.

Students of international bargaining have argued that a host government's bargaining power relative to the foreign investor is likely to increase if the investment (1) is actively sought by competing firms, (2) requires a relatively low technology with multiple substitute sources, (3) requires the commitment of large sums of fixed capital that once in place are not easily liquidated or moved, and (4) requires the involvement of government as a principal financier, a principal consumer, a principal distributor of outputs, a principal supplier of inputs, or a principal regulator of either inputs or outputs (Encarnation and Wells

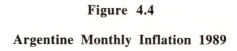

Figure 4.4

Argentine Monthly Inflation 1989

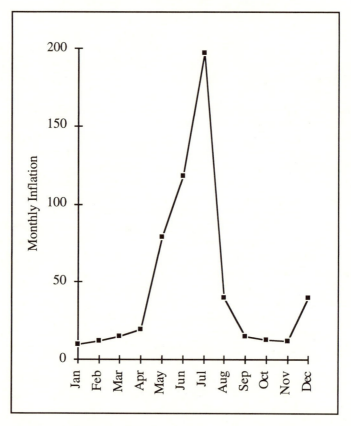

1985, 51). None of these conditions seemed to favor the Argentine government in the ENTel sale.

Despite the initial interest shown by more than a dozen foreign firms, the turbulent political environment, the unsettled and often contradictory regulatory framework, the large investments required to upgrade ENTel's network, and the blurry future of the Argentine economy discouraged participation and the government soon found itself scrambling to avoid a massive retreat of prospective bidders. The Argentine government began to realize that it would not be easy to achieve privatization unless the deal was sweetened. As an immediate consequence the five-year guarantee of exclusivity in basic services were extended to ten years.[61] A similar fate followed the segment of value-added network services and international services which, in early 1990, were included in the exclusivity packet to enhance the attractiveness of ENTel's offering.[62]   Only the least profitable services—such as naval radio communication and national telex—and those liberalized prior to privatization—such as cellular telephony and national data transmission—were left open to competition.[63]

By combining liberalization of the Argentine telecom market with the privatization of ENTel, the fate of most telecom services was inexorably linked to the sale of the SOTE. The new operating companies now control and monopolize most telecommunications services in the country.[64]

Simultaneous with its efforts to reform the monopoly status of basic and value-added network services, the government aimed at further liberalization by dismantling state regulatory agencies. The underlying assumption behind the creation of CNT was that the commission would intervene to guarantee the free and fair play of telecom actors in the marketplace. Yet, the irony of the Argentine regulatory reform is that, when the privatization process concluded, CNT's main functions became the regulation and protection of two private monopolies.

The story of the Argentine telecom liberalization suggests that the financially weak condition of the country's economy led the government to a "desperate" search for foreign investment. Dependency on foreign capital to revive the Argentine economy improved the bargaining position of private investors while undermining the preferences of state officials. This basic condition was reinforced by other factors. Argentina was classified in the international financial community as a risky market. Additionally, ENTel was rated very poorly vis-à-vis other more attractive companies in the burgeoning international privatization market.

CONCLUSION

The saga of telecommunications reform in Argentina in the 1980s is an excellent testing ground for the hypotheses presented in this study. A comparative study of reform at different periods throughout the decade offers rich material to understand how different political and economic settings in each administration affected the success of telecom reform initiatives.

During the military regime, although the government was able to insulate policy making from pressures of domestic coalitions, reform advocates nevertheless failed to achieve cohesion among the governing elite around issues such as privatization. The leadership failed to concentrate sufficient power to discipline followers and to block dissidents within the state apparatus. Consequently, in the specific case of ENTel, privatization projects emerged but languished for several years until they were canceled in 1982 with the demise of the military administration.

The Alfonsín government revived the idea of a privatized ENTel. It faced similar problems to those confronted by the military. The Alfonsín administration, however, lacked the necessary policy coherence and cohesion needed for an administrative and proprietary reform of that magnitude. Reform implementation was carried forward by different agencies with conflicting interests; the president was not personally involved in the process and lacked control over the federal bureaucracy in regard to privatization issues. More importantly the Radical administration operated in a highly participatory and open political environment. Historical conditions imposed on this transitional democracy made state autonomy or insulation of the policy process a task beyond the government capabilities. Alfonsín's failure to privatize ENTel was mostly rooted in the inability of the government to block opposition arising from domestic political coalitions.

Menem's reform process stands in clear contrast to these two previous administrations. This is not to say that the president alone was able to craft state restructuring that avoided the weaknesses and deficiencies of previous administrations. Structural factors spurred by the peculiar socioeconomic and political conditions during the early stages of the Menem government cleared the road for a quick and almost unchallenged program of privatization.

The unprecedented economic crisis that hit the country in the last year of the Alfonsín government dismantled preexisting interest group coalitions and granted the new administration a period of relative autonomy and insularity from the traditional Argentine backlash politics. Furthermore, the Radicals, the main opposition party, were in no condition to block policies that they themselves had initiated. Menem thus gained the compliance of Congress through special legislation that granted the executive all the legislative power needed to carry out state reform through presidential decrees. Potential threats from the judiciary—in particular the Supreme Court—were diluted by increasing the number of members to achieve a majority that supported the government. And, finally, labor opposition, the only remaining significant challenger to the privatization of ENTel, was blocked and dismantled by Menem through skillful political maneuvers.

At the state level, the sale of the national carrier was carried out by a small group of ad hoc state officials appointed by the president for the specific task of privatizing ENTel. They operated outside bureaucratic channels, and they counted on the full support and direct participation of the president.

With most of the opposition under control and an integrated and insulated group of state officials in charge of selling the company, Menem was able to achieve what the two previous administrations had failed to do: transfer ENTel to private hands. However, since the insulation of the policy process and the sharp increase of presidential powers were temporary phenomena and not structural elements in Argentine politics—as was the case in Mexico and Malaysia—the privatization of ENTel was indirectly affected and shaped by what the government did and did not do to avoid the resurgence of strong political challenges to the official project.

Besides being a rich arena in which to explore the validity of the proposed analytical approach, the Argentine case also offers important insights into the weaknesses of a political explanation of telecom reform. The failure of the Menem administration to open telecom services to competition calls into question the generalizability of a statist approach and highlights the role of the domestic economy in shaping a new profile for the sector.

If state autonomy and power concentration in the head of the state were adequate variable to explain liberalization, then we would expect Menem's government to succeed, while other governments lacking those characteristics— such as Thailand—should fail in their liberalization efforts. However, we find the opposite, that is, that "weak" governments, such as Thailand, have been able to open the market to competition, while "strong," autonomous governments, such as Argentina under the Menem administration, have failed.

The explanation offered in this study points to the attractiveness of the domestic market and its impact on the bargaining capabilities of the host government. While in countries such as Thailand, the attractiveness of the domestic market granted the government the required leverage to open the telecom market to competitive entry, in Argentina the government closed the sector, recreating a private monopoly in order to comply with the interests of potential private investors.

In summary, Menem was able to sell the Argentine national carrier ENTel because he could insulate the policy process from the pressures and interference of domestic opposition interest groups and because he tightly controlled the central bureaucracy. Yet, Menem failed to accomplish his original plan for a liberalized Argentine telecom market due to the government's failure to resist private investors' demands for a closed market.

NOTES

1. Interview with Carlos Menem, *La Nación*, 6 April 1992, 1.

2. This is the way that Argentines and students of Argentine politics have interpreted Peronist philosophy. However, since Perón was a pragmatic leader ready to change or even reverse political decisions according to the dominant political climate, he often made extremely contradictory ideological statements and political actions. In 1954, for example, he sent a bill to Congress that, under the label of "Administrative Emergency and State Restructuring Law," contradicted most of his previous positions on the role of the state in the economy. In statements that supported the legislation, Perón argued that, due to the need for national recovery, the state had in the past taken over economic sectors, including public services, that should have "normally" been in the private realm. He concluded that having already fulfilled the purposes that justified state-interventionist policy, "the executive branch had the intention to restitute those entities to their natural domain: the private sector." Law 14380/54.

3. See *Ambito Financiero* 9 February 1988; *Tiempo Nuevo* 16 May 1989

4. The privatization strategy not only ran against the electoral campaign discourse, but it also reversed the publicly advertised position of the Peronist party, which fiercely opposed the Radical's privatization initiatives in Congress.

5. Once in power Menem published a book to support state reform. In a chapter titled "The Incommensurable Growth of the State" he developed a rationale for privatization. See Menem and Dromi 1990, 108. Other studies of that period showed that the Argentine public sector grew in the 1980s only 0.1 percent, while other developing countries had an average growth of approximately 6 percent. See Oszlak 1990.

6. An *interventor(a)* under the Argentine legal system is a temporary executive director with special powers appointed by the Argentine president. Law 23696, Art. 2.

7. The local law firm of Mairal-Klein was appointed as legal advisor, while Deloitte, Haskins & Sells, Touche & Ross, and Ruival, Otone & Asociados, did the financial evaluation of ENTel (The valuation was initially assigned to Banco Nacional de Desarrollo [Banade], but was later transferred to consulting firm—presumably because Banade did not have the personnel or time required for the task). Coopers & Lybrand and Hartenech & López provided technical advice, while Morgan Stanley & Co. and Banco Roberts provided financial advice.

8. On the role of state actors in the sale of SOEs, see Waterbury 1992.

9. The Minister of Services and Public Works and the Minister of Economy gained some control of the process in the final stages when a crisis emerged between the government and the new operators over tariff levels.

10. Initially it was thought that ENTel could be divided for sales purposes into the existing five administrative regions. These five regions were a hangover from the days of military governments in which ENTel was split in five to reflect and respond to the command of the five operational regions in which the army was organized.

11. Value-added services are, according to the government's definition, all those not included in the definition of basic services, while basic services are defined as the provision through the public network of all voice messages, be they local, regional, or international. Decree 62/90, 5 January 1990.

12. As shown later, this commitment to privatize in a short period of time gave the government the required initial push and inertia to overcome domestic political opposition, but it also weakened the administration in its bargaining with private investors.

13. Menem was the candidate of a coalition (Frejupo) consisting of the Peronists and three other small political parties. Menem came to power with the support of 47.3, while the second candidate—the Radical Eduardo Angeloz—gained 32.4 percent.

14. *La Nación*, 22 May 1989, 8.

15. The Public Sector Reform Law was designed to last one year with an optional extension to a second year. One of the most important features of the legislation was that it banned the possibility of any legal action against the state during the period of its enforcement and two years after expired.

16. Law 23696, Art. 11.

17. Although the legislation was initially restricted to state reform, it went later far beyond its initial boundaries, with the president "governing by decree" almost every aspect of Argentine economic, social, and political life. Using an exceptional legislative power known as a decree of "need and urgency"—granted to the executive only on very rare occasions—Menem ruled by decree on extremely important issues (such as the deregulation of a large number of economic activities) and on minor ones (such as the donation of small amount of money to the government of Bolivia). Both of these legislative acts would normally have been in the purview of Congress.

18. *Clarin*, 21 September 1992, 3.

19. There were previous national strikes but no significant political effect. See *Telephony*, 23 April 1990.

20. During the Alfonsín administration (1983—1989), for example, urban unemployment grew by 70 percent.

21. Menem's confidence in overcoming opposition within his own party led him to argue that, "If Gorbachev can dismantle the whole of communism to im-

prove the Soviet Union's economic performance, surely we can do the same with Peronism in Argentina." *Business International* 1991, 83.

22. Popular support for telecommunications privatization cannot be taken for granted. In some countries, such as New Zealand, 90 percent of the public opposed the private provision of public services. Tucker 1991.

23. Mora y Araujo, Noguera y Asociados 1990.

24. It is important to remember that consumers were not the only ones to protest the tariff increase. Businesses, politicians of every party, unions, and community organizations also rejected the increase. Therefore, it is hard to determine how much the administration's retreat can be attributed to consumers protests. "Argentina Cancels Boost of 433 percent in Phone Rates," *Wall Street Journal*, 22 March 1990, 15.

25. For a study on the impact interest-group politics in the regulation of telecommunications services, see Teske 1990b.

26. The Inspector General of Justice raised questions about inconsistencies and illegal procedures taking place during ENTel's privatization, but the central issue leading to his resignation was his opposition to the valuation of ENTel and the price assigned to the company.

27. For more details see the sections in Chapters V and VI devoted to the financial reform in Mexico and Malaysia.

28. Decree 62/90, Art. 12.2.

29. In September 1990, Resolution 199/90 established a tariff increase based on raises in the prices of telephone equipment. Coming in the midst of monthly increments to keep pace with inflation, this 42 percent hike did not have the same upsetting effect as did the 400 percent attempted by the administration in March of the same year.

30. RPI-X is a rate-of-price-increase formula that includes a variable (X in this case) to account for technological improvements in the industry. In the case of ENTel, X was set at 2 percent for the first seven years, and if the period of exclusivity is extended to ten years, X will be brought down to 4 percent for the three remaining years.

31. Under this new scheme, rate increases are based on the domestic consumer price index. However, if the dollar or the domestic consumer price rises more than 25 percent while the other remains fixed, then tariff will be adjusted according to a combined formula—40 percent based on the dollar and 60 percent on domestic consumer prices. In November 1991 this mechanism was replaced by one in which the increase of tariff is based on the Consumer Price Index of the United States.

32. To avoid future backlashes related to this measure, the government included an article in the privatization law that allowed the executive to absorb all debts of the SOEs. Law 23696, Art. 15.1.

33. Most of the US$900 million owed by ENTel was in the form of debts contracted by the last military regime to install a sophisticated telecom network aimed at worldwide broadcasting of the 1978 World Soccer Cup.

34. Prior to the transfer, the debt of ENTel had reached almost US$2.2 billions.

35. The official commitment to avoid the likelihood of a future monopoly in telecommunications translated in legislation written to avoid having the same bidder win both regions (Decree 62/90, chapter V).

36. Initially the notion was that after five years of exclusivity the Argentine market for basic services would be open to competition.

37. In the only case in which there was keen interest on the part of investors was when the country was divided in three regions: north, south, and Buenos Aires. The only problem was that everybody was interested in Buenos Aires, which concentrated 59.2 percent of the nationwide traffic, and little or no interest was manifested for the other regions. For the initiative in splitting ENTel into five companies, see "Dividirán a ENTel en 5 Subempresas," *Ambito Financiero,* 21 July 1990.

38. Decree 59/90, Art 2, and Decree 62/90, Annex VIII, 5 January, 1990.

39. The creation of separate companies in most of the world is aimed at blocking cross-subsidies between different services provided by the same firm. In the case of Argentina, however, the government argued that the network was not mature enough to survive and expand without subsidies, and, therefore, Decree 62/90 (art. 7.8.5.) incorporated the practice as a legal requirement on the companies.

40. Decree 1185/90, Art. 6 (a).

41. Tariff regulation is determined by the Ministry of Economy and not by CNT.

42. Interview with top government official. Ricardo Zinn, *Entelequia* no. 23, Enero-Febrero 1990, 13.

43. *El Cronista Comercial,* 21 October 1990.

44. The irony of the Argentine telecom privatization process is that ENTel ends up being purchased by three European SOTEs: Telefonica, France Telecom, and STET.

45. In "debt-equity swap" operations, private investors redeemed public foreign debt for equity shares in new or existing state-owned companies. On the effects of debt equity swaps on Latin American privatizations see, Abdala 1992a, Bergsman and Edisis 1988, and Petrazzini 1993.

46. *Clarin,* 22 December 1989.

47. Interview with Argentine congressmen, and *World Telecoms Research,* 30 March 1990.

48. *Communications International,* August 1990, 22.

49. Some of these companies were BellSouth, Bell Atlantic, G.T.E., Nynex International, US West, Cititel, Continental Telephone (all U.S. firms), STET (Italy), Telefónica (Spain), Cable & Wireless (England), France Cable et Radio (France), and Siemens (Germany).

50. The government had to modify once more the conditions for the acquisition of ENTel to accommodate the particular situation of Bell Atlantic. The American company could not meet the minimum 10 percent capital participation initially required by the Argentine government because domestic regulations in the USA did not allow Bell operating companies to own more than 5 percent of telephone companies abroad.

51. Personal letters addressed by both companies to the government. See also *Clarin,* 3 October 1990, and *La Nación,* 2 October 1990.

52. Citibank was at that time one of Argentina's main international creditors and head of the Committee of Argentine creditors. Telefónica de España is owned by the Spanish government with (34.1 percent) a large number of small domestic investors (43.9 percent), and foreign investors (22 percent). Although the Spanish government does not have the majority of ownership, it controls the firm because other shareholders—most of them small and highly dispersed investors—do not have ability to form coalitions large enough to mantain control of the business.

Techint is an Italian multinational corporation whose Argentine branch—created in 1947—soon became one of the main service providers of the Argentine state.

53. France Cable et Radio is the international branch of the state-owned France Telecom, a powerful conglomerate that provides domestic and international telecommunications services throughout France. STET (Societa Finanziaria Telefónica) is part of the Italian IRI (Institute for Industrial Reconstruction). Compañía Naviera Pérez Companc is one of Argentina's most powerful economic groups. Morgan Bank is one of the most important creditors of the Argentine foreign debt.

54. Based on the value of the debt papers in the secondary market at the time of the sale (approximately 19 percent of the face value), the total price paid for the company comes to US$955 million.

55. The highest rate was achieved by Telekom Malaysia with US$3,357 per main line, followed by CANTV of Venezuela with US$2,900, Teléfonos de México with US$1,653, and Telecommunications of Jamaica with US$850, while ENTel Argentina raised a revenue of only US$800.

56. Decree 731/89, art. 10, 11 and 17. Prior to these initiatives the only segments of the domestic telecom sector that were liberalized were the equipment market (1987) and, in limited fashion, mobile services (1988).

57. Manufacturers Hanover Trust Company, "Telco North Syndication Preliminary Information Package," Confidential Report, New York, 7 September 1990.

58. *Business International* 1991, 85.

59. Investors' reluctance to take risks with new investments in the Argentine market is also one of the factors that contributed to the administrations decision to give up the request for fresh currency and to accept, instead, debt-equity swaps.

60. *El País*, 14 June 1990. It is not clear whether this was a truthful statement of Telefónica's position—since the company remained in the bidding process all the way through and intended to purchase both areas of ENTel—but it was the perception of most other companies that dropped from the process.

61. Decree 59/90, art. 10. The argument to extend the period to ten years was that the new companies would need at least two years to adapt to the new market, five years to recover investments, and an extension of three years would follow if all initial quality and quantity targets were achieved.

62. Decree 59/90, Art. 17.

63. Decree 62/90, Art. 9.11. Both cellular telephony and national data services were liberalized by presidential decrees during the Alfonsín administration. Cellular telephony is provided in the Buenos Aires area by the new private company, comprising Telefonica and Telecom (Startel) and Movicom, a consortium made up of by BellSouth (31 percent), Motorola (25 percent), Citicorp (8 percent), and two local companies—Socma (16 percent) and BGH (20 percent). National data is provided by Impsat, Satelnet, and recently Alcatel. Two other companies (Keydata and Tecsel) hold licenses to operate but are presently out of the market.

64. The closed nature of the Argentine telecom market is so notable that the country emerged in the General Agreement on Trade in Services (GATS)—held parallel to the Uruguay Round GATT negotiations—as one of the few nations that rejected any possibility of opening their domestic telecom market in the near future. See Government of Argentina 1991.

5

Mexico 1988–1991: A Sweeping Reform

This chapter looks in detail at Mexico's successful privatization of its national carrier, Teléfonos de México, S.A. (TELMEX), and the liberalization of its domestic telecom market. The Mexican case offers fruitful comparison with the Argentine case, because both countries share certain economic and political features as well as the initial goals of their telecom reform programs; however, the Mexican administration was able to achieve without major sacrifice what was impossible or difficult in the Argentine case (i.e., privatization of their state-owned telecommunications enterprise [SOTE] and significant liberalization of the local market). A comparison of the Salinas and Menem governments' privatization efforts reveals common characteristics in regard to state-society relations and hierarchical relations within each administration that contrast sharply with those of the 1980–1989 Argentine governments. Hence, an analysis of the contrasts in Mexico's and Argentina's privatization and liberalization experiences provides rich material to help understand the divergent outcomes of reform.

This chapter further extends the arguments outlined earlier: successful privatization is highly dependent on the nature of state-society relations and level of cohesiveness within the state at the moment of the sale, while telecom market liberalization is strongly linked to economic conditions in the country.

THE MEXICAN POLITICAL SYSTEM

In formal institutional terms, Mexico resembles other modern Western democracies. The system is a presidential one, with three independent powers (executive, legislative, judicial) with their respective checks and balances, and federalist structures with fairly autonomous local governments. In practice, however, Mexico is governed by an extremely centralized and powerful state, which holds tight political control over most of Mexican society through the official party, the Partido Revolucionario Institucional (PRI) (Cornelius and Craig 1991).[1]

In practice, Mexico's federalism is not much more than a formal institutional arrangement between the central administration and state and municipal governments. Historically, the federal government has controlled 85 percent of all public revenues, while state governments control less than 12 percent and municipal governments only 3 percent.[2] Redistribution of resources has been highly discretionary and dependent on the president's will.

Centralism is also evident in the survival of high political figures at the state level, such as governors. Although governors are elected through free competitive elections, candidates of the PRI are handpicked by the president and a small group of personal advisors. Centralized control over the political life of the state extends to the point that the president has the ability to dismiss and replace elected governors. If the governor intends to resist the decision of the central administration, the president can always request the PRI-controlled senate to "dissolve" the state government.

Political centralism is also apparent in the percentage of high-level government officials who were born and raised in Mexico City. The presence in the federal administration of Mexico City-based interests has been growing since the late 1920s. During the 1930s approximately 5 percent of the cabinet came from the capital, but in the last two administrations that number rose to over 60 percent. The fact that the last five presidents were from Mexico City reinforces this conclusion.

Institutional centralization at the national level is replicated in the organization and distribution of power within the state. Mexico, like Argentina and most other countries in Latin America, is a presidential system; some authors, however, describe it as "presidentially centered" to highlight the particular characteristics of the Mexican case. In fact, based on the powers held by the president, that label appears particularly appropriate.

The president's control over Congress is striking. The tacit network of clientelism and informal hierarchies and loyalties that link the president and Congress has been in place since the 1930s and has led to automatic ratification by both chambers of executive decisions. This dynamic is also reflected in the other "independent" power—the judiciary. As with the Congress, important and sensitive political decisions tend to require first an implicit presidential approval.

As in the case of governors, the president has full control over the appointment and dismissal of juries, something that has never been questioned by Congress.

In the Mexican case, political parties have played a nonconventional role in politics. There is only one major party in the country—the PRI (Partido Revolucionario Institucional)—and one significant opposition party—the PAN (Partido de Acción Nacional).[3] The PRI is a stunningly efficient political machine. Since its creation in 1929 no opposition party has held power in Mexico. And whenever the opposition has posed a serious electoral threat, the government, supported by its powerful corporatist system, simply refused to recognize electoral defeat (Meyer 1989). The dominance of the PRI is so overwhelming that it had won every election from 1946 to the mid-1980s with an average popular support of 83.5 percent of the electorate. The PAN has achieved an average of only 12.5 percent of voter support in the last twenty years (Molinar Horcasitas 1991). Yet, despite this overwhelming presence, the PRI has no independent influence on public policy. Created as an appendage to the powerful Mexican state, the party's main function is to channel and organize the complex network of clientelistic relations that dominates Mexican politics.

At a societal level the PRI acts as a buffer between civil society and the central administration, granting little or no room for popular participation in the decision-making process. Social demands are channeled through a sophisticated architecture of interest representation. Interest groups, and even individual citizens, have only one mechanism to bring their demands to the higher levels of the state: through one of the political structures "licensed" by the state to organize and represent sectors of society—peasants, urban unionized workers, businessmen, teachers, and so forth.[4] As Cornelius and Craig point out,

> the structures that aggregate and articulate interests in Western
> democracies (political parties, labor unions, and so on) actually
> serve other purposes in the Mexican system: limiting the scope
> of citizen's demands on the government, mobilizing electoral
> support for the regime, helping to legitimate it in the eyes of
> other countries, distributing jobs and other material rewards to
> select individuals and groups (Cornelius and Craig 1989, 27).

Ultimately this means that Mexican politics occurs in the context of an extremely complex and sophisticated network of tightly controlled clientelistic relations that grant the president a far-reaching control over interest groups and social organizations of various kind.

This concentration of power at high levels of the state indicates that policy making is a closed business limited to the presidential circle. Most public policies are initiated, elaborated, and implemented by high-level government officials with the full support of a highly professionalized bureaucratic elite. The professionalization of civil servants and bureaucrats—a feature that is often absent in other LDCs—dominates the Mexican policy-making system. A unique combination of personalized relations and meritocracy have generated a powerful and effective state, in which control is exercised through patron-client networks, while legitimacy and efficiency is achieved through merits and professional training. Party and state complement each other in quite efficient ways. While the PRI's main function was to organize and absorb social demands skillfully, the federal bureaucracy's job is to effectively implement policy directives set by the president and his advisors.

While in Argentina there is much debate about the origins of political instability, in Mexico there is scant disagreement about the source of political stability. Most arguments tend to emphasize the role of the Mexican Revolution in engendering a powerful state apparatus and the effective mechanisms of social rewards and penalties set thereafter by the governing elite. The revolution was a major social disruption in Mexican history that erased pre-existing social arrangements, institutions, and embedded interests in society. It granted revolutionary leaders a unique opportunity to a strong, centralized state apparatus.[5] Mexico's six decades of political stability and institutional continuity stand in sharp contrast to the experience of Argentina over the past half century.

THE MEXICAN TELECOM SECTOR

As in Argentina, telecommunications services in Mexico were initiated by local entrepreneurs but soon dominated by large foreign companies. Differing from Argentina, Mexico's services provision was not nationalized in a single event but instead went through a progressive change in ownership until a majority of the shares came under state control in the early 1970s. Following worldwide reforms in the sector, the Mexican government sold the company to private investors in the late 1990s.

The privatization of TELMEX constitutes, in terms of ownership, a return to the early days of telecommunications services in the country. The first telephone connection in Mexico was launched in 1878, as a local private initiative.[6] The license to lay out a local telecommunications network was granted to Alfredo Westrup, an entrepreneur of Mexican nationality. Three years later, another Mexican, A. G. Greenwood, was offered a federal license to build a national network that would interconnect the already growing local networks.[7]

Even though the initial steps establishing a telecom sector in Mexico were under local control, it did not take long for the business to go into private foreign hands. Differing from the Argentine experience, in Mexico it was not the pressure of overseas companies that turned the market to foreign control, but the initiative of Greenwood himself. Faced with technical and financial constraints, the Mexican businessman sold the concession to the American-owned Continental Telephone Company (CTC) only a year after the business was launched. In 1882 the company was transformed into Mextelco and grew to become a central player in the Mexican telecommunications sector.[8]

Although Mextelco held a federal license to provide services nationwide, the company did not enjoy exclusive rights and, therefore, had to face competition in various regions of the country. The Mexican government was very keen to create a competitive marketplace in telecommunications services. However, the American company had enough financial and technical leverage to drive it out of the market or absorb most of the entrants. Throughout the 1880s small companies sprang up throughout the country offering local services yet, by the early 1890s, Mextelco had acquired most of them and had consolidated the Mexican market under its control.

The government remained firm in its policy of encouraging competition in the telecommunications market. In 1903 it granted a new license to a local entrepreneur—José Sitzenstatter—to operate in Mexico City.[9] Sitzenstatter followed Greenwood's path, and two years later the license was sold, this time to one of the largest European telecommunications equipment manufacturers: the Swedish firm, L. M. Ericsson & Co. In 1907 Ericsson began operations under the commercial name of Mexeric.[10]

During the Mexican revolution (1910–1917) the Swedish company, despite its recent entrance in the local market, managed to avoid nationalization. While Mexeric remained private and foreign throughout the revolutionary years, Mextelco was overtaken by the government in 1915 and returned to the private sector ten years later.

Mextelco was reprivatized in 1925, and, as in the case of Argentina, it was the rapidly growing American International Telephone and Telegraph Corporation (ITT) that bought it. Although ITT had a powerful technical and financial support, it was not as easy as in Argentina to gain control of the market. During the years in which Mextelco was under government control, Mexeric rapidly expanded its market share. By the time ITT came into the market, Mexeric controlled 53 percent of the Mexican market.

This distribution of market share led to strong competition between the two companies and to the development of isolated networks. Although the government ordered the companies to interconnect their networks, the official initiative did not have any effect until the late 1940s when government involvement in the sector threatened the autonomy of the companies.

The Birth of TELMEX

The Mexican government, unlike other governments in LDCs, did not participate actively in the telecommunications sector in its early years. The first communication law was published in 1932, and not until the late 1940s did the government intervene in an effective way to shape the evolution of the market. The main factor driving government intervention was the lack of interconnection between the two dominant service providers—Mextelco and Mexeric.[11]

Government pressure led to much more than network interconnection. In 1947, under official "incentives," Ericsson along with Swedish and Mexican investors created a business conglomerate that drove the creation of Teléfonos de México, S.A. (TELMEX)—the dominant provider of telecommunications services in Mexico during the following four decades. On January 1, 1948, based on Mexeric's existing infrastructure, TELMEX began operations. The control of the new company was in Mexican hands, with Corporación Continental, S.A.—a one-man company owned by the Mexican national Alex Wenner-Green—holding 409,000 shares and Ericsson owning 389,950

shares.[12]   The government also managed to place two high officials of the
Alemán administration on the executive board of TELMEX.[13]

Ericsson's willingness to allow the participation of Mexican investors and
government officials in the executive board of the new company granted the
government strong leverage to demand interconnection of the networks of
Mextelco and TELMEX. This time, direct government involvement in one of the
companies convinced ITT executives that it would be wise to comply with the
official mandate. A few weeks later Mextelco interconnected its network, and
Mexico achieved for the first time an integrated national network.

Network interconnection and the active involvement of the government in
the sector made Mextelco increasingly vulnerable to TELMEX's decisions and
strategies. The weakness of Mextelco was enhanced even further by the fact that
Mexeric—now TELMEX—owned minority shares in Mextelco. In 1950 in a
government-supported business takeover, TELMEX acquired Mextelco,
bringing under its control most of the existing telecommunications system of
Mexico. By 1957 TELMEX controlled 96 percent of all telephones in service,
served 98 percent of the customers, accounted for 91 percent of the telephone
workers, and operated 95 percent of the switching systems in the country.

During the 1950s government involvement in the sector grew slowly but
steadily. In 1952, for example, the Telephone Services Tax Law was created,
setting a 15 percent tax on local services and 10 percent tax on long-distance
services. In 1954 the government took the lead again by implementing a
financial scheme to solve TELMEX's shortage of funds. The financial strategy
required that new subscribers purchase shares of the company in order to get
new telephone connections. The approach solved much of TELMEX financial
constraints, but tilted ownership distribution. In the next three years some large
shareholders, like Ericsson, dropped significantly their participation in the
company.[14]

Government's role in shaping the sector did not stop there. In August 1958
a mixture of government coercion and persuasion led both foreign companies—
Ericsson and ITT—to sell their shares to a group of Mexican investors.[15] From
1958 to 1972, TELMEX's ownership remained private and Mexican. The
company grew at a quick pace: the number of lines tripled by the mid-1960s, and
the number of telephones increased fourfold. By 1967 Mexico was the third
fastest growing telephone system in the world.

TELMEX Under State Control

During the 1960s the government remained highly involved in the
development of the Mexican telecommunications infrastructure. Through official
loans and investment programs the state gradually expanded its participation in
TELMEX.

By the early 1970s, the rapid modernization of the Mexican economy and a
deepening of nationalism and statism among governing elites led President Luis
Echeverria to argue that government control of TELMEX was needed if the
company was to play a key role in national development and security. At that

time the Mexican state already controlled 48 percent of TELMEX. On August 1972, the Mexican government bought the remaining 3 percent of the company's shares needed to reach the 51 percent ownership of the firm.[16]

Under state control TELMEX kept its rapid pace of development. Foreign commercial loans and government commitment to network expansion led to yearly average growth of 12.8 percent. Consistent with its social policies, and in an attempt to compensate for years of biased development in favor of urban telecommunications, the government created the first long-term plan for nonurban areas. Later administrations implemented renewed plans for rural telecommunications. But in the late 1980s the skewed regional distribution of services was still evident: 50 percent of all lines were concentrated in the three largest metropolises—Mexico City, Guadalajara, and Monterrey—and more than 10,000 rural communities (under 500 inhabitants) had no access to any telephone service.

Aside from extending the network to the countryside, TELMEX aimed at technological innovation and upgrading of the system as a whole. A turning point for the modernization of the network came in 1985 with the earthquake that swept Mexico City. The quake deeply affected the existing infrastructure, forcing TELMEX to replace and upgrade a considerable percentage of the network. The renewal consisted largely in the replacement of old manual switchboards and mechanized exchanges with electronic switchboards and digital exchanges. [17]

TELMEX's own innovation strategy was boosted by specific demands from the business community operating in Mexico. In 1985 the demands of large multinationals operating at the U.S.-Mexico border led to the installation of digital private networks in three industrial parks in northern Mexico (Barrera 1990). A year later the company began a long-term plan to lay out fiber optics in Mexico City. By 1990 the project was extended to other major metropolitan areas with plans for the installation of approximately 9,000 miles of long-haul fiber optic.[18] The company's expansion program involved also the creation of twenty-four subsidiaries that carried out business in areas as diverse as publishing, real estate, radio telephony, satellites, and construction (Mier y Terán 1991).[19]

Although TELMEX's services and infrastructure expanded during the 1980s, the company was also affected by a variety of problems that hindered the overall performance of the firm. The growth of telecommunications services suffered due to high taxes, limited financial resources, a low investment profile, a distorted pricing structure, and low labor productivity.

The sharp growth of taxes over telephone services was an important factor that affected TELMEX's performance. On local services, for example, the tax was set in 1980 at 69.64 percent of the tariff; yet, by 1989 it accounted for 90.48 percent of the tariff. Taxes on domestic long-distance services showed a similar evolution, while taxes on international services fluctuated at an average of approximately 45 percent of the tariff.[20]

In spite of high taxes, local telephone tariffs remained low, compared to the price charged for long-distance and international services.[21] This was a consequence of the notion that telecommunications was a public service, and therefore international and long-distance users should subsidize local users. As a consequence local services absorbed 52 percent of the company's costs and contributed 15 percent of its revenues. The goal of achieving universal services was also at the basis of a tariff freeze from 1954 to 1975 driving TELMEX revenues down by 94 percent in real terms.[22] Despite the distorted tariff structure, TELMEX had a reasonable rate of return during the 1970s and 1980s. The company had an average of US$193 million net profit between 1982 and 1987.[23]

Although the company was profitable, it faced investment restrictions due to the fact that revenues were channeled to SHCP before the company received its annual budget. The government, based on general political and economic criteria, decided how much should be assigned to new investments in telecommunications. The company generally received much less of what it originally submitted to the Secretaría de Hacienda y Crédito Público (SHCP).[24] For this reason TELMEX relied heavily on foreign loans for investments in infrastructure and services. This financial support was effective until the early 1980s when the foreign debt crisis led to near halt of all foreign loans. The crisis deeply affected TELMEX's ability to borrow from abroad, thus dropping capital investments and the growth rate of the public network from an average of 12.8 percent in the 1970s to 6 percent throughout the mid-1980s (Figure 5.1).[25]

Figure 5.1

TELMEX Performance Indicators (1985–1991)

Year	Lines installed (Mill.)	Annual average growth	Digital lines % of total	Public phones (Mill.)	Invest. per line (Mill US$)	Annual average growth
1985	3,586	na	na	na	145.7	na
1986	3,776	5.20	10	34	117.5	-19.3
1987	3,984	5.53	14	42	114.1	-3.0
1988	4,261	6.94	34	46	156.1	36.8
1989	4,702	10.34	39	64	202.1	29.5
1990	5,189	10.36	46	83	327.8	62.2
1991	5,841	12.56	56	101	320.8	-2.1

Source: TELMEX

During the 1980s, while TELMEX expansion slowed down by half, the pace of growth of its labor force increased. In the 1970s the company's work force grew by 6 percent; by the mid-1980s, it was rising by an average of 8 percent a year. The size of the company's labor force which, by the late 1980s surpassed 49,000 employees, rendered the company with a ratio of 105 main lines per employees affecting TELMEX productivity. Compared to the leading telecommunications companies elsewhere in the world, TELMEX had a very low labor productivity (Figure 3.4).[26]

Advocates of state reform have argued that much of the poor performance of state-owned enterprises (SOEs), such as TELMEX, is due to the distorted incentive mechanism that built up throughout the years in the realm of public sector administration. In the case of TELMEX the institutional relation between the company and the state seemed, at least on paper, not to have been the source of the firm's deficiencies. TELMEX was, by law, an autonomous commercial corporation in which the state participated as a shareholder like private investors. In practice, however, the company was under the tight control of the Secretaría de Comunicaciones y Transportes (SCT), which held the presidency of the executive board and other key positions. SCT not only controlled operations; it also set the general policies of the sector and performed more specific regulatory functions—that is, determined technical norms and standards, controlled procurement, decided investment plans, and set tariffs for all services.

Despite efforts to upgrade and expand telecommunications services, TELMEX could not meet demand. The number of unfulfilled connection requests rose from an average of 43 percent in the 1970s to approximately 60 percent in the 1980s, and by 1989 Mexico had only six main lines per 100 people, while only 16 percent of its households were connected to the public network.

The problems faced by the company during the 1980s, the prospects of increased demand—in the quantity, quality, and diversity—for new services, and the rise to power of a group of government officials with a strong commitment to state reform led to the announcement in September 1989 of a broad privatization program. The sale of state-controlled telecommunications business was in Mexico, as in many other LDCs, one of the first large transactions. As in the case of ENTel, TELMEX's transfer to the private sector was as much an economic as a political event. However, in contrast to ENTel's privatization, the sale of TELMEX and the reform of the Mexican telecom sector was much less politicized. The reason for this difference lies in the uniqueness of the Mexican political system rather than in some intrinsic characteristic of TELMEX's sale.

THE SOCIOECONOMIC CONTEXT OF REFORM

Despite Mexico's stunning political stability, which has greatly enhanced its economic development, in the 1980s the country faced a reversal of the impressive economic growth of previous decades. This crisis, which led Mexican leaders to review their economic strategies and adopt state reform and privatization of SOEs, highlights the fact that policy making is not a purely political phenomenon and that economic conditions are as important as politics when explaining policy adoption, implementation, and outcomes.

Mexico grew rapidly after World War II, reaching averages of 6.6 percent annual growth from 1960 to 1976, and 8.4 percent from 1977 to 1981. During these years the public sector also expanded rapidly. By 1982 the Mexican state controlled 1,155 SOEs, which produced more than 15 percent of gross domestic product (GDP) and accounted for over 40 percent of total investments.

Yet, in 1982 a deep economic crisis ushered in a period of stagnation and recession.[27] In subsequent years the burden of a mounting external debt, a decline in international prices for petroleum, rising inflation rates, and the convergence of various other negative factors signaled Mexican leaders that it was time for a change. The failure of early, minor reforms showed that, due to the magnitude of the crisis, major structural changes were required.

In its effort to overcome the crisis, the government implemented a profound restructuring of the economy based on three transformations: state reform (mainly privatization of SOEs), opening of the economy (liberalization and trade reforms), and incentives for private-sector growth (relaxation of regulations on foreign and local private investments).

From 1983 to October 1992 Mexico's privatization program reduced the number of SOEs from 1,155 to 221, with 57 more slated to soon be privatized, liquidated, merged, or dissolved.[28] As in the case of Argentina, the program initially targeted small, formerly private enterprises, which were mostly liquidated due to their indebtedness and lack of economic value. From 1983 to 1988, 154 SOEs were "disincorporated or disengaged."[29]

In 1989, with the change of *sexenio*—Mexican word referring to the six year period of a presidential term—the Mexican state underwent important political changes. While in the past there has always been tension in the distribution of power and control of the state between traditional and technocratic politicians—*políticos* and *técnicos*—with the Salinas administration the balance tilted markedly in favor of the latter. Incoming technocratic elites shared, among other things such as training abroad, a neoliberal view of the economy. The continuing economic and fiscal crisis and their common understanding of solutions to the problem led them to deepen even further the state reform program initiated by the previous administration. With the nonviable SOEs already liquidated or dissolved, the Salinas government moved decisively to sell larger and sometimes profitable SOEs, such as TELMEX.

THE PRIVATIZATION OF TELMEX

Telecommunications was a key element in Salinas's modernization strategy (Cowhey, Aronson, and Székely 1989). In Mexico, the decision to restructure the sector was not solely tied to downward economic cycles. Current telecom reforms mirrored a shift in the development strategy of the country from inward-looking, import-substitution industrialization to one of export-led growth. Reflecting this new conception of development, president Carlos Salinas de Gortari officially announced on September 18, 1989—during the annual meeting of the telephone workers' union—his intention to privatize TELMEX.[30]

TELMEX, the second largest company in the country and one of the thirty largest telephone companies in the world, was a profitable business and had grown rapidly in last twenty years.[31] Why would the government want to sell a company that had provided an important source of public revenue?

Three factors seem to underlie this puzzling decision. First, TELMEX's privatization should be viewed as only one piece in the overall Mexican state reform program. In that sense, the sale of a profitable and attractive SOE, such as TELMEX, played a critical role in signaling the commitment of the Mexican government to structural reform in the national economy.

Second, it was expected that the sale would bring large amounts of needed cash to lessen fiscal constraints, and, simultaneously, the public flotation of TELMEX's shares would enhance the infant local capital market. Further, TELMEX's attractiveness would probably set a "high-price mood" for the upcoming sales of SOEs targeted for privatization.

Third, the existence of a public monopoly in the telecommunications sector did not fit well with the new outward-oriented economic program of the government. TELMEX would not only have to grow at an extremely quick pace to satisfy infrastructural requirements for entrance into the global market, but also it would have to diversify in ways that required technological expertise and capital beyond TELMEX's capabilities.[32] These considerations led to the official decision to sell the telecom firm.

One of the characteristics of the Mexican privatization program was the high degree of centralization in the management and control of the whole process. The sale of every Mexican SOE was managed by one government office, the Department for the Disincorporation of Parastatal Entities (Unidad de Desincorporación de Entidades Paraestatales - UDEP).

This office was created by President Salinas in 1988 and reported directly to the Secretary of Finance. UDEP was headed by Jacques Rogozinski—a Ph.D. in economics trained in the United States—and consisted of six director-generals and a handful of administrative staff. Like other state officials in the Salinas administration, the director generals were all highly trained specialists and most of them came from outside the national bureaucracy. As a consequence they had little stake in protecting the SOE's status quo. The office had full presidential support and was institutionally insulated from the everyday political pressures suffered by other state institutions.

Shortly after the official announcement of the pending TELMEX privatization, the sale of the company was placed under the jurisdiction of UDEP. As in the Argentine case, the government would have to dilute any potentially harmful opposition to the project, and the institutional and financial restructuring of Mexican telecom sector. The latter, of course, was highly dependent on the achievement of the former, since little restructuring can be achieved in the face of widespread opposition.

Buffering the Opposition

In societies organized around the presence of an overarching interventionist welfare state, privatization becomes a highly politicized and socially sensitive issue. In most LDCs the sale of SOEs has ignited some degree of political opposition. Mexico is no exception. The government confronted the resistance of labor and political groups in the sale of several of SOEs—Aeromexico and Minera de Cananea are telling examples in this regard. However, thanks to the stability of its political system, privatization has been generally smooth and manageable compared to other cases such as Argentina, Thailand, Colombia, Brazil, and South Africa.

A long tradition of tight clientelism, hierarchical relations, and power concentration gave the Salinas administration the needed political space to maneuver during the privatization process. However, these conditions were not taken for granted, and Salinas and his predecessor, Miguel de la Madrid were very careful to realign forces among different coalitions to dilute any meaningful resistance to the privatization of major SOEs. While the government sought political support from the PRI, the telecommunication union, and state managers, it blocked some opposition parties and interest groups from entering the process.

Getting the PRI mobilized to support TELMEX privatization was one of the government's first moves. Given that the PRI's political philosophy vindicated an interventionist welfare state, a centrally managed economy, subsidization of universal public services, and an implicit distrust of the private sector, one would have expected resistance to state retreat in key economic sectors such as telecommunications. This expectation seems reasonable given the actions of Argentina's populist Peronist party that, based on similar political and economic principles, resisted Menem's privatization of ENTel. However, there is a crucial difference between the PRI and the Peronists. While the PRI is characterized by a long tradition of party discipline and clear hierarchical relations, for several decades the Peronists had been a loose conglomerate of groups with conflicting interests and ideologies and little party discipline. As a consequence, while Menem struggled to keep his party under control, Salinas had the solid support of most PRI constituents.

The only resistance from the PRI appeared in late December 1990 when a group of PRI deputies joined the opposition and requested that Communication Secretary, Andrés Caso Lombardo, appear before Congress to clarify aspects of TELMEX's sale.[33] However, this dissent arrived too late since, by that time, the sale of TELMEX was already concluded. Exposure of the Communications Secretary to the incisive questions of opposition deputies had no impact on the reform process itself.[34]

In contrast with Argentina's party system, opposition parties in Mexico were very weak. The 1988 election that brought Salinas to the presidency was the first time in sixty years that the PRI saw its hegemony in serious jeopardy.[35] But, a year later, when TELMEX was put up for sale, the political crisis was largely over, and opposition forces were retreating.[36]

In the particular case of the sale of TELMEX, the Salinas administration confronted the opposition of the Partido Revolucionario Democrático (PRD) and the Partido Popular Socialista (PPS). These parties hoped to influence the privatization process in Congress, but the administration used several legal instruments to bypass the legislature and introduce regulatory reforms in the sector. Most conditions for TELMEX's sale were included in an amendment to the company's Concession Title. And, general regulatory reforms in the telecom sector were introduced by issuing a Communications Law Ruling.[37] Due to their status as minor rulings, neither of these two pieces of legislation needed congressional approval, and therefore, Congress was bypassed and lost its only chance to influence TELMEX privatization.[38]

Telecommunication workers—a political force that confronted governments elsewhere—assented to TELMEX's sale. The labor movement in Mexico has been a traditional constituent of the PRI and a main supporter of the Mexican state. The Sindicato de Telefonistas de la República Mexicana (STRM) was no exception. As the telecom sector's main union, it counted in its ranks 41,521 of the 49,000 working for the company. In 1976, however, there was a profound realignment of political forces within the organization. A new, younger generation of labor leaders, headed by Francisco Hernández Juárez, took over the union, with the result that STRM became one of the most independent labor organizations in the country. For two years the union was combative and struck several times to protest government policies.

When the idea of privatizing TELMEX was first announced, STRM strongly opposed it, arguing that such reform was not necessary and workers would fight it.[39] For a while it appeared that the union had succeeded in holding its position. In March 1989, STRM's leader announced that the plans for privatization of TELMEX were "definitely discarded."[40] However, as political events unfolded throughout the year the union was challenged by a revival of an official initiative to privatize TELMEX. Aware of the growing presidential commitment to the sale of the SOTE and the power of the state to enforce presidential orders, the union shifted towards a more lenient position. By July 1989 union leaders left the final decision on TELMEX privatization in the president's hands. In September, union leaders publicly announced their support of privatization arguing that the state was in no financial condition to modernize and expand TELMEX's operations at the speed required by the new economic program.[41]

Despite this official union announcement—which coincidentally mirrored the government's arguments for the sale—observers have claimed that the workers' position was affected by recent political events in the labor movement,[42] and what its members had come to perceive as the "irreversible nature" of privatization.[43] It made no sense for the union to resist the inevitable.[44] Opposition would bring worse outcomes for workers than would bargaining a reasonable position in the soon-to-be privatized firm. In this way the union traded its support for the privatization in exchange for participation in the ownership of the company,[45] employment stability, and the continuance of certain labor rights.[46]

In the case of the privatization of TELMEX, government strength in bargaining with the union was enhanced by the wealth of information that the administration had about the internal operations of the company and the role of labor within it. In 1987, the government implemented the "Program for the Intensive Improvement of the Service," which presumably aimed at identifying and overcoming deficiencies in the company. Intentionally or not, the program served to collect data and valuable information that was later used to bargain with the union (Fernández Christlieb 1991, 35).

Falling in line with the union position, most TELMEX managers and government officials in charge of the telecommunications sector consented to the administration's initiative. Most officials were members of the PRI and loyal followers of the government line. Although some voiced disagreement with the administration's policy, it would have been professional suicide to oppose the program. Moreover, potential resistance at the top of the company was ameliorated by offering TELMEX managers a long-term loan to allow them to purchase 1.4 percent of the company's stock.

The local and international business community responded to Mexico's privatization as it did elsewhere: applauding and cheering the new business-oriented policy. Yet, not all of the private sector logically fell into the support category—some, like telecom equipment providers, had incentives to block the privatization of their secured client. However, for some unknown reason, local equipment suppliers like Ericsson and Alcatel did not rise up as they did in Argentina during the Alfonsín administration.

Finally, Mexican consumers did not resist the program in any significant way, in spite of being harmed by price increases. The political culture of each country and the conditions faced by each president in selling the national telecom enterprise are reflected in the different attitudes of Mexican and Argentine consumers to tariff increases.

Restructuring TELMEX

The restructuring of TELMEX was carried out in both the financial and institutional spheres. For the government to be able to restructure TELMEX on time, it was crucial that no political interference or bureaucratic struggles develop. With the creation of UDEP the government blocked the possibility of any bureaucratic infighting.[47] And with a variety of political measures directed at different parts of the political spectrum, it succeeded in dismantling or blocking potential political opposition to the project.

Financial Restructuring

The financial restructuring of the company affected the capital of the firm, service tariffs, telephone taxes, and TELMEX debt. Prior to the sale of TELMEX, one key financial challenge for the Mexican privatization team was arranging to keep the privatized TELMEX in Mexican hands while simultaneously getting a purchase price for the company that probably no

Mexican business group could afford to pay. To achieve this the government implemented a sophisticated and creative capital restructuring of the company.

Until privatization, TELMEX had only two classes of stock: AA shares (which could be owned only by the government) and A shares (open to private ownership). In the months just before the sale, the government's 55.9 percent AA shares were split and reassigned voting rights.[48] Up to 4.9 percent of AA shares were converted into A shares. Utilities of the first semester of 1990 were capitalized, and with this capital upgrade new L shares were issued.[49] Since L shares had no voting rights, the company was left under the control of shareholders of AA and A shares, which constituted 40 percent of the stock. This ultimately meant that 20.4 percent of AA shares (offered in the initial bid) constituted 51 percent of the controlling stock. The government then ruled that 51 percent of AA shares (or 10.4 of the stock) must be held by a Mexican group and that AA shareholders could only vote together.[50] A Mexican group controlling 51 percent of 20.4 percent of the company thus could control the whole company.

Another crucial event in TELMEX's preprivatization restructuring was the sharp and unprecedented tariff upgrade carried out in the two years prior to the sale of the company. Until late 1987 real prices of telephone services declined steadily.[51] However, in January 1988 the government implemented a drastic tariff hike for all services.[52] Tariffs were adjusted differently according to the type of service (local, long-distance, and international) and the nature of service consumption (business or residential). Local basic service, for example, went up 186 percent, while connection charges rose fivefold in real terms.[53]

In January 1990 Mexicans experienced another stiff tariff upgrade. This tariff reform was clearly related to the upcoming privatization of TELMEX. President Salinas had announced only a few month earlier the official decision to sell the SOTE, and by early 1990 the public started to suffer the consequences of "preparing TELMEX for sale." Local rates skyrocketed 620 percent, while international tariffs dropped several points.[54] These tariff hikes provided TELMEX a 126.54 percent profit increase during 1990 (Corona 1992, 3).

Direct and indirect taxes on telephone service were also restructured prior to privatization. High taxes were previously included in the price of telephone service (90.48 on local services and 57.82 on domestic long-distance services in 1989) as part of the telephone tariff. The government now created a new tax of 29 percent on TELMEX's revenues from rental charges, local, and national long-distance calls. But it allows TELMEX to offset 65 percent of that against investments (as long as investments were above the total amount that the company owed in that tax year).

TELMEX debt was also transformed prior to the sale. The Mexican government took over most of it from foreign banks in a 1990 debt-renegotiation agreement. TELMEX canceled the debt with the government a few months prior to the sale, and was transferred to private investors with a short-term debt amounting to approximately 5 percent of its total operating assets.

Institutional Restructuring

Prior to the TELMEX offering, the government carried out a variety of institutional and proprietary reforms that affected the control of certain segments of the market.[55] In 1989, Telecomunicaciones de México S.A. (TELECOMM), a new state-owned telecom company was created to provide services. Due to a constitutional mandate, satellites must remain under state control.[56] The provision of fax, telex, and telegrams, and the ownership of the national microwave transmission network, was also transferred to TELECOMM. The transfer of the national microwave network to TELECOMM resulted from the government's attempt to create competition between TELECOMM and TELMEX in the provision of long-distance services. But investors set the condition that the privatized TELMEX would have the microwave network under its control. In December 1990, TELMEX bought the network from TELECOMM, thus becoming Mexico's sole provider of long-distance telecommunication services until 1996.

Existing telecommunications legislation was updated in the preprivatization period. Unlike the Argentine case, the Salinas administration developed a fairly sophisticated regulatory framework to govern the privatized telecom sector.[57] The *Reglamento de Telecomunicaciones*, a legal reform of the Communication Law of 1932, established the general regulatory framework for any telecom business in Mexico.[58] The regulation of TELMEX's operations was updated in a revision of the 1976 Concession Title to the company.[59] The Concession Title, although specifically aimed at regulating TELMEX operations, nevertheless had become central to the evolution of Mexican telecommunications due to the company's overwhelming dominance in the sector.[60] The norm includes the establishment of monopoly and competitive segments of the market, periods of exclusivity, the establishment of quantity and quality goals to be met by TELMEX, a new pricing regime, interconnection rules, and norms to avoid cross-subsidies and predatory behavior in the sector.

According to the Concession Title, which extends until the year 2026, private TELMEX enjoys a monopoly on long-distance services until 1996.[61] Basic local services were opened to competitive entry from the moment the new concession was granted, but TELMEX was not obliged to interconnect new entrants to the market and, therefore, it was imposible for potential competitors to survive in the market. The Mexican government also reserved the right to open to competition all basic services if TELMEX did not comply with the expansion and efficiency goals set in the Concession Title.[62] After 1996 TELMEX must also permit the resale of idle capacity of leased private lines.

TELMEX must meet certain improvement goals in a limited period as well. Lines in service, for example, must expand at an average of 12 percent per year. Before December 31, 1994, all towns with more than 500 people must have basic service. All cities of more than 5,000 people must have automatic switched services. Public phones must increase from the current 0.9 per 1,000 people to 5 per 1,000 people by 1998. The waiting period for new service must drop to six months in 1996, with a reduction by one month in each subsequent year, with the goal of a waiting period of only one month by the year 2000.

Repairs should be accomplished within eight hours of notification. Credit must be awarded to any customer deprived of services for more than seventy-two hours.

Pricing policy and interconnection rules were also reformed under the new concession. The pricing in Mexico now follows the RPI-X formula. Factor X has been set at 3 percent for the period 1991–1996 (when TELMEX's long-distance monopoly expires) and will be reset, thereafter, every four years according to incremental costs. In addition the concession regulates the conflictive issues of interconnection.[63] TELMEX has been required to adopt an "open-network architecture" (ONA) to allow interconnection of customers and competitive carriers.[64]

The concession also carefully regulates the potential ability of TELMEX to extend its monopoly power over liberalized segments of the market. TELMEX has been asked to spin off separate firms for the provision of competitive services—such as value-added network services (VANS), cellular, data services, private networks, telecom equipment, and so forth. The new ruling is aimed at dismantling potential cross-subsidization that TELMEX might implement to establish predatory prices and crowd out incoming competitors.

Furthermore, the concession has not modified those parts of the Communication Law that grant the Secretaría de Comunicaciones y Transportes (SCT) considerable control over TELMEX. Accordingly, the Mexican common carrier is obliged to make available to SCT technical plans of the company. The Communication Secretary may request modifications to those plans if third parties set legitimate requirements in that regard. TELMEX has to report to SCT every quarter on quantity and quality improvements, and SCT has a variety of penalty faculties—which include cancellation of the concession—if the goals established are not fulfilled.

Despite SCT's considerable policing power, agency officials recognize the difficulty in preventing business transgressions, such as the horizontal and vertical integration of TELMEX's operations.[65] SCT's powers and legitimacy have also been diminished by the intervention of SHCP, which, operating as the president's right arm and bypassing SCT's jurisdiction, have made deals directly with TELMEX.

The inability of SCT to deal with emerging problems in the sector highlights one of the main lacunae in the new legislation: the creation of a new, adequate regulatory agency. In this sense Mexico's reform differs from countries such as the United Kingdom, Argentina, and Venezuela, where restructuring has also rearranged the institutional structure of regulatory agencies.[66]

In Mexico, SCT still carries out regulation of telecommunications with similar infrastructure, finances, and powers that it had prior to privatization. But now there is a major difference: SCT must control the balanced evolution of a sector that is far more complex and diversified than what it was historically. For instance, during the past two decades, SCT's main goal was the self-regulation of TELMEX; in the future it will have to regulate a firm that operates independently. Furthermore, SCT customarily regulated an absolute monopoly, but in the future it will have to craft norms aimed at a market, in which companies operate in both regulated and liberalized segments, and in which services do not fit clearly into either.

One might argue that SCT's status quo is a reflection of Mexican political culture. The fact that the telecom regulatory agency has not gained financial and operational autonomy—as they have in other countries that privatized, such as Argentina and Venezuela—can be attributed to the centralized, hierarchical structure of the Mexican political system. The Mexican president is not ready to decentralize the regulation of a critical economic sector such as tele-communications. It has also been suggested that the direct intervention of LDC presidents and economics ministers in the control of privatized SOTEs and the weak presence of regulatory agencies can be attributed to the fact that privatized telecom firms have boosted local capital markets. Introduction of competition or the appearance of stringent regulations for the carriers would harm the attractiveness of the newly privatized companies on the stock market. In aiming at the development of infant domestic capital markets, governments have protected the privatized firms at the expense of creating sectoral improvements through competition.

TELMEX for Sale

The privatization of TELMEX, along with that of Argentina's ENTel, emerged in 1990 as one of the most outstanding worldwide privatization events. As the vice president of Nynex International asserted: "the privatization of TELMEX is a unique opportunity in life; it could become the deal of the century."[67]

The bidding process for Mexico's telephone company initially attracted sixteen of the most qualified international telecommunications companies, such as Nippon Telegraph and Telephone, Cable and Wireless, Southwestern Bell, Nynex International, GTE Telephone, Bell Canada, Singapore Telecom, U.S. Sprint, Telefónica de España, France Cable et Radio, STET, and United Telecommunications.

Most consortiums dropped out of the process due to financial difficulties. As a consequence only three groups—Grupo Gentor, Acciones y Valores, and Grupo Carso—all headed by Mexican investors presented bids for TELMEX. Although the government considered issues such as management, technology, quality of services, and financial capability in selecting the winning bid, it was the price offered for TELMEX that ultimately counted the most. On December 13, 1990, one month after the November 15 bidding deadline, TELMEX was sold to the consortium comprised by the Mexican financial conglomerate, Grupo Carso,[68] and two foreign common carriers, Southwestern Bell (U.S.)[69] and France Cable et Radio (France) (Figure 5.2).[70]

The government sold 20.4 percent of the company's privileged type AA shares for US$1.76 billion.[71] Due to restrictions imposed by the Foreign Investment Law, Grupo Carso has the majority control of the company with 10.4 percent of the shares, while Southwestern Bell and France Cable et Radio own 5 percent each.

Salinas also scored a victory in the second stage of TELMEX privatization. By mid-June 1991, the government sold 1,745 million L shares, representing 16.5 percent of the company, on foreign stock markets in the form of American Depository Shares (ADS). The shares went for US$27.25 each.[72] The government realized US$2.27 billion from the sale.[73] In May 1992, the government sold 500 million L shares (representing 4.7 percent of the company) in a public offering and earned US$1.35 billion.[74] After this sale the Mexican government kept 4.8 percent of the company's shares, to be floated in a public offering in the near future.[75] The privatization process deeply transformed the ownership profile of the company. Before privatization the government held 55.9 percent of the firm, private domestic shareholders 21.3 percent, foreign private shareholders 22.8 percent, and TELMEX employees did not own any shares in the company. By May 1992, the government participation had been reduced by 4.8 percent, while domestic private shareholders had grown to 35 percent and foreign private shareholders to 55.7 percent, with employees owning 4.4 percent of the business.

Figure 5.2

**Composition of TELMEX Share Ownership
as Percentage of Total Shares (September 1991)**

Owner	Share Type	Percentage	US$ Millions
Grupo Carso	AA	10.4	US$860
Southwestern Bell	AA	5.0	US$425
France Cable et Radio	AA	5.0	US$425
TELMEX group*	L	5.1	US$701
TELMEX employees	A	4.4	US$325
Foreign investors	L	16.5	US$2,270
Mexican government	L	9.5	US$1,307
TOTAL	AA,A,L	55.9	US$6,313

Source: *El Nacional* and the Mexican Secretariat of Finance and Public Credit
* Constituted by Grupo Carso, Southwestern Bell, and France Cable et Radio.

The privatization of TELMEX and these public offerings in the local and international capital markets have been so successful that the company had increased, by 1992, thirty times its preprivatization value.[76] By May 1993 the value of the company had dropped slightly but it had become the number one firm—based on its market value—among the top 100 companies in developing countries (Figure 5.3).

LIBERALIZING THE MEXICAN TELECOM MARKET

Mexico, unlike Argentina, has substantially liberalized the telecom service market. The Mexican government has been able to introduce competition in all nonbasic services in the country, and TELMEX must comply with new regulations (such as the establishment of separate subsidiaries with separate accounts, network development for easy interconnection, and the sharing of network information) to avoid unfair competition in the provision of these services.

Wireless communication, such as cellular telephony and paging, has been liberalized. Cellular telephony is provided on a competitive basis in the nine regions into which the country has been divided.[77] Despite the stringent bidding requirements, which included a minimum of US$1.5 million in capital plus proven technical expertise, SCT received 106 cellular telephony applications. Figure 5.3 shows the distribution of companies throughout the country. The ninth region corresponds to Mexico City, which already had two companies providing cellular service.[78] Seventeen new radio licenses have been granted for paging service—including several with nationwide coverage in the 900 MHz range. Radio telephony permits have also been granted for services in central Mexico and other regions of the country. SCT still controls the concession of licenses for the operation of cellular, radiotelephony, and paging systems. Considering the inadequacies of the public network to fulfill the telecom needs of a rapidly growing economy, the Mexican government expects a burst of new wireless services provided by private operators.[79]

The government is also permitting the installation of overlay digital private networks. Data services are provided under market conditions by Telepac (a state-owned company), TELMEX, and by various private companies. In preparing the Mexican market for further liberalization, the Salinas administration included in the TELMEX concession the obligation to allow the resale of idle capacity in private, leased lines after 1996. The government has also reserved the right to open to competition all basic services if TELMEX does not fulfill the efficiency goals and competition rules established in the Concession Title.[80]

The government has kept—under the corporate organization of TELECOMM—state ownership of satellites,[81] telex, fax, and telegram services. However, TELECOMM has to compete with private firms in the provision of fax, telex, and, soon, in satellite services. Despite constitutional restrictions, the Salinas government has carried out regulatory reforms to allow installing and operating of private satellite communication (Mody and Borrego 1991).[82] In this way, TELMEX, private telecom companies, and large users will be able to own and operate earth stations for data transmission, rural telephony, and other services. Generally these services are operated through the modern technology

Figure 5.3

Regional Cellular Telephone Concessions in Mexico

Region	Company	Owners
1. Baja California Norte Baja California Sur	Baja Celular Mexicana (Bajacel)	Tecelmex General Cellular
2. Sonora, Sinaloa	Movitel del Noroeste (Movitel)	McCaw Cellular Comm. Contel Cellular
3. Chihuahua, Durango, and Torreón	Tel. Celular del Norte (Norcel)	Domos Int. Motorola Centel Cellular
4. Nuevo León, Tamulipas, and Coahuila	Celular de Telefonía (Cedetel)	Millicom Inc. Protexa
5. Jalisco, Colima, and Michoacan	Com. Celulares de Occidente (Comcel)	Racal Inc. BellSouth Iusacell
6. Aguascalientes, S.L.P., Sacatecas, Guanajuato, Querétaro, and various cities and towns	Sistemas Telefónicos Portátiles Celulares (Portacel)	Bell Canada Iusacell Alarcon
7. Puebla, Tlaxcala, Veracruz, Oaxaca, and Guerrero	Telecom. del Golfo, S.A. (Telecom del Golfo)	Bell Canada Iusacell GMD
8. Chiapas, Tabasco, Yucatán, Campeche, and Quintana Ro	Portatel del Sureste (Portatel)	Ass. Communic. LCC Co.
9. Mexico City	Iusacell	Bell Atlantic Iusacell
All the regions	TelCel	SouthWest. Bell France Telecom Grupo Carso

Source: PNUD-UIT/SRE-IMC 1991 and Lehman Brothers 1994.

of very small aperture terminals (VSAT). Some companies such as Princeton Consulting, Incorporated and Satellite Applications Engineering Corporation, have already applied for government licenses to install a national satellite mobile systems.

The obvious question that arises in the presence of these market transformations in Mexico is, Why has the Mexican government been able to open most of the market to competition while the Argentine administration failed to do so? Considering that both countries achieved complete privatization of their SOTEs, what explains this difference in outcome of attempts to liberalize?

As suggested before, I argue that the attractiveness of each market determined the bargaining power of local governments to achieve desired goals. In other words, while the unattractive profile of the Argentine market weakened Menem's bargaining power, the bright outlook for the Mexican economy enhanced Salinas's leverage to achieve proposed goals.

While Mexico suffered a considerable decline of private investments throughout the 1980s, the trend was dramatically reversed during 1990. In that year, foreign direct investments alone reached US\$5.2 billion.[83] Investor confidence in the Mexican economy was rooted in some encouraging macroeconomic events of late 1989 and 1990. Inflation, for example, dropped from 51.7 percent in 1988 to 19.7 percent in 1989, while GDP grew from 1.7 percent in 1988 to 3.2 percent in 1989 and 4.4 percent in 1990.

In September 1989 Mexico reached an agreement on its foreign debt rescheduling—commonly know as the "Brady Plan." The approval of international financial institutions to reschedule debt under those conditions was an international signal of the country's trustworthiness. The rescheduling was announced in the same month in which the privatization of TELMEX was officially publicized. The coincidence of these events sharply improved Mexico's standing in the international privatization market.

External confidence in the country's political and economic prospects was reinforced with important changes in investment legislation. In May 1989, the existing 1973 Law to Promote Mexican Investment and Regulate Foreign Investment was modified to "increase the volume and accelerate the flow of investment capital by providing legal certainty and by simplifying and clarifying the administrative rules and procedures that apply to such transactions." These new regulations were an effort to liberalize the investment environment.[84]

The prospect of a North American Free Trade Agreement (NAFTA) consolidated even further Mexico's allure for the international business community. With NAFTA, investors in Mexico would not only benefit from the country's competitive advantages (such as cheap labor, lower taxes, loose regulations, etc.), but they would also gain direct access to the world's most important market, the United States. Private investors from the United States also expected that NAFTA would tend to unify legal treatment of local and foreign businesses, granting foreign companies benefits that are now absent in the Mexican market.[85]

More specifically, in the telecommunications market, the prospect of NAFTA brightened TELMEX's privatization and the overall future of the sector. Since it was expected that NAFTA would bring about a sharp increase in economic activity among the three partners to the agreement, the consumption of telecom services would, therefore, increase geometrically with the boosting of trade and related economic activities. For companies that are well aware of the long-term benefits of early market entrance, TELMEX's privatization appeared as an excellent opportunity to be ahead of the game were NAFTA to be fully implemented.[86]

Liberalizing the economy was another major economic reform that enhanced Mexico's position in the competition for private investments in the telecommunications sector. While in 1983 the percentage of import value subject to licensing was approximately 83 percent, by 1990 the Mexican economy qualified as one of the most open economies in the world, with the average tariff at approximately 13.1 percent.[87] Lowering custom entry barriers was important for the cost structure of potential future owners of TELMEX. The opening would allow the import of telecom hardware, granting TELMEX considerable leverage to bargain for better conditions with local equipment providers. But, more importantly economic liberalization—and regional economic integration— is expected to increase international trade and commerce, thereby boosting the demand for long-distance telecom services.

NAFTA and economic liberalization were not the only elements that made Mexico an attractive investment. If NAFTA failed, Mexico's allure for telecom investment would continue since its border with the United States generates important flows of international calls to and from the United States granting TELMEX revenues for approximately US$1 billion a year (Devlin and Guerguil 1991, 49). As economic events converged, Mexico's attractiveness to the international business community grew.[88]

In political terms, Mexico has not always been a secure place for investments. Successive governments, responding to demands from various sectors of society and seeking political stability, followed a state-interventionist / freemarket pendulum that placated political interests but scared away capital and discouraged investments.[89] This trend, however, was reversed after the mid-1980s when the Mexican administration took a clear stand in favor of private sector development. With President Salinas, the trend was reinforced and, by the time TELMEX was privatized, there was little political threat to new private investments in the country.

These improvements in the Mexican economy, the particular attractiveness of the telecom sector, and the progressive dilution of any major political threat to the reform project, gave the Salinas administration considerable bargaining power to achieve both the privatization of TELMEX and a significant liberalization of the telecom market at the same time.

However, the opening of the Mexican telecom market was not to be taken for granted. Private investors applied heavy pressure to keep the market as closed as possible. The best example in this regard is the intended liberalization of long-distance services. While the government initially transferred the national microwave network to TELECOMM, with the intention of turning the state company into a competitor of TELMEX on long-distances services, investors required the network to be transferred to TELMEX and long-distance services to be kept closed a number of years.

CONCLUSION

In Mexico, as in Argentina, telecommunications services developed under private foreign ownership. In most Latin American countries service was nationalized in the 1930s or 1940s, but in Mexico telecom remained a private business until 1972, when the government gained control of 51 percent of the company's shares. Even then, TELMEX remained a corporate entity. In other words, it was never a traditional PTT—operating as a branch of the secretary of communication—as was the case in many other LDCs. The long-standing presence of private business in telecommunications sector contradicts the widespread notion that the Mexican state was one of the most interventionist in the world. Yet, although the state never had full ownership of the firm, successive governments since the 1930s managed to control and shape the evolution of telecom service. One of the clearest examples of this was the "Mexicanization" of the company in the mid-1950s.

Telecom services grew quickly during the 1950s, 1960s, and 1970s, regardless of whether the company was under majority private or state control. In the 1980s TELMEX performance suffered along with the rest of the national economy. In response to the economic crisis of the 1980s the Mexican government implemented an overarching state reform program that positioned the telecom sector—as then-presidential candidate Carlos Salinas put it—"as the cornerstone to modernize Mexico".

In Mexico, as in other less developed countries, the privatization of large public utilities, such as TELMEX, was a politically controversial process. However, when compared with other cases, Mexico shows a puzzlingly untroubled privatization. Neither a long tradition of strong nationalism and revolutionary pride nor socially entrenched welfare policies and state interventionism proved an impediment for the Mexican state in fully reversing its long-term telecom policies and moving towards widespread privatization and liberalization of the sector.

Resistance to this "revolutionary" shift was not absent. Yet, the particular arrangements of the Mexican political system granted the Salinas administration the needed insulation and concentration of power required to implement the sale of the national carrier. Contrary to the Argentine case, the Mexican government paced and shaped the reform to meet most of its initial goals. Cohesion among state officials, a disciplined bureaucracy, considerable presidential power, and an insulated policy process, gave the Salinas administration most of the political tools absent in the privatization attempts during Argentina's military regime and the Alfonsín administration.

While the privatization and liberalization of TELMEX during the Salinas administration bears little resemblance to early privatization attempts in Argentina, it does share important elements with the efforts of Menem's government to sell ENTel. In both cases the process was insulated from the interference of Congress, opposition parties, labor, and local interest groups. Both sales were carried out by a small group of government officials, who operated in a politically insulated environment, enjoyed full support of the president, and counted with direct presidential intervention when necessary. The power assigned to these officials endowed them with the power not only to privatize the national carrier but also to completely restructure the telecom sector.

Nevertheless, there were important differences. While ENTel's privatization was carried out from "within" the company by the appointed head of the firm, TELMEX's sale was managed through the Finance Secretariat. And while in Argentina the last stages of the sale suffered from bureaucratic struggles between the Minister of Public Works and Services, the Minister of Economy, and the privatization team, TELMEX's sale was a smooth event in which other sectors of the state never challenged the privatization team. Finally, by concentrating responsibility for the sale of all state enterprises in one state agency, the Mexican government benefited from the specialization and experience gained by the few actors involved. In contrast, Argentina's privatization team was dismantled once the task was accomplished and no "body of knowledge" was ever amassed as a result of the experience.

There is a more substantive and crucial difference in the outcomes of the attempted liberalization of the domestic telecom markets of Mexico and Argentina. While the Salinas government has opened most services to competition and reserved the right to do so with those to which a temporary monopoly was granted, the Menem administration conceded a monopoly over all services—with the exception of the least profitable ones or the ones that were already liberalized.

This study argues that the answer to this intriguing divergence in policy outcome results from the attractiveness of the local market. In Argentina, where the economic and political environment was risky for private investment, liberalization goals were sacrificed in order to attract enough capital for a successful privatization of ENTel. Although the Mexican government granted minor concessions—such as the delay of competition in long-distance services—the country's stable economic and political environment and its potentially large telecom market gave the Salinas administration enough leverage to protect and implement market liberalization.

In sum, the Salinas and Menem governments enjoyed considerable state autonomy vis-a-vis domestic pressures. Both presidents had a tight rein on the administrative and political process within the state apparatus, and both pushed through the sale of the SOTEs, overcoming various obstacles along the way. However, Mexico's market outlook allowed the Salinas government to "protect" its planned liberalization, while Argentina's market prospects led the administration to relinquish its intention to introduce competition in order to achieve successful privatization.

NOTES

1. For the section on Mexican politics, I rely largely on the work of Cornelius and Craig.

2. On average a municipal government depends on the federal administration and state governments for approximately 80 percent of its income.

3. It has been argued that opposition parties "gave the regime a loyal opposition in the Congress, provided an outlet for the protest vote (people so dissatisfied with the government's performance that they could not bring themselves to vote for PRI candidates), and served as vehicles for dissident political leaders, keeping them within the government-sanctioned arena of political competition" (Cornelius and Craig 1991, 73).

4. The three main organizations are the Confederación de Trabajadores de México (CTM), the Confederación Nacional Campesina (CNC), and the Confederación Nacional de Organizaciones Populares (CNOP).

5. The history of several East and Southeast Asian countries show a comparable correlation between major historical social dislocations and the emergence of a powerful and autonomous state apparatus (i.e., Indonesia, Malaysia, Vietnam, Korea, etc.). See Neher 1991.

6. The network was set up to link the main police stations of Mexico City with the Ministry of Government.

7. This historical account relies among others on the work of Enrique Cárdenas de la Peña (1987), and Fátima Fernández Christlieb (1991).

8. The legal name of the company was Compañía Telefónica Mexicana, S.A.; however, throughout its years of operations it was known by other names such as Compañía Telefónica de México and Mexicana.

9. Mexico City concentrated at that time—as it still does today—by far the largest number of subscribers in the country.

10. The legal name of the company was Mexikanska Telefonaktiebolager Ericsson, and it was comprised of L. M. Ericcson (60 percent), Stockhomls Allmanna Telefon AB (20 percent), and the Swedish banker, Marcus Wallenberg (20 percent).

11. The coming to power of the Miguel Alemán Valdés administration in the late 1940s reinvigorated government intervention in the Mexican telecommunications sector.

12. Other small private investors, such as Bruno Pagliai, Octavio Fernandez Reynosos, and José Joaquín César, held fifty shares each.

13. The government representatives were Antonio Martinez Baez (Secretary of Economy) and Abelardo Rodríguez (ex-president of Mexico).

14. Ericsson's participation, for example, dropped to 37 percent.

15. Ericsson and ITT would remain the Mexico as equipment providers for several years more.

16. When the company was nationalized in 1973, there were approximately one million telephone lines in the country; when it was privatized in 1990 it operated 5.27 million lines.

17. To avoid the vulnerability that is attached to the centralization of operations, TELMEX operations in Mexico City were split into four centers (a strategy that was later replicated through the country). Each of these centers were individually connected to national long-distance and international services, and were interconnected through twenty fiber optic routes and nine digital microwave systems (Fernández Christlieb 1991, 32).

18. TELMEX also provided nine systems for public data communication.

19. This conglomerate of companies accounted by 1990 for US$3.5 billion in revenues. Some of these subsidiaries were Anuncios en Directorios, S.A.; Compañía de Teléfonos y Bienes Raíces, S.A. de C.V.; Construcciones Telefónicas Mexicanas, S.A. de C.V.; Canalizaciones Mexicanas, S.A. de C.V.; Construcciones y Canalizaciones, S.A. de C.V.; Alquiladora de Casas, S.A. de C.V.; Editorial

Argos, S.A.; Fuerza y Clima, S.A.; Imprenta Nuevo Mundo, S.A.; Impulsora Mexicana de Telecomunicaciones, S.A.; Industrial Afiliada, S.A. de C.V.; Operadora Mercantil, S.A.; Radio Movil Dipsa, S.A. de C.V.; Renta de Equipo, S.A. de C.V.; Sercotel, S.A. de C.V.; Servicios y Supervisión, S.A. de C.V.; Teleconstructora, S.A.; and Teléfonos del Noroeste, S.A. de C.V.

20. Taxes on long-distance services started at 43.99 percent of the tariff in 1980 and rose to 57.82 percent by 1989, while taxes on international services started at 43.99 percent in 1980, reached 50.53 in 1986, and dropped to 40.30 in 1989.

21. After the nationalization of TELMEX, telephone tariffs were set by the Secretaría de Hacienda y Crédito Público (SHCP) in consultation with Secretaría de Programación y Presupuesto (SPP), Secretaría de Comunicaciones y Transportes (SCT).

22. In 1976 a devaluation of the Mexican peso and efforts to reduce the external debt of the company led to the first tariff increase (24 percent) in more than two decades. Since then tariffs have been raised frequently, becoming a yearly pattern after 1981.

23. According to government officials this tariff structure (consisting of low basic telephone rates coupled with high taxes) had a dual purpose supposedly benefiting both SHCP and TELMEX. Government officials claimed this arrangement provided large revenues for SHCP, while keeping local-service costs low enough to allow TELMEX to expand basic services at subsidized prices. Only the high SHCP revenues were assured, however. Benefits to TELMEX were less apparent, since low telephone rates negatively affected the company's revenues and its ability to undertake new investments (Pérez Escamilla 1989).

24. In 1987, for example, TELMEX transferred to SHCP US$500 million from the company's revenues; however, it received back only US$150 million for the next fiscal year from the central administration.

25. In preparing the company for privatization, overall investment and growth improved.

26. However, TELMEX's worker per line ratio was not so bad, when compared to other telephone companies in the developing world.

27. In 1982 the fiscal deficit reached approximately 17 percent of GDP.

28. Although in quantitative terms, the number of SOEs "disengaged" is impressive, one should keep in mind that in financial terms some of the largest Mexican SOEs still remain in state hands. PEMEX alone, for example, accounts for more than half of all SOE revenues. (PEMEX is the fifth largest oil company in the world.)

29. Reduction of state sector enterprises can occur via mergers, liquidation, and dissolution as well as through privatization. The Mexican government has thus avoided the politically sensitive term "privatization," replacing it with the less-loaded concept of "*desincorporación*"—that can be translated as "disengagement" or "de-incorporation."

30. TELMEX privatization had been discussed publicly for more than a year at this point.

31. More specifically, TELMEX contributed to state revenues with 1.02 percent of all public-sector income (Corona 1992, 6).

32. The implementation of overlay private digital networks, for example, was a consequence of TELMEX's technological limitations. The company could not provide reliable and state-of-the-art high-speed lines (Barrera 1990, 14).

33. *La Jornada*, 8 December 1990, 12.

34. *El Nacional,* 22 December 1990, 1; and *El Día,* 22 December 1990, 1.

35. The two parties that posed serious threats to the PRI were the Partido de Acción Nacional (PAN) and the Partido Revolucionario Democrático (PRD).

36. Improvements in the economy, the implementation of large social welfare programs for the low-income population (which preempted the leftist agenda) and the promise of "democratization" (which lured discontented middle and upper classes) favored the PRI and the governing elite. In the 1991 elections the PRI regained much of its historical voter base.

37. A *reglamento* is a body of very specific rules that regulate the operationalization of the general principles set by law. Yet, since there is no legal body overseeing the telecommunications sector other than the outdated 1934 law, this new ruling has gained the force of the main telecom regulatory body in Mexico.

38. It has been argued that this official approach might have hindered commitment of private investors, since the two major pieces of legislation that govern the Mexican telecom sector are based on presidential decrees and not on federal laws. However, there is no significant evidence of that in the first years of TELMEX operations.

39. *El Nacional,* 26 February 1989, 5.

40. *El Nacional,* 24 March 1989, 4.

41. *El Nacional,* 10 September 1989, 1.

42. When Salinas came to power, the decision to keep labor under control was reinforced by clear government signals, such as the incarceration (on charges of corruption) of the head of the powerful oil workers' union.

43. In an article on the issue, the head of the union argued that, "the privatization of public enterprises has become a dominant feature of the economies of most countries around the world. It is a process that does not discriminate against the political or economic orientation of each nation, nor does it distinguish among various ideological positions or levels of development" (Hernández Juárez 1991, 43).

44. There is a Mexican saying that reflects political actors' perceptions when they have to bargain with the state: "it is better to have 50 percent of something, than a 100 percent of nothing." This is probably how the union perceived their chances in the process.

45. TELMEX workers gained access to 4.4 percent of the company's stock— of which 1.76 percent are A share with voting rights.

46. The size of the Mexican market, its actual and potential growth rate, its position in the international economy, and the prospect of its integration into larger North American trading block, turned TELMEX privatization into an attractive deal, granting the government some bargaining leverage to request employment stability and the permanence of certain workers' rights.

47. By removing TELMEX restructuring tasks from the control of the Secretary of Communication the government guaranteed that no bureaucratic infighting or embedded interest would slow down or block the restructuring process.

48. TELMEX capital was restructured on June 15, 1990, in a shareholders' general assembly.

49. L shares are worth one-and-a-half times less than an AA or A share.

50. The specific conditions for the sale of TELMEX shares was established by the Esquema de Desincorporación de Teléfonos de México, S.A. de C.V. (TELMEX), approved by the government on September 7, 1990.

51. Two factors seem to have affected this trend. First, when the government took over TELMEX in the early 1970s, it began to subsidize low tariffs with the aim of achieving universal service of public telecommunications. Second, during the 1980s, the approval of tariff increases did not keep pace with spiraling inflation. Prices for basic telephone services declined fast, since during that period taxes added to the basic tariff of telephone services rose sharply, eating up large portions of the general tariff increase.

52. It has been argued that the upgrade had the double purpose of adjusting tariffs to inflation and gaining genuine revenues for renewed investment plans. Pressumably, it was not related to the prospect of TELMEX privatization. However, considering the closed nature of Mexican politics it is hard to tell if the privatization was already in the minds of a few in the inner presidential circles.

53. For a detailed analysis of TELMEX price and tax reforms, see Tandon and Abdala 1992.

54. Accumulated increases from 1986 to 1990 equated to a tariff increase for local services of 1,240 percent.

55. Although some important regulatory reforms were introduced to privatize TELMEX, there was no need for any constitutional reform—as will be the case in Brazil if privatization of Embratel and Telebras ever proceeds.

56. Art. 28 of the Mexican Constitution.

57. The existence of a clear regulatory framework was one of the factors that contributed to the development of a transparent reform in which the announced set of rules were not modified during the process. This element—which contrasts sharply with the Argentine case—has been fleshed out by some analysts as a crucial factor in the success of TELMEX privatization. See Tandon and Abdala 1992, 16.

58. The Reglamento de Telecomunicaciones was published in *Diario Oficial*, 29 October 1990.

59. The new Concession Title was published in *Diario Oficial*, 10 December 1990.

60. For a detailed study of both legal bodies, see Martínez 1992.

61. There are several national and foreign companies waiting eagerly to enter the profitable long distance market in 1996. AT&T, for example, has increased its presence in the Mexican market dramatically in the last few years. In April 1992 the North American company bought a Mexican telecom company—Informática y Telecomunicaciones S.A.—that provided data,video, and voice integrated systems to the business community. Among the local concerns interested in the market is PEMEX—which owns a long-distance telecom network for its own operations. The SOE is looking forward to expanding its services to other customers when the market opens in 1996.

62. See *Modificaciones al Titulo de Concession de Telefonos de Mexico, S.A. de C.V.,* Art. 2-4.

63. Barriers to interconnection can emerge due to the refusal of the public network operator to connect other users or providers. Reason for denial can range from the lack of tariff agreements to the mere abusive behavior of the dominant carrier. For some examples of this latter situation, see Chapter VII, section on service providers. But problems of interconnection can also arise due to the technical interoperability of the systems. In this second case interconnection deficiencies may arise from large fixed investments in systems with incompatible standards, software packages that are not compatible, and the existence of applications that are designed to operate only in isolation.

64. Open network architecture is a private network arrangement that emerged as an alternative to ISDN. It was developed to counter the possibility that ISDN would recreate PTT's monopoly over most telecom services. ONA's standards and protocols allow users interactive management of telecom services. The network, which is organized in seven hierarchical layers, customizing them according to customer's particular needs. Through ONA users can become providers also. See Smith and Pitt 1991, and Minoli 1991, 57.

65. Ironically, one of the most publicized penalties applied to TELMEX was applied by the consumer protection agency (PROFECO)—and not by SCT. PROFECO applied the penalty based on consumers' complaints about the quality of company's customer services.

66. In the United Kingdom, for example, the telecom regulatory agency, Oftel, was created as part of the reform of the sector. In Latin America Argentina has created Comisión Nacional de Telecomunicaciones (CNT), and Venezuela has set up also its Comisión Nacional de Telecomunicaciones (Conatel).

67. *El Nacional,* 18 October 1990, 21.

68. Grupo Carso is the sixth largest economic conglomerate in Mexico. Headed by Carlos Slim Helú, it controls companies operating in mining, copper manufacturing, auto parts, paper products, retailing, insurance, stock brokerage, food, and tourism; and it employs approximately 30,000 people. During 1990 Grupo Carso had US$1.5 billion in sales and US$81 million in net profits. Profits for the group has skyrocketed due to TELMEX's purchase, since by 1992 annual net profits for the telecom company reached US$2.6 billion (*Notimex,* 22 July 1993, and *La Jornada,* 23 July 1993).

69. Southwestern Bell is one of the regional Bell operating companies (RBOCs) that emerged as a consequence of AT&T divestiture. The carrier operates 11.3 million lines, provides employment to 66,700 people, and has sales of approximately US$8.9 billion. Profits of the company come not only from Southwestern Bell itself, but also from the eight subsidiaries that the company controls. These firms provide cellular telephony, research and development (R&D) operations, telecom-equipment provision, and are involved in the publishing business.

70. Information about France Cable et Radio can be found in Chapter 4, section on ENTel's sale.

71. The consortium headed by Acciones y Valores, comprising GTE and Telefónica de España, offered US$1.68 billion for TELMEX. The amount received by the Mexican government for TELMEX went far beyond anybody's expectations. Yet, one should keep in mind that the TELMEX sale was enhanced by including in the deal most of the twenty-four subsidiaries mentioned above.

72. Each ADS contains 20 L type shares.

73. Telephone workers and the new private owners also purchased TELMEX shares. The union, using a credit of US$325 million provided by the Mexican government, bought 187 million type A shares through Nacional Financiera (Nafin). That represents 4.4 percent of TELMEX's capital. Grupo Carso, Southwestern Bell, and France Cable et Radio had access to 5.1 percent of the capital through type L shares. In this way, Southwestern Bell, for example, bought US$467 million worth of L shares, doubling its participation in TELMEX.

74. This offering had similarities to the May 1991 sale. There was an overdemand for shares—in this case of approximately 70 percent— and most of them were sold in the United States, with smaller offers in the stock markets of Mexico, France, Switzerland, Canada, and the United Kingdom.

75. The proceeds of the TELMEX sale were initially used to create a Contingency Fund to overcome fluctuations in the international oil market. But, in October 1991, most of the fund was used to reduce internal public debts.

76. The value of TELMEX went from US$1.2 billion in late 1988 to US$29.8 billion in May 1992 (Tandon and Abdala 1992).

77. There are two operators in each region.

78. One of the companies is Intelcel, a subsidiary of TELMEX; the other one is IUSACEL.

79. Explosive diffusion of wireless communication to bypass the deteriorated public network in LDCs will reinvigorate traditional domestic and international struggles on proprietary rights and allocations of radio frequency spectrum. For implications of recent increases in the provision of wireless telecom services, see "Airwave Wars," *Business Week,* 23 July 1990. For an elaborate historical analysis of the international politics of radio spectrum allocation and the role of LDCs, see Savage 1989.

80. Mexico is among the few countries that promised in its initial commitments to the General Agreement on Trade in Services (GATS) to liberalize basic telecom services (Pipe 1993, 40).

81. Satellite remained under state ownership. In 1982, article 28 of the Mexican Constitution was modified to include the explicit statement that satellite communication was a strategic tool for the nation, and should, therefore, be kept under exclusive control of the state.

82. Satellite services are currently provided through two domestic satellites (Morelos I and II). The government is planning to add a third satellite, to provide services to all of Latin America. The system has forty-four transponders that make possible the operation of 361 telephone circuits, 230 telex circuits, satellite telephone communication with forty-three countries, telex communication with seventeen countries and two video channels.

83. In the first half of 1991, FDI reached US$8 billion. This impressive figure for the first half of 1991 is due in some part to the US$2.7 billion TELMEX stock sale.

84. Under this new legislation, foreign investors may own up to 100 percent of those businesses classified as unrestricted. Projects in most economic sectors are no longer subject to CNIE (National Foreign Investment Commission) approval. Authorization is automatic as soon as the project meets certain basic requirements: investment should not exceed US$100 million; funds should come from abroad; the project must not be located in one of Mexico's largest metropolitan areas; there should not be significant foreign exchange inflows or outflows during the project's first three years; and the project must utilize adequate technology, satisfy environmental requirements, create jobs, and offer employee training and personnel development programs. See Secretariat for Commerce and Industrial Development of Mexico 1990. For other studies on Mexico's foreign investments, see Peres Núñez 1990, and Huss 1991.

85. The impact of NAFTA on the Mexican economy and on the flow of private investments from the United States is even more relevant when one takes into account that 66 percent of all Mexican foreign investment comes from the United States.

86. For new investors, the balance between important advantages and high risks is quite delicate since the implementation of NAFTA will also bring greater competition and a more unstable market for TELMEX.

87. Import licensing was required on only 2 percent of the tariff items, and the economic sectors that still required import licensing (automobiles and pharmaceuticals) were gradually being liberalized.

88. By 1991 Mexico was the largest recepient of foreign direct investment (FDI) in Latin America, attracting one-third of all foreign capital. Sustained economic recovery, elimination of most foreign ownership restrictions, the prospect of NAFTA, and the impressive privatization of SOEs were indicated as the main reasons that boosted investors confidence in the country (Jasperson and Ginarte 1992).

89. Nationalization of the banking system is probably the most outstanding event in this respect.

6

Generalizing the Argument

Are the central premises of this study applicable to countries other than Argentina and Mexico? In the case of telecom privatization attempts, do we find in other cases a correlation between privatization success and autonomous government with high concentration of power in the executive? In other words, when less developed countries (LDCs) attempt to privatize their telecommunications industries, does success correlate with governmental autonomy and a powerful chief executive? When liberalization and privatization are attempted simultaneously, does success correlate with attractive domestic markets? To test the arguments presented earlier and to see if the causal links apparent in the experiences of Argentina and Mexico also occur elsewhere, this chapter briefly examines the experiences of other developing countries where telecom reform—even though attempted during this same historical period— followed different paths. That is, some succeeded and some failed in their reform attempts.

The chapter looks at the experiences of five Latin American countries (Chile, Colombia, Jamaica, Venezuela, and Uruguay), two Southeast Asian countries (Thailand and Malaysia), and an African nation (South Africa).[1] In all of these cases, the governments formally announced their intention to (partially or totally) privatize the national telecommunications enterprise. Most of the privatization efforts took place in the late 1980s. In the final section, arguments about the viability of market liberalization offered in previous chapters are extended to the cases of Malaysia, Thailand, and Jamaica.

THE POLITICS OF FAILED PRIVATIZATIONS

The governments of Thailand, Colombia, South Africa, and Uruguay attempted and failed to sell their state-owned telecommunication enterprises (SOTEs).[2] This section explores these cases and briefly draws correlations between politics and telecom privatization. Among the cases presented, Colombia and South Africa show interesting similarities with the Thai case in the sense that organized labor played a central role in dismantling privatization. Uruguay is a somewhat different and peculiar case since the failure of privatization was rooted in the activism of political and civil organizations that— through a grassroots movement—gained enough support to call a national plesbicite and defeat the government's telecom privatization project.

Thailand

The Telephone Organization of Thailand (TOT) and the Communications Authority of Thailand (CAT) were at the time of privatization attempts the two main service providers in Thailand. TOT operated the domestic telephone network, leased circuits for point-to-point domestic communication, and provided certain long-distance and international services to neighboring countries. CAT provided international telecommunications and all nonvoice domestic services. The Post and Telegraph Department (PTD)—which functions under the Ministry of Transport and Communication (MTC)—was in charge of the regulation of the sector.

Pressured by a booming economy and rapid urbanization, the government concentrated its efforts on the development of basic infrastructure. Domestic telephone service increased by an average of 26 percent a year in the mid-1980s while the number of connected subscribers rose by 18 percent.[3]

In spite of this impressive growth rate, in the late 1980s Thailand still had one of the poorest telecom service records in Southeast Asia. Lack of long term planning, financial constraints, managerial and technological problems, poor coordination between the two companies, and other deficiencies plagued the country. By the end of 1990, the waiting list for subscriber lines had climbed to 992,496. Customers waited from six months to ten years to get connected to the public network. Although CAT and TOT launched new telecom services and diversified their operations, neither was able to keep pace with growing demand and diversification of services.[4] As a consequence, in 1990 the country had 1.8 telephones per 100 people—one of the lowest telephones-to-population ratios in the region.[5]

Economic development in the 1980s brought up pressures for improvement of the system. In 1985, the government of Prem Tinsulanon put forward the first attempt to reform the sector by proposing the separation of postal and telecommunications services in the country. The initiative met the opposition of telephone workers who went on strike. This was the first step in a long and uneasy attempt to reform and privatize telecommunications in Thailand.[6] The failure of the Thai telecom privatization attempt lies in the political dynamics created by powerful interest groups that successfully battled the project each time it appeared on the political agenda.

Thailand—reflecting the institutional profile of other countries that failed to achieve state reform—has suffered from government instability and political disorder throughout the last fifty years. In 1932 a military coup (the first of what would become a recurrent feature of Thailand's political life) put an end to the two-hundred-year-old Chakri dynasty (Yoon 1990). Despite the coup, the monarch remained as the formal head of the state, and Thailand was reorganized as a constitutional monarchy. In contrast with the stability of the monarchy, the government has suffered instability and lack of continuity. Nineteen prime ministers have occupied power and thirteen different constitutions have been adopted since the early 1930s.

It has been argued that this pattern of political instability was an unconventional mechanism for political renovation (Wilson 1962, and Riggs 1966). However, in the last two decades Thailand has undergone profound restructuring of its social and economic institutions with major consequences for Thai politics.[7] A benchmark of this transformation was the student rebellion of 1973 that, it is commonly believed, removed the last true military strongman (Hewison 1989). From 1973 to 1976, Thailand was ruled by a civilian government, and popular participation in public affairs surged. Despite another regressive coup in 1976, there is a consensus that in Thailand post-1973 politics has been increasingly open and decentralized. A reflection of this is the controlled parliamentary government created in 1977 by Prime Minister General Kriangsak Chomanan. General Chomanan stepped down from power three years later under popular and parliamentary opposition to his economic policies and was replaced by Prem Tinsulanon, who was selected by a wide coalition of civilian politicians.

Tinsulanon was the first to attempt an initial reform of the sector. Yet the project was postponed due to labor opposition. In August of 1988, Chatichai Choonhavan took office and revived Prem's reform initiatives. The new program not only renewed the plans of the previous administration, but also made them fully compatible with the Sixth National Economic and Social Development Plan of Thailand (1987–1991), which proposed that "the role of the private sector in national development should be enhanced both in production and in provision of infrastructure of services hitherto provided by the government." In the particular case of communications, the state should "encourage private sector participation in investing and operating public communications services. For example, joint investments, leasing and partial or total takeovers will be allowed."[8]

During 1988 the government lobbied managers of state-owned enterprises (SOEs), state employees, and the public in general to gain political support for its privatization program.[9] In May 1989 the Choonhavan administration was ready to launch a plan to privatize 49 percent of TOT's shares, but the timing for reform was not right. The government was attempting to introduce reform without having gained enough insulation from social pressure or achieved strong hierarchical support within the state.

At the legislative level, the government confronted a bicameral legislature in which many of the 357 members of the lower house and 268 members of the Senate had vested interests in state-owned enterprises. Since the 1979 election, Parliament has consisted of numerous political parties, none of which have ever attained a majority. The six-party coalition that has led the government not only has faced opposition from other political forces, but often encountered conflicts and serious disagreements within the coalition itself.[10] The diverging interests of different fractions of the legislature and the weak support of the parties within the governing coalition, played an important role in the progressive erosion of the reform program.

Reflecting the political dynamics present in Parliament, managers of SOEs challenged mandates of high state officials. In the telecommunications sectors this became obvious in late 1989 when TOT top managers, in clear disobedience to orders from the prime minister, granted a contract to a Japanese firm.[11] Although the action of TOT officials constituted a direct violation to the power hierarchy within the state, no disciplinary action was taken against them. According to analysts, official inaction arose from a latent "fear of rocking the government's stability."[12]

Although this event revealed the power of TOT's managers, the most important element in the government's retreat was the opposition of the unions and the military. The unions acting overtly and the military working behind the scenes, efficiently dismantled the privatization project.

In terms of sheer numbers, the strong union role is puzzling. Only 5 percent of Thai workers are unionized. At least two factors appear to contribute to the public sector's union strong role. First, Thailand's largest unionized sector consisted of state employees—more than 260,000 workers. Second, state workers' salaries and benefits were much better than those of their counterparts who worked in private companies.[13] Fear of losing the status quo ran high and led to a huge mobilization against the government.[14] Two massive strikes, in July 1989 and in February 1990, led by one of the state unions and joined by workers of the other sixty-three SOEs, resulted in the government announcing the indefinite suspension of all privatization plans.[15] The outcomes were predicted by a local political analyst, who argued that

> privatisation here is simply an economic and political impossibility. The unions' ferocity is only matched by its organisation. No government, including a military junta can hope to follow through on even the smallest aspect of privatising. As Chatachai is rapidly discovering, pursuing the programme is tantamount to political suicide.[16]

Besides the unions, the army constituted the other most important player in the process. The military stake in blocking TOT privatization was based on the fact that the army saw the privatization of national telecommunications as a threat to national security and a considerable loss for its control over the communication system of the country. Furthermore, both TOT and CAT had high army officials on their board of directors, positions they would likely lose with the transfer of the company to the private sector. For those reasons the military, led by army commander Chaovalit, built up a close alliance with public sector workers to dismantle privatization initiatives.[17] Despite their small number, the military were a very powerful political force in Thailand and their opposition to the reform program had a definitive impact on its fate.[18]

By March 1990 it became clear to Prime Minister Choonhavan that the privatization program was unfeasible. In a meeting he told other political leaders, "I may be the last prime minister in the democratic system. I have less confidence than ever in democracy ... the privatization issue has weakened it and we (his party coalition) are now plagued with difficulties."[19] On February 1991, only a year after his assessment, the first successful military coup since 1977 overthrew the Chatichai administration, canceling all potential privatization plans.

In summary, an increasingly open political system and a progressive decentralization of power weakened the Thai government in its ability to enforce controversial economic reforms, such as privatization. The outcome was the indefinite suspension of TOT's sale.

Colombia

The Colombian government struggled for two years to restructure and privatize its Empresa Nacional de Telecomunicaciones (Telecom), state-owned since 1943. The dynamics of resistance to Telecom's privatization greatly resembles the case of Thailand. In both countries a government with limited political support, dispersed power, and strong worker opposition had to retreat from privatization efforts.

In 1989 Congress passed legislation granting the president special powers to reform the telecommunications sector.[20] Only a few days after assuming office in May 1990, President Gaviria used these powers to craft a decree that liberalized the provision of long-distance services and allowed private overlay networks.[21] The presidential ruling met immediate resistance from telecom workers, whose strike forced the government to cancel the project. The only reform that the administration was able to introduce at that time—with the consent of the union—was the opening of the market to the provision of cellular telephony.[22]

In February 1992, Gaviria tried again to send a new telecommunications bill to Congress. Organized labor again moved to block the initiative. They were supported by politicians who also opposed the project.[23] For several weeks workers marched in the streets and protested in front of the Communication Ministry. Mobilization against the project reached its peak on April 24, 1992 with the calling of a general, indefinite strike that cut off all communications in the country. The strike concluded six days later with the resignation of the communication minister and the definite cancellation of the privatization initiative.[24]

Much of the Colombian experience provides evidence supporting the central argument of this study. Like Argentina and Thailand, Colombia has a long history of political struggles and violence. The two major contenders have been the Liberal and Conservative parties. Clashes between the two groups led to widespread national violence that left 250,000 people dead in the decade between 1948 and 1958. In the early 1960s a social pact was forged and gave birth to the National Front. This political coalition was able to put a stop to political violence. Until the late 1980s Liberal and Conservative parties alternated in power every four years.

Tight political control by the National Front led to political apathy among most of the population and to the resurgence of political violence carried out by various guerrilla groups. Spreading political violence led the government to negotiate the incorporation of guerrilla groups into the national political system in the mid-1980s. During 1989–1990 most guerrilla groups demobilized and entered the political arena, marking the beginning of a new era. In May 1990, César Gaviria, the Liberal candidate, was elected.

Behind this seemingly *deja vu* electoral result, the Colombian political system was undergoing a deep transformation characterized by the crumbling of the old coalition and the emergence of new, confrontational political forces.[25] Shortly after assuming power, the Liberals suffered a schism dividing the party into several antagonistic groups. The conflict diminished the ability of the government to influence and shape through representatives of the governing party the new national constitutional that was to be up for reform in the coming months.[26] As a result, the new constitution (approved on July 5, 1991) retained Colombia's presidential system but profoundly diminished presidential powers, strengthened the role of Congress, and decentralized control of the political process.[27]

Gaviria attempted the privatization of Telecom in this context of political decentralization and lack of presidential authority.[28] Colombian political transformations not only led to a weakening of the executive, but also ignited popular political activism and participation. As a consequence, the government not only faced the resistance of telecom workers, but also the support that they gained from other unions, political groups, and citizens in general who mobilized against the sale of the firm.

South Africa

South African's telecom system was operated until the early as a traditional PTT. The South African Posts & Telecommunications (SAPT), which held a monopoly in service provision and a monopsony in equipment procurement, provided all telecom services in the country (Horwitz 1994).

In the mid-1980s the South African state began to face serious fiscal problems, for which privatization was the most widely recommended solution.[29] In 1986 the Economic Advisory Council of South Africa called for the implementation of a broad privatization program—which was later articulated in the "White Paper on Privatisation and Deregulation on the Republic of South Africa."[30]

From 1987 to 1990 the Botha administration embarked on restructuring several of the major SOEs, whose privatization was the ultimate goal. In early 1990, under grave domestic and international political pressure, the new president, F. W. de Klerk, announced the legalization of the African National Congress party (ANC) and other banned organizations. He also announced the government's intention to proceed with the privatization of state-owned firms. The strategic attempt to sneak in privatization of SOEs behind the bright lights of the announcement of the dismantling of apartheid was not missed by most of the opposition. The ANC publicly warned the government that they would have no other option but to nationalize all SOEs privatized prior to political normalization and it would be without compensation.[31]

Although the ANC did not support nationalization as a general policy,[32] it nevertheless viewed privatization not so much as a mechanism to overcome fiscal problems, but as a political strategy by the white minority to remove from the public domain a considerable portion of public wealth, and to transfer crucial sectors of the national economy—such as telecommunications—to white hands.[33]

While the privatization of SAPT would have been an easy task to achieve a few years earlier, the project now became impossible. After many decades of an exclusionary and repressive apartheid regime, the white minority, which had tightly controlled the politics and economics of South Africa since 1910, found themselves in the 1980s facing unprecedented domestic and international pressure to open the political system to the black majority. Unable to control growing demands and opposition, the government legalized previously banned political parties, called black leaders in to negotiate an opening of the political process, and progressively dismantled the laws that governed the apartheid regime for so many years.

In the midst of this profound political transformation and under the burden of a stagnant economy, the weakened de Klerk government attempted to move forward with the sale of SAPT. Yet, strong opposition from empowered anti-apartheid political organizations blocked it and forced the government to rescind on all privatization attempts. As in Thailand and Colombia, workers played a central role in canceling the project. In an effort to overcome worker opposition, the government offered shares to SAPT employees. However, while workers in other countries supported the arrangement, South African telecom workers rejected it. Leaders of the telecommunication union, such as Mr. Mashele, advised SAPT employees not to accept the offer, because "workers who take shares will be reluctant to take industrial action."[34]

Led by the Congress of South African Trade Unions, thousands of black workers in Pretoria, Johannesburg, and Port Elizabeth demonstrated against privatization on March 29, 1990. A few days later, Dawie de Villiers, minister of Public Enterprises, announced that SAPT and other SOEs would not be sold as initially planned. The government feared that pushing privatization further might jeopardize negotiations with the ANC and other black organizations and disrupt the fragile political equilibrium achieved up to that point.

Furthermore, the government knew Parliament would have to pass legislation to reform current regulatory arrangements if SAPT were to be sold. In Parliament the Conservative party (CP), a strong political group consisting mainly of right-wing Afrikaners, opposed the government.[35] CP members viewed privatization as a direct threat to the job reservation system, which had long granted public service jobs to the Afrikaner population. The prospect of a privatized SAPT running on commercial principles would also hinder cheap telephone service for rural Afrikaners—the main constituents of the party (Horwitz 1994, 27). Aware that the privatization of SAPT had become a highly sensitive political issue, the government shelved the project.[36]

Uruguay

Uruguay offers a similar, yet distinct, case. Privatization of the national carrier, Administración Nacional de Telecomunicaciones (ANTEL), had to be suspended because of a popular vote against the project.[37]

On September 27, 1991, the Uruguayan Congress passed law 16211 to restructure and privatize SOEs. Broadly known as the Public Enterprises Law, the new legislation included as one of its main targets the sale of ANTEL. According to official arguments, the government was attempting to attract new capital to double the company's current US$50 million annual investment in order to satisfy unmet service demands. Several foreign firms—Telefónica de España, France Cable et Radio, STET, Nynex, Bell Atlantic, and BellSouth— and some local groups showed interest in the project.

In late 1991 political groups and citizen organizations began a campaign against the privatization of ANTEL. According to Uruguayan law, citizens who seek revision of government initiatives must pass through three different legal phases. First, they have to collect 12,000 signatures. This grants them the right to call a referendum, the second phase, in which 600,000 votes must favor revision.[38] In the third stage, the government calls a national plebiscite in which the winner must achieve a simple majority of votes.[39]

Despite the success of the movement to call a referendum, the government—counting on the support of an important segment of the main opposition party—did not take seriously the grassroots opposition. The privatization schedule for ANTEL was maintained as initially planned. Yet, a few months later, the government was forced to retreat from the sale of ANTEL when 72 percent of the voters in the national referendum, held on December 13, 1992, opposed the sale of the state-owned telecom company.

Participatory mechanisms, such as the referendum, gave the citizenry the ability to affect the policy-making process, thus blocking the government's attempt to implement unpopular policies.[40] In the case of ANTEL's privatization, the population's resistance to the reform was reinforced by the nature and dynamics of party politics. Uruguay's political system historically has been dominated by two political parties—the Colorados and the Blancos—a loose gathering of diverse factions with strong ideological differences and disparate political preferences.

On November 1989 general presidential elections brought to power Luis A. Lacalle of the Blanco party. The lack of congressional majority led Lacalle to invite the opposition Colorado party to form a national governing coalition (*Coincidencia Nacional*). However, the privatization program and other controversial presidential initiatives progressively eroded the agreement. As a consequence national leaders of the two main parties struggled to keep the support for privatization of lower-rank political leaders and party constituents. Midlevel politicians are a crucial bridge between political elites and citizens. They build popular consent for government policies. However, in the case of ANTEL's privatization, this chain (which operates so effectively in countries like Mexico and Malaysia) was not only broken, but also snapped back on itself, as midlevel party members started to actively campaign against the official project.

THE POLITICS OF SUCCESSFUL PRIVATIZATIONS

The following section briefly explores the experience of four countries that successfully privatized their national telecom enterprises: Malaysia, Chile, Jamaica, and Venezuela. Malaysia—the first Southeast Asian country to privatize its SOTE—shows strong similarities with Mexico.[41] Chile—the first developing country to carry out complete privatization of its SOTEs—is probably an extreme case in regard to the workings of this study's basic premises. In Jamaica, the privatization of the national carrier was a closed deal between a private telephone company and the government, with little or no participation by political actors. Venezuela, on the other hand, is particularly puzzling: a seemingly weak government, with an unpopular head of state who confronts considerable popular resistance to structural adjustment policies, nevertheless achieves the privatization of the national carrier. The ambiguity of the available evidence and the limited data at hand renders the Venezuelan case an enigmatic "black box."[42]

Malaysia

Malaysia was a British colony until 1957. Reflecting colonial infrastructure patterns, the communication system of Malaysia was developed in a way that allowed the British to monitor the economic, political, and social evolution of the colony (Onn 1989). In the early days of the colonial empire telecommunications services were provided by an office under the supervision of the superintendent engineer. After 1946 the office gained regulatory and operational functions in the provision of services throughout the peninsula, and became the Malayan Telecommunications Department. Later, in 1963, the Department of Telecommunications (DoT), controlled by the Minister of Works, Telecommunications, and Posts, and operating under the name of Jabatan Telekom Malaysia (JTM) became the main provider and regulator of services in the country.

From 1947 to 1957 telecommunications services in Malaysia grew at a very rapid pace, reaching growth rates of 16 percent per annum. During the 1960s and 1970s the pace of growth diminished, but it nevertheless remained high with annual averages of about 8.5 percent. The pace of network development is reflected in statistics: in the early 1970s there was 1 telephone per 100 people, in 1980 there were 2.9 per 100, and by the late 1980s there were 10 telephones per 100 people.

Throughout this period the company added a variety of technologies and services. In 1975 most crossbar exchanges were replaced by electronic exchanges, which led to the introduction of International Subscriber Dialing Service in 1979. By the late 1980s, 80 percent of subscribers had access to the service, giving them direct dialing to over 150 countries. Data services were introduced in 1984, when Malaysian Packet-Switched Public Data Network (MAYPAC) and Malaysian Circuit-Switched Public Data Network (MAYCIS) launched their operations.

However, network development could not keep up with the booming economy. The waiting list for new services grew from 14,000 in the early 1970s to 365,000 in 1987.[43] In 1972 the Telecommunications Act of 1950 was amended to introduce institutional and administrative reforms to DOT. One of the key events in the restructuring of the sector was the mandate to DOT to operate on "commercial principles." To accomplish this, accounting and financial matters were separated from the central administration. The goal was to make the DOT financially autonomous and self-sufficient. The reform did not work very well. From the mid-1970s to the mid-1980s operating expenditures were always higher than revenues, up to the point that by 1984 only 52.9 percent of the department's expenditures were funded by genuine revenues. Providing telecommunications services had become a costly operation for the government.[44]

The deficient performance of most SOEs and the economic decline of the early 1980s gave rise to official programs to reform the state.[45] With a political philosophy strongly resembling that of the Thatcher government, the administration of Prime Minister Datuk Seri Dr. Mahathir Mohamad, borrowed a considerable number of ideas and strategies for state reform from England. The privatization of Malaysian SOEs became a crucial element in this state reform initiative (Government of Malaysia 1989). As in other cases described here, local politics and the state's role in the domestic political system remain a crucial element in the unfolding of Malaysia's privatization initiative.

Politically, Malaysia is a constitutional monarchy that gained independence from British domination in 1957.[46] Five years later, in 1963, the Federation of Malaysia was created.[47] A multiracial coalition, known as Barisan Nasional has governed the country since its independence.[48] Prime Minister Mahathir Mohamad, is the country's fourth prime minister since 1957.[49] Politics in the country was organized very much along ethnic lines (Muzaffar 1989, and Datar 1983).[50]

Ethnic diversity, wealth disparities, and the pursuit of national development brought into the forefront of Malaysian political and social life a strong, centralized, and insulated state, capable of achieving ethnic integration, economic redistribution, and national growth.[51] In regard to the distribution of power and openness of the system, Malaysia displays striking formal differences but substantive similarities with Mexico.

Malaysia is a constitutional monarchy with a parliamentary system. Mexico, instead, is a presidential system with a bicameral Congress. Despite these institutional differences they share key political features. Malaysia, like Mexico, is internationally recognized as a democracy. However, both nations have not had the renewal of government control that is characteristic of most other democracies in the world. They both, instead, have been governed by one political party since the current political regime took power: Barisan Nasional in Malaysia and the PRI in Mexico. In both countries the opposition has been very weak.[52] And both political systems are structured to integrate a diversity of interest groups into a broad coalition under the patronage of the party in Mexico and of the electoral front in Malaysia.[53] In both countries the boundaries between the state, the government, and the party were, until the early 1990s, an institutional fiction.

Malaysia's bureaucracy is stable and professionalized, with demarcation of roles and hierarchies and a strong concentration of power in the hands of the prime minister (Puthucheary 1987). Malaysia also has a long tradition of politically aware and technically trained state officials that constitute the Malaysian Civil Service.[54] Its members belong to the same ethnic, educational, and kinship background as the political elite creating an "administrative state" that sets the political tone of the country (Esman 1972, 72).[55]

Clear hierarchical relations in all segments of the political system, strong concentration of power in the executive, discipline within the party system and within the state, and a politically dismembered society (in which demands are channeled through the specific power structures to which the state has granted representational legitimacy), makes Malaysia a highly integrated political system in which state control permeates civil society and national politics.

Political opposition to top-level decisions has been generally futile within the Barisan coalition and even outside of it. However, during the years of JTM privatization the government confronted for the first time in its long hegemonic history serious challenges not only from opposition forces, but also from factions within the Barisan coalition. Although these events were not directly related to the privatization of JTM but to general government policies, they are, nevertheless, illustrative of the government's ability to control the opposition and insulate the policy-making process.

In 1986, with his re-election as prime minister, Dr. Mahathir Mohamad led Barisan Nasional to a sweeping victory in national elections.[56] However, a few months later, he nearly lost the leadership of the United Malay National Organisation (UMNO) party, in what was the first challenge to the party's leadership. An alliance between Tengku Razaleigh Hamzah, then trade and industry minister, and Datuk Musa Hitam, a former deputy president of UMNO, cast serious doubt on Mahathir's ability to lead the country. Soon after, dissidents questioned the validity of the elections on juridical grounds, arguing that the operations of UMNO were illegal because thirty of its branches were improperly constituted.

Intraparty struggles were reinforced by new challenges from other parties, within and outside the Barisan Nasional coalition. Privatization of SOEs revived the important issue of official economic discrimination against Malaysia's Chinese population which was institutionalized in the National Economic Program (NEP).[57] Following the guidelines established by the NEP, the privatization program was conceived as a proper mechanism for the redistribution of wealth between the Chinese and Malay populations. For example, Malays had preferential access to state subsidies and public sector benefits and opportunities—like public sector employment—while Chinese were implicitly excluded from the redistributive program. This, and other economic and political issues, caused resentment among the Chinese. During the 1986 elections, the Malaysian Chinese Association (MCA), the Chinese party within the Barisan Nasional and second largest in the coalition, lost considerable support. Simultaneously, the Democratic Action Party (DAP), another predominantly Chinese party outside the coalition, won 20.8 percent of the votes, becoming the largest opposition party in the country. Further conflicts within the MCA and growing loss of support from its constituents resulted in the party leader threatening the government with a possible MCA withdrawal from the coalition if the state maintained its discriminatory policies against the Chinese community.

In response to these challenges, Mahathir moved decisively to dissolve growing resistance to official initiatives. First, under the Internal Security Act, approximately one hundred opponents were arrested, various demonstrations and political rallies were banned, and three newspapers were closed. Second, the court decision that UMNO was operating illegally was displaced via the formation of a new party, UMNO Baru, from which opponents were excluded. Third, constitutional amendments reformed jurisdiction and functions of the judiciary, making it more difficult for judges to take independent action. Fourth, a variety of political pressures led to the dissolution of the Supreme Court, and a new one, acquiescent to the official line, was convened. Finally, several laws were amended to limit political freedom and strengthen the power of the executive.[58] By early 1989 intraparty struggle had disappeared, opponents had formed new parties that were not a serious threat to the regime, and Chinese protest was in clear decline. By the end of the same year, UMNO Baru and its leaders had regained full control of the Malaysian political scene. All of the above illustrates the tight integration of the Malaysian political system. Therefore it is not surprising that the government was able to implement widespread state reform despite a troubled political environment.

The roots of telecom reform in Malaysia can be traced back to 1983 when the government, in its effort to overcome a deepening fiscal crisis and unprofitable, slow-growing telecommunications services, designed a plan to implement a long-term restructuring of the telecom sector (Government of

Malaysia 1985). In early 1984 the administration announced its intention to privatize the company, and in March of the same year the proposal was formally approved by the cabinet. The announcement was met with resistance from telephone workers and other economic and political groups with vested interests in the sector.

Telecommunications workers constituted the most relevant and perhaps the only significant opposition to the project.[59] They feared losing jobs if JTM were to operate under profit-maximization and efficiency principles. They also feared loss of exclusive rights and benefits. However, powerful union resistance in Malaysia was unlikely since unionism in the country is largely underdeveloped (Deyo 1989).[60] In the telecommunications sector in particular, two factors diminished worker's resistance. On one hand abundant surplus labor diminished workers' bargaining power. On the other hand the government guaranteed that the new company would retain employees for a period of five years (Isahak 1990).[61]

Diverging from telephone workers, JTM managers and government officials, lacked incentives to oppose the project. The professionalization of the Malay state offers a clear and encouraging career path for state officials, but at the same time it leaves scant space for dissent. To resist a decision emanating from the head of the government would be a major professional mistake. In the case of JTM, privatization managers also had little fear of job instability. The state would remain the largest owner of the company, and although there could be job instability due to commercial efficiency in the long run, in the short term there was no unemployment threat.

The government's tight control over the Malaysian political system enabled it to dismantle potential opposition and quash further challenges. In August 1985, Parliament passed the Telecommunications (amendment) Bill and the Telecommunications Services (Successor Company) Bill, providing the regulatory framework needed for further reform.[62] In January 1987 the new company, Syarikat Telekom Malaysia (STM) was corporatized with the government retaining 100 percent ownership.[63] STM began its operations under a twenty-year license issued by the Minister of Works, Telecommunications, and Posts (Woon 1990).[64] In November 1990, STM was listed in the Kuala Lumpur Stock Exchange (KLSE), and 13 percent of the company's shares were sold to the public.[65] STM employees and several Malay institutions later acquired a number of new shares created to increase the company's capital base. After this sale state ownership shrank to 81 percent of STM capital (Onn 1994).

Corporatization of state-owned telecom services and partial privatization of the company were probably among the most important measures that the Malay government adopted to upgrade the sector in its attempt to meet the needs of a booming national economy. Reform has turned STM into a profitable business, whose listing on the Kuala Lumpur Stock Exchange made it by May 1993 the most-valued enterprise in Malaysia, with a market value of US$11.6 billion.[66]

Successful transformation of JTM into a private business should not be taken for granted. The Malay government faced a variety of challenges throughout its privatization efforts. However, the autonomy of the Malay state and the heavy concentration of power in the head of the executive played an important role in making the sale of JTM a successful venture.

Chile

State reform in Chile began in 1974 during the military regime of General Augusto Pinochet, making it the earliest privatization program initiated in Latin America.[67] The process can be divided into two clearly defined stages from 1974 to 1978 and from 1985 to the present.[68] Privatization in the telecommunications sector began in 1982, when the Pinochet administration sold a majority of shares in the National Telephone Company (CNC) and Coyhaique Telephone Company (CTCOY).[69] Between 1985 and 1987, shares of the two major national carriers—Compañía de Teléfonos de Chile (CTC) and Empresa Nacional de Telecomunicaciones (ENTEL)—were sold to private local investors.[70]

In January 1988, 30 percent of CTC was sold to the Bond Corporation Chile, S.A.[71] Bond Corporation increased its participation in CTC capital stock throughout 1988 by buying shares in various other offerings. By the end of that year it had gained control of 50 percent of the company. When the Bond empire collapsed two years later, Bond Corporation Chile sold its shares in CTC to Telefónica de España.[72] During this period the government offered the remaining shares on the Santiago and New York Stock Exchanges.

The history of the dominant Chilean long-distance carrier, ENTEL followed a similar pattern. During 1988 the government sold to private interests its majority control in ENTEL, and completed the sale of the remaining shares during 1989. By 1990 the company was owned by Telefónica de España, Chase Manhattan Bank, Banco Santander, employees, and small private investors. By mid-1990, when the new democratic administration took office, both CTC and ENTEL were owned and controlled privately.[73]

The unchallenged privatization of the entire Chilean telecommunications system can be seen as an extreme case of power concentration and state autonomy. In September 1973 a military coup toppled the socialist government of President Allende. For the next sixteen years Chile was governed by a harsh authoritarian regime, headed by a military junta whose role was defined by a statute giving them absolute executive and legislative power. Political activities and parties were banned, constitutional rights suspended, and, under the aura of a new political era, the country was submerged in a prolonged period of repression and state-led terror.[74]

The Chilean regime was notable for the single-handed management of the government by General Augusto Pinochet. However, Pinochet's one-man leadership did not go unchallenged. Early on, the high command of the air force hoped to replace Pinochet's free-market approach with a more corporatist, nationalistic program based on a strong state sector. However, Pinochet skillfully displaced his opponents and consolidated his power.

Social uprisings and popular protests during the early 1980s also posed a threat. Deep economic crisis and years of heavy political repression brought civilians into the street. Lack of cohesion among opposition groups, a return to widespread political repression, and a recovering economy eroded support for popular mobilizations. By 1986 the country was again under Pinochet's absolute control.

With no opposition in the armed forces, a weak and dispersed resistance in civil society, and an extreme concentration of power in the president's hands, the privatization of Chilean SOTEs was not a difficult task. Similar to the Mexican experience the process was enhanced by concentrating the management of the sale in one state agency, the Development Corporation (Corporación de Fomento a la Producción—CORFO).[75] As a consequence, Chile stands out as one of the few cases in the developing world in which the attempts to privatize SOEs were not paired with any significant resistance to the program.

Jamaica

Jamaican SOTE privatization was unconventional. Jamaican Telephone Company (JTC)—a wholly state-owned firm—provided domestic telecom services until 1987. International services were offered by Jamitel—a joint venture between Cable and Wireless (C&W) and the government of Jamaica. In 1987 the companies merged their shares creating Telecommunications of Jamaica (TOJ). At that point the Jamaican government controlled 82.7 percent of the shares, with C&W holding the remainder. Through a variety of public offerings and direct purchases by C&W, the government sold all its interest in the company. By late 1990 C&W controlled 79 percent of TOJ, while the remaining 21 percent was in hands of private shareholders. As in other cases, the particular organization of the Jamaican political system and its workings during TOJ's privatization provided important elements to understand privatization success.

Jamaica is a parliamentary system dominated by two parties—the Jamaican Labor Party (JLP) and the People's National Party (PNP)—that have controlled national politics and alternated in power since the early 1940s.[76] Curiously the two parties held similar constituency profiles and political programs. Leaders were from the educated middle class, while loyal followers were largely poor population—which constitutes approximately 50 percent of the electorate and were evenly divided between the JLP and the PNP. Since both parties have shared similar political programs during most of their history (with the exception of the period roughly between 1970 and 1985), electorates from upper- and middle-income groups fluctuated between one party and the other and, on occasion, supported both at the same time.

In terms of political control, the parties were hierarchically organized with a fairly sophisticated system of patronage. The control of the party resided largely with the national leaders. Elections have strengthened this pattern of power concentration by giving the winning party a solid majority in Parliament. Power concentration in the prime minister and his inner circle was based on two factors. First, a parliamentary majority crowds out potential interferences from the opposition party. Second, the only remaining threat to executive hegemony, that is, the possibility of intraparty challenges, was greatly diminished by the way in which patronage and clientelism were organized in national politics. The party in power tended to deliver benefits to its followers directly through local bosses, excluding from the process parliamentary representatives. This marginalization has progressively weakened Parliament's position in national politics. The decision-making process has become highly concentrated in the executive, and Parliament has become merely a forum for discussion rather than a central actor in policy making.

In the particular case of TOJ privatization, the convergence of several factors led to a relatively uncontested sale. The market-oriented administration of Edward Seaga, which came into power after eight years of Manley's socialist government, made the initial moves toward privatization. A clear electoral mandate in favor of greater market dominance in the national economy gave Seaga the space to maneuver and launch the first stage of TOJ's privatization. The next stage was carried out by a second Manley administration. One possible explanation in regard to Manley's success in selling the majority of the company's shares is that, as with Argentina's Menem, the new administration profited from the disorientation of his followers and the lack of a strong opposition from Seaga's party. Manley, as did Seaga, remained personally involved and kept tight control of the progress of the initiative. And, finally, the process was removed from the government's privatization entity, the National Investment Bank of Jamaica, and was instead carried out in isolation by a small group of government officials (Wint 1995, 11).

Worker participation in the company's ownership also led to low levels of opposition. Ownership has often been an important element in the dismantling of labor's challenge to the sale of SOTEs. Another factor is the buffering of consumers: granting C&W an absolute monopoly over all services kept local tariffs low while meeting universal service goals through cross-subsidies. Tariffs did not increase for business either. The volume of international traffic rose dramatically during the 1980s allowing the company greater profits, which were used to fulfill its universal service mandate, without having to raise long-distance and international services prices.

In sum, Jamaica's reform was viable due to the structure of national politics, the ways in which both the Seaga and Manley administrations dealt with the issue, and the simple fact that the transformation had scant negative social-welfare consequences. In structural terms the successful privatization seems to be based on the tight control that the party in government achieved over the Jamaican political system as a whole. This was enhanced by the direct involvement of the presidents themselves, both of whose privatization teams worked largely in secret. In regard to welfare effects, users—residential or business—were not hurt since tariffs have remained stable, and low-income users will continue to benefit from cross-subsidies used to support expansion of universal services. Finally, most workers have kept their jobs and have gained access to a limited number of shares of the company.

Venezuela

The privatization of Compañía Anónima Nacional de Teléfonos de Venezuela (CANTV), was launched in April 1991 by the government of Andrés Pérez.[77] The program initially proposed the sale of 30 percent of the company. Arguments related to the urgent need to tackle fiscal problems and to upgrade the performance of national telecom services gave impetus to the government initiative. In the following months conditions for the sale were modified and the number of shares to be sold in a public bidding was raised to 40 percent. In November 1991 CANTV was sold to Venworld Telecom C.A.—a consortium made up of GTE, AT&T International Inc., and Telefónica Internacional de España S.A., C.A. La Electricidad de Caracas, and Consorcio Inversionista Mercantil.[78] The new private owners have full management and operational control of the company. Yet, the ownership control of the firm remains in Venezuelan hands, since the remaining 60 percent of shares are owned by the Venezuela Investment Fund, representing the Republic of Venezuela (49 percent) and CANTV employees (11 percent) (Frances 1993).

This seemingly smooth privatization of a public utility in a country in which welfare-state benefits are widespread is intriguing. It is even more puzzling given that, during the two years prior to privatization, the Pérez administration faced popular uprisings protesting its structural adjustment policies. In February 1989, for example, riots broke out in Caracas against the government's recently adopted austerity measures. Clashes between protesters and government forces caused more than 300 hundred deaths. In the following two years the government had to confront several other popular disturbances that challenged the authority of the administration. Based on this widespread discontent, in February 1992 a group of junior army officers led a military rebellion. The plotters were successful in most of the country but failed to control Caracas or to capture the president. While most Venezuelans rejected the idea of a military rule, there was little support for President Pérez.[79] Venezuelans blame the government and politicians in general for falling living standards, dilapidated public services, and widespread corruption.[80] After the military uprising, Pérez's legitimacy was damaged and discontent grew among various factions of the two dominant parties. Pérez spent most of 1992 fighting off attempts to shorten his term.

Although these events took place a few months after the privatization of CANTV and did not directly challenge the privatization process, it illustrates the existence of popular discontent during the privatization period. Some observers even argue that privatization played an important role in stirring up the military rebellion.

This macropolitical picture contrasts with the specific political dynamics related to the privatization of CANTV. Although some small political parties and organizations protested the sale there was no significant opposition. Several factors seem to have contributed.[81]

First, as in the case of ENTel Argentina, there was considerable support for privatization among the population. The company performed poorly in years prior to privatization, and quality indicators dropped considerably.[82] A survey carried out a month prior to the sale showed that 81 percent of the interviewed population was in favor of privatization and only 10 percent opposed it.[83] This support probably influenced the reaction of other societal actors—political parties, the unions, and so forth. Second, after the negotiations, the two main political parties reached an agreement in favor of privatization.[84] Since these two political parties control Congress there was no major challenge to the legislation proposed by the executive. Third, the Venezuelan labor movement, controlled by the Confederación de Trabajadores de Venezuela (CTV) has long been a member of the governing party.[85] In September 1991, the CTV announced its support for CANTV's sale.[86]

This rosy picture of CANTV's privatization contrasts markedly with the gloomy political scenario described above. Given the scant available information, the Venezuelan case is a black box waiting for more in-depth research to unravel the intricacies of CANTV's privatization.[87]

LIBERALIZING LDC'S MARKETS

Based on the experiences of Argentina and Mexico, this work has argued that privatization and liberalization are different though interrelated processes, and hence are influenced by different forces. If telecom privatization depends primarily on political dynamics, market liberalization seems to rest on the health of the local economy (which heavily influences government bargaining power) and on whether market entry is granted simultaneous to privatization. The cases of Malaysia, Thailand, and Jamaica illustrate this correlation.

Malaysia

Like Mexico, Malaysia is another LDC that has successfully opened its telecom market. In the mid-1980s the Mahatir government implemented a broad liberalization program that allowed competitive entry into data and value-added network services, paging, cellular telephony, radio telephony, and a variety of other specific services.[88]

In data services the main operators were MAYPAC and MAYCIS. Both were operated by STM and were introduced in 1984. The government, however, granted permission for the leasing of private lines to provide businesses with timesharing services, thus offering cheaper and more efficient routes.[89]

Value-added network services were also provided by private companies in competitive conditions. Information Networking Corporation Sdn Bhd provided data services, access to databases, electronic mail, and fax messaging. Electronic data interchange services were provided on a competitive basis by Electronic Data Interchange (M) Sdn Bhd and Value Added Network Services. Komtel, owned by the Sapura Holdings Group, offered value-added network services such as wake-up, message check, and appointment reminder. More recently, other services such as domestic and international messaging have become available. Skytel, a joint venture of Mobile Telecommunications Technologies, offered access to alphanumeric messaging, voice mail, and international messaging.

Malaysia also liberalized its wireless communications. Paging services were provided by forty different companies throughout the country. The government granted thirty-two licenses to companies operating locally in different areas of the country, seven licenses to firms that operated on a nationwide basis, and one license to an international paging operator. An interesting element in the liberalization of paging services is that STM was initially not allowed to enter that segment of the market.

In the area of cellular telephony, in 1992, there were twelve private mobile radio systems in operation, and thirteen additional companies applied for licenses for the provision of CT2 systems.[90] The government also carried forward considerable liberalization of its mobile telecommunications market. Cellular services were first introduced to Malaysia in 1985, when STM launched its Automatic Telephone Using Radio (ATUR), making it the first of its kind in the region. ATUR held a monopoly for few years, until a new license was granted to Cellular Communications (Celcom)—a telecom company owned by the Fleet Group.

In Malaysia we find both telecom liberalization and a booming local market in a politically stable environment, yet this successful telecom opening does not offer solid evidence for the argument offered in this work. The Malaysian government kept control of the majority of STM stock, and, therefore, did not face any major pressure for a closed market from private investors. A booming local economy made it possible for the government to privatize the company without relying heavily on large private investors.

Under such conditions, the only other potential opposition to the government's intention to grant competitive entry to third parties comes from STM. Two factors make this unlikely. First, STM was still government controlled and, due to the political dynamics described in the privatization section, it had little chance to successfully oppose government initiatives. Second, several of the new telecom corporations competing in the market were economic conglomerates with links to the governing coalition. The Mahatir administration, therefore, has few incentives to protect STM's monopoly. To sum up, in Malaysia the absence of complete privatization and the complex politics around market liberalization have complicated what were, in the case of Argentina and Mexico, fairly straightforward bargaining dynamics between private investors and the government.

Thailand

Thailand is an interesting case because previous administrations failed to privatize national carriers, yet successfully introduced competition in several segments of the market.[91] Cellular telephony, paging, national data transmission, and VSAT/satellite were provided by Telecommunications

Organization of Thailand and Communication Authority of Thailand (TOT and CAT) and private companies in a competitive environment.

Cellular services offered a quick solution to Thailand's scarcity of telephones. Despite its high cost (approximately US$3,500 per unit), the service, originally provided by both CAT and TOT, quickly oversold and became congested. The government, in its effort to improve infrastructure services, opened the market, granting licenses to companies like Ucom (a Thai Motorola subsidiary), whose subscribers' list reached 55,000 in the mid-1980s.

Paging services were initially operated by CAT in Bangkok and surrounding areas. In 1986 the company had more than 8,000 subscribers and was encountering difficulties in handling surging demand. In 1987, the government granted a franchise to Pacific Telesis Thailand, Limited (a subsidiary of Pacific Telesis International) to operate a second system. Since then, paging has been opened to competitive entry by third-party providers, with the government controling the granting of concessions.[92]

Lack of an official master plan for telecom expansion led to an overlapping of CAT and TOT jurisdictions in the provision of data communications. Each company offered high-speed data lines that can handle sixty-four kilobits of information per second. In response to pressures from the Bangkok business community, the government broke the duopoly and granted two private firms— Compunet Corporation, Limited and Samart Communications—licenses for the provision of satellite-based domestic data services. The former company has been operating since 1989, offering two data communication services: Datasat and Satlink. The latter has targeted the financial community and plans to offer three network configurations to its customers: Samartnet, Samartlink, and Samart Broadcast Service.

The progressive liberalization of national data services had been replicated in the satellite sector. The government granted a thirty-year concession to a Thai communication company—Shinawatra—to operate two telecommunications satellites, with an eight-year monopoly in the provision of services.[93] Shinawatra's first satellite was launched in 1993.

Thailand highlights the interdependence between privatization and liberalization, and between the latter and the status of the national economy. First, it reveals that carrying out liberalization in the absence of total privatization is more feasible than trying to open the market simultaneously with privatization. As in Malaysia, and in contrast to Argentina and Jamaica, the absence of private investors requiring a closed market in exchange for purchasing the national SOTE, relieves the government from a considerable burden in its liberalization efforts.

Second, Thailand shows how a booming economy can provide the national administration with enough bargaining power to override monopoly demands from the national carrier—during 1989, for example, the economy grew at 12 percent of GDP. Pressure from local and foreign businesses operating in the country and the inability of CAT and TOT to respond to skyrocketing service demand gave the government leverage to overcome opposition to the erosion of the national monopoly. Finally, the rapidly growing Thai economy provided enough revenue, business, and employment possibilities for CAT and TOT to make it unnecessary for the companies to battle for control of services that were not central to their operations.[94]

Jamaica

The evolution of liberalization in the Jamaica telecommunications service market strongly resembles that of Argentina. The core of TOJ's privatization occurred between late 1987 and mid-1988, a period in which TOJ's license for the exclusive operation of long-distance services was about to expire. The government had the choice of renewing the license or of refusing the license renewal and opening the service to competition. To pursue the latter course, however, the government needed a private telecom investor to overcome fiscal problems and to provide a strong financial and technological basis for the development of the sector; this led the Seaga administration to relinquish potential market liberalization on behalf of strong investment commitment on the part of C&W. Consequently the government not only renewed the license but made it exclusive for twenty-five years (renewable for another twenty-five) and included the provision of all telecom services and equipment in the country.

The C&W monopoly in the Jamaican telecom market was one of the conditions demanded by the private firm prior to making a capital commitment. C&W also rejected the possibility of RPX-I pricing formula and pressed the government for a real pretax rate of return on equity of approximately 19 percent.

Since the government made no explicit announcement about its intention to introduce free-market mechanisms in the Jamaican telecom sector, it is uncertain if that was its initial aim. However, considering Seaga's strong ideological commitment to the workings of the free market, it is likely that the government would have introduced competition in the sector if it could carry out both privatization and liberalization simultaneously.

The Jamaican case, like Argentina's, illustrates the exclusionary dynamics generated between privatization and liberalization in the context of an unattractive market.

CONCLUSION

This chapter has applied the basic theoretical premise of this study to other countries in the developing world that have attempted the privatization of their telecommunications carriers. The fact that several countries, after announcing their intentions to privatized, failed to achieve their goal, while others succeeded in privatization initiatives, offers a rich ground to test the generalizability of the hypothesis.

The first part of the chapter explored the failed cases: Thailand, Colombia, South Africa, and Uruguay. Mirroring the outcome of the first Argentine privatization attempts, in which the lack of policy-making insulation from domestic opposition groups and the negative consequences of bureaucratic infighting created significant obstacles, the four cases analyzed here denote the importance of state autonomy and power concentration in the head of the executive.

In Thailand the government failed to sell major SOEs—including the national carrier—due to worker opposition and the lack of support from other groups with vested interests in the sector. A similar profile can be found in South Africa and Colombia, where telecom worker mobilization defeated official privatization plans. Uruguay is a variation on the theme of state permeability and vulnerability. In this case it was not workers but organized domestic coalitions that blocked privatization. In all four cases, workers and civil organizations were supported by various segments of political organizations and parties that opposed the sale of SOEs. In summary, Thailand, Colombia, South Africa, and Uruguay provide evidence of failure to privatize in political systems where state officials and the policy process are not insulated from strong societal pressures against reform initiatives.

The experiences of Malaysia, Chile, and Jamaica, on the other hand, illustrate the correlation between an insulated political system and successful privatization. Jamaica represents an interesting example of policy-making insulation and executive strength in a democratic system. Malaysia—portraying a similar political profile to Mexico—illustrates the dynamics of privatization in a country with a highly centralized political system, in which concentration of power in the hands of the prime minister and the tight control of the policy-making process granted the government the required institutional tools to achieve the restructuring of its telecommunications services. Chile during the authoritarian military regime depicts the most extreme case of power concentration. Pinochet was not only able to insulate the policy process—a feature common in authoritarian regimes—but he was also able to gain the discipline of state officials—the lack of which is mainly responsible for the two first privatization failures in Argentina. Finally, Venezuela challenges the hypothesis. A seemingly vulnerable administration achieved the reform of its telecom system in the midst of widespread opposition to the government. Given the scarcity of data, the case remains a puzzle and calls for further research and analysis.

The cases explored in this chapter, which constitute most of the LDC telecom privatizations attempted up until 1993, complement the cases of Argentina and Mexico and provide strong evidence in support of the central argument of this study. That is, they all point to the importance of state autonomy and the relevance of cohesion among state official, or, in its absence, the existence of concentration of power in the head of the government.

In regard to liberalization, the cases analyzed point to the links between the privatization of SOTEs and the opening of the market. Thailand illustrates the viability of liberalization in the absence of privatization. While the Thai case strongly resembles Argentina's initial privatization attempts, it departs markedly from the privatization and liberalization experience of the Menem administration. The Menem administration was successful in privatizing the national carrier where the Thai government failed, but Thai liberalization efforts were far more successful than those of Argentina. Two factors seem to explain the difference. First, the Thai government did not have to bargain with potential private investors, who might have demanded a closed market as a condition for investment. Second, a booming national economy placated resistance from domestic interest groups and granted the government leverage to overcome opposition to market liberalization.

Malaysia also indicates that the relationship of simultaneous liberalization and privatization matters, but shows that the kind of privatization is important, too. If the government—instead of private investors—becomes the main shareholder of the company, the need for a closed market as a risk guarantee disappears. In spite of the fact that Syarikat Telekom Malaysia operated as a private business, the government still exercised important control over both the firm and the market. While there may be resistance on the part of the new company managers and workers in the new company, the likelihood of bending government initiatives was low. With Malaysia's "strong," insulated state, the chances are even lower since local interest group opposition will probably follow the patterns observed for privatization.

Finally, Jamaica again illustrates the price of privatization under unattractive market conditions. The possibility of competition in the local market has now been postponed for fifty years in exchange for a commitment by private investors. The government gave up the potential benefits of a competitive market in exchange for a slow, but secure, development of the public network and basic universal services.

NOTES

1. Included in this list are almost all LDCs that have attempted reform of their telecom sector as of mid-1993. Latin American countries predominate because that is where most telecom reform has taken place.

2. Brazil and Greece are other LDCs that have been struggling with privatization initiatives. In Brazil, the Collor administration, which took office on March 15, 1990, announced a sweeping privatization program. The privatization of the dominant national common carrier—Embratel—would require a constitutional reform, which common sense would dictate is why it hasn't been sold. However, it might be argued that it is not the constitutional impediment but the peculiar dynamics of Brazilian national politics that have blocked telecom privatization. The Collor government enjoyed only limited support for its privatization program. He controlled only 5 percent of Congress, had to confront union opposition, and faced divisions within his own coalition, in which, for example, the then-vice-president of the country, Itamar Franco, resisted the idea of a broad privatization program. Greece is also a case of telecom privatization failure. According to the information available, the Greek experience strongly reflects the political dynamics present in Thailand, Colombia, and South Africa. For a study of the Brazilian case, see Molano 1995, and Wohlers 1994.

3. International calls increased by a rate of approximately 50 percent during the final years of the 1980s.

4. For growth rate, customer waiting lists, and other data, see Paul Handley, "Progress by Numbers," *Far Eastern Economic Review*, 23 March 1989, 83. For waiting period and installation charges, see Hukill and Jussawalla 1989, 51.

5. In terms of main lines Thailand had 25 lines per 1,000 inhabitants, while more developed countries in the region had over 300 lines per 1,000 people. Taiwan, for example, had 375, South Korea 304, Singapore 370, and Hong Kong 424 (International Telecommunications Union 1992b).

6. *The Economist*, 23 February 1985.

7. Rapid and high economic growth, migration from the countryside, higher levels of education and health, a growing middle class, and the penetration of foreign cultural and political values are some of the driving forces of social change in recent years in Thailand (Morell and Samudavanija 1981, and Ross 1985).

8. National Economic and Social Development Board, Government of Thailand 1987, 5 and 285, cited in Hukill 1990.

9. The official plan to open the telecom sector to private ownership was strongly backed by the United States, which had been a long-term ally of Thai governments. Through the National Telecommunications and Information Administration (NTIA), the U.S. government called for the merger of CAT and TOT and the privatization of both companies.

10. Most political parties in Thailand were generally organized around a few key leaders who represent particular interest groups in business and commerce. Permanent personality clashes and interest conflicts among heads of the parties led to permanent realignment in the structure of coalitions.

11. The contract was for the installation of a digital transmission system. The decision of TOT's managers provoked protests from other bidders, who argued against TOT's method of evaluation. The government ordered a review, but— deliberately ignoring the prime minister's orders—TOT closed the deal with the Japanese company.

12. Economic Intelligence Unit 1989, 15.

13. In mid-1989, Thai workers in the private sector were making approximately US$3 per day (the lowest salary in Southeast Asia, after Indonesia).

14. While unions in other LDCs were in decay during the 1980s, those in Thailand were gaining influence. Unionization in the country grew under the leadership of the Thai Trade Union Congress, which has been battling congress for social security benefits and other labor rights. See Rodney Tasker, "Improving Slowly," *Far Eastern Economic Review*, 27 July 1989.

15. The strike in July 1989 was initiated by workers of the Electricity Generating Authority of Thailand (EGAT), and it was the first public evidence of the difficulties that the government had in reforming SOEs. In February 1990, Bangkok port workers won the important concession of a government guarantee not to privatize the new deep-sea port of Laem Chabang. With the support of other state unions, they got a written commitment from the government that privatization was on hold for all SOEs. See Paul Handley, "Port in a Storm: Strike Stalls Thai Privatisation Plans," *Far Eastern Economic Review,* 15 February 1990; and "Thai Privatization in Trouble," *Wall Street Journal*, 15 February 1990.

16. "Power Asia: EGAT Privatisation Scheme Suspended as Crisis Deepens," *The Financial Times,* 26 March 1990.

17. A public statement by General Sunthorn Kongsompong, a close ally to army commander Chaovalit, reveals the relation between workers' resistance and the military. The officer warned the government that if it didn't back down in its

plans "there will be further industrial action among state enterprise unions protesting the government's privatisation programme" (Rodney Tasker, "Bracing for Change," *Far Eastern Economic Review*, 15 February 1990).

18. The armed forces' political influence in Thai society is out of all proportion to their numerical strength. The army numbers only 190,000 (of whom 80,000 are conscripts). The navy and the air force combined are only 93,000 (*Economic Intelligence Unit* 1989, 5).

19. *The Financial Times*, 26 March 1990.

20. Law 72/89.

21. Decree 1900.

22. On Colombian restructuring and the privatization of Telecom, see, for example, Fonnegra and Osorio 1992, and Uricoechea 1992.

23. Worker resistance was joined by the Liberal party, the Communist party, the Socialist party, M-19, and some members of the Conservative party.

24. It is said that the success of the strike was largely due to the experience gained from workers resistance in other countries. To avoid the experience of Argentina—where the strike was broken by calling in the army to operate the system—telecom workers in Colombia took with them crucial hardware and software components in the system thus avoiding the possibility of any takeover by third parties.

25. The Conservative party, for example, fractured, nominating two presidential candidates. This helped the candidate of the ex-guerrilla movement, M-19, to gain third place in national electoral results—with 12.6 percent of the votes.

26. In this election, for example, the ex-guerrilla M-19 party won 27 percent of the votes.

27. Congress can curtail the presidents' ability to declare a state of emergency and rule by decree. The president has also lost control over the appointment of governors (now elected directly by the population) and over a considerable part of tax revenues, which will be collected and managed directly by departments and municipalities.

28. Besides structural and institutional factors such as those described above, the privatization of Telecom also suffered—as in the Alfonsín administration—from the lack of a centralized privatization agency (the project was managed by the Ministry of Communication), and the inadequate personal involvement of the president in the project.

29. According to the government, privatization would reduce the fiscal burden by increasing the tax base, shrinking state involvement in the economy, pushing the privatized firm to improve its efficiency, and stimulating the economy through private shareholding.

30. Much of the information and data on the telecommunication reform in South Africa is borrowed from Horwitz 1992.

31. See Christopher S. Wren, "Pretoria Retreats on Privatization," *New York Times,* 13 November 1990.

32. The ANC endorsed a mixed economy in which state, cooperatives, and private ownership would coexist.

33. Max Sisulu, head of the ANC's economic department, compared privatization to "selling the family silver without even consulting the family." See Christopher S. Wren, "Pretoria Retreats."

34. By industrial action, Mr. Mashele means a strike against the government. Wren, ibid.

35. Afrikaners are descendants of Dutch settlers who first occupied the Cape peninsula in the latter half of the seventeenth century. Along with the descendants of the British settlers who seized the Cape in 1806, they constitute the white population of the country. Whites (i.e., British and Afrikaners) account for only 13 percent of the South African population.

36. The government has, nevertheless, "corporatize" the company.

37. For further information on the privatization of ANTEL, see De Leon 1992, and Rebella 1993.

38. A majority of more than 600,000 votes constitutes 25 percent of the country's electorate.

39. At this stage votes are secret and obligatory.

40. As in many other countries in the developing world, the Uruguayan government faced strong opposition from a number of interest groups and the population at large, all of which resisted the prospect of losing benefits traditionally granted by an interventionist, welfare state.

41. Considering that the state still holds the majority of shares in STM, we might argue that it is somewhat different from the Argentine and Mexican cases. However, in regard to the success or failure of governments in significantly reforming their telecom sectors, Malaysia can be clustered with the Latin American cases for the following reasons. First, the transformation of a company into a private business has important consequences for workers who lose public-sector benefits and for high-level managers, who are generally replaced by managers from the private sector. Second, under a new regime operating on commercial, competitive principles, politicians and civil servants lose control over the sector and advantages stemming from it, residential users (the majority of customers) suffer tariff increases, and equipment providers lose their captive markets. Finally, although the majority of shares did not end up in private hands, these structural reforms and their consequences should create political incentives and resistance just as if the company were being placed under complete private ownership. For these reasons I considered the politics of privatization in Malaysia to be very similar to those of Argentina and Mexico.

42. The analysis of the following cases draws on limited and incomplete research. More in-depth field work and secondary data is needed to convincingly confirm or reject the suggested theoretical premises and causal correlations.

43. As a proportion of subscribers, the number of backlogged requests surged from 7.8 percent in 1970 to 32.3 percent in 1987.

44. Further, providing services to the large rural population was an obstacle to sound financial and technical management of the company. While rural customers accounted for 40 percent of all expenditures, they contributed only 10 percent of total revenues.

45. International economic recession in the early 1980s caused a decline in prices of LDCs' raw material. Malaysia was particularly affected by these downturns in the international economy.

46. The head of the state is the king, who is elected every five years by the nine ruling sultans of peninsular Malaysia.

47. At that time, the federation comprised Peninsular Malaya, Sarawak, Singapore, and Sabah. In 1965 Singapore left the federation and became an independent country.

48. Barisan Nasional translates as National Front. The main parties in the coalition are the United Malays National Organization (UMNO), the Malaysian

Chinese Association (MCA), the Malaysian Indian Congress (MIC), the Gerakan party, and the Pesaka Bumiputra Bersatu (PBB) party.

49. Mahathir Mohamad was also the head of UMNO (United Malays National Organization), the Malay party that has headed the governing coalition since independence. For studies on Malaysia's political system, see, also Ahmad 1987, and Milne and Mauzy 1978.

50. Malaysia's population is composed of 55 percent Malays and other in- digenous population, 34 percent Chinese, and 11 percent Indians. Ethnic conflicts have dominated the country since the British left the peninsula, and until today race remains the single most important aspect of politics. Unequal income distribution between Chinese and Malays has been a key issue in racial friction.

51. For a study on the role of state relative autonomy in the development process of Malaysia, see Leong 1991.

52. Both governments faced a decline in hegemony in the late 1980s, but they quickly regained control of their respective political arenas and by the early 1990s were again in solid control of politics in their countries.

53. While Barisan Nasional integrates conflictive ethnic groups and diminishes racial tension, the PRI integrates different professional and income groups and reduces economic-based tensions.

54. The MCS comprises only 15.5 percent of the Malaysian civil service.

55. An administrative state is, in the words of Esman, one in which "the state is the dominant institution in society, guiding and controlling more than it responds to societal pressures, and administrative (bureaucratic) institutions, personnel, values, and styles are more important than political and participative organs in determining the behavior of the state and thus the course of public affairs."

56. Much of the information about political events in Malaysia is based on the Economic Intelligence Unit 1992.

57. Although the Chinese population is a minority, it has controlled business and trade for decades. The Malays (or Bumiputra—"the sons of the soil") are traditionally the largest, yet less affluent, ethnic group in Malaysia. In 1971, after ethnically driven national revolts, the government instituted a National Economic Policy (NEP) to balance the distribution of wealth among different ethnic groups. The main goal of the program was to increase by 30 percent the stake of the Malay population in the country's equity share.

58. The laws reformed were the Official Secrets Act, the Police Act (both regulate public meetings), the Printing Press and Publications Act, the Internal Security Act and the Societies Act (which governs the formation of political parties and other societies).

59. Although worker opposition was the only visible significant challenge to the project and would not seem to jeopardize the privatization of JTM, one should not underestimate its relevance. As can be seen in cases such as Thailand, Colombia, and South Africa, the labor movement can be a decisive player in blocking privatization.

60. The political weakness of labor in the context of some East and Southeast Asian countries can be attributed to several factors. First, a common Confucianist cultural heritage emphasized hierarchy, paternalism, cooperation, industriousness, and the subordination of the individual to the state, all of which effectively suppress opposition movement by labor. Second, rapid economic growth is a strong disincentive for labor opposition. And, third, strong states, through the

control of political parties, unions, and the media, have suppressed labor organizations.

61. The government also offered retirement packages to those willing to leave JTM. In this way, almost 400 of the 28,724 employees dropped out of JTM.

62. The Telecommunications (Amendment) Act of 1985 restructured Jabatan Telekom Malaysia as a state regulatory agency, while the Tele-communications Service (Successor Company) Act of 1985 regulated the operations of the new company, Syarikat Telekom Malaysia.

63. Through corporatization, the company became a private business regulated by the 1965 Companies' Act.

64. The state has kept the prerogative of reviewing the companies' monopoly in the provision of basic services.

65. Some of the factors that delayed the public flotation of STM shares were related to managerial and financial issues. The company had to adjust its operations to the logic of private markets, and restructure its accounting system to meet the requirements of Malaysia's Capital Issues Committee (CIC). But more importantly, STM, according to regulations of the CIC, had to show a record of continuous profit during three years to be able to list its shares on the Kuala Lumpur Stock Exchange.

66. The company announced a thirty-six-fold increase in net income for 1988. By 1991 the company was earning US$333 million, which represented a sharp increase over the US$203 million in profits of the previous year. In 1992 the company posted a profit of US$361 million. The value of STM shares has climbed steadily from the US$1.80, at which it was issued, to US$4.25 in late June of 1991. See Michael Westlake, "Ringing the Changes," *Far Eastern Economic Review* (July 1989), 66; Nick Ingelbrecht, "Privatisation Doubles Profits," *Asian Business* (September 1991), 13; and *Business Week*, 12 July 1993, 98.

67. On the Chilean privatization program see, for example, Hachette and Luders 1993, and Larroulet 1991.

68. The state sector, and in particular the number of SOEs, grew at an impressive rate in the early 1970s during the socialist administration of President Salvador Allende. The number of companies run by the state grew from 64 in 1970 to 498 by the end of the Allende administration three years later. In reaction to this nationalization of the Chilean economy, the authoritarian Pinochet government reprivatized many SOEs. During the first months of the program 250 companies were returned gratis to their previous owners, and 232 other companies were sold to the private sector during the following few years. By 1980 the state controlled only forty-three enterprises. Despite their small number, most were large SOEs and accounted for an important share in Chile's economy. The program was halted from the early to the mid-1980s, with the state taking back some of the privatized SOEs due to bankruptcy. In 1985 privatization was revived and important SOEs were sold.

69. These two companies accounted for 4 percent of the telephone lines in the country and served almost 8 percent of the population.

70. CTC, which became state-owned in 1974 when the Chilean government acquired 80 percent of the company's shares, provided local telephone service to 77 percent of the national territory, and owned 94 percent of all phone lines in Chile.

71. The corporation, which was part of a holding with interests in gold, beer, yachts, and finances, was owned by Australian business tycoon Alan Bond, and offered US$114.8 million for CTC shares.

72. Telefónica paid US$392 million for the controlling shares of CTC.

73. For further information on the privatization of the Chilean telecom system, see, for example, Salomon Brothers, Inc. 1990, Galal et al. 1992b, Melo 1991, and Agurto 1991.

74. It is estimated that 15,000 people were killed and 10,000 political refugees left the country.

75. Within CORFO, privatization was controlled by the "Normalization Unit."

76. My analysis of the Jamaican political system relies heavily in the work of Spiller and Sampson 1992.

77. The Pérez administration came into office in February 1989, two years prior to the privatization proposal.

78. The consortium paid US$1.88 billion. GTE controls 51 percent of the consortium shares; Telefónica de España, 16 percent; AT&T, 5 percent; and the remaining 28 percent is shared between Banco Mercantil and Electricidad de Caracas.

79. The high level of popular discontent with the government enabled the Venezuelan military to move to the forefront of the political scene. To regain authority and control, President Pérez appointed the highly regarded defense minister, General Ochoa Antich, as foreign minister.

80. The Economic Intelligence Unit 1992, 6.

81. Much of this analysis of the politics of CANTV's privatization has been drawn from Frances 1993.

82. Rate of completed domestic calls, for example, dropped from 45 percent in 1987 to 39 percent in 1990. The average of time for customers out of service grew from forty-six to ninety-three hours in the same period. And the percentage of failures repaired in seventy-two hours dropped from 85 percent in 1988 to 72 percent in 1990. Data from Frances 1993.

83. *El Diario de Caracas*, 22 October 1991, 20. Cited in Frances 1993, 23.

84. These two parties—Acción Democrática (AD), and Comité de Organización Política Electoral Independiente (COPEI)—have alternated in the presidency and generally dominated Congress since 1958. In the last election, for example, AD and COPEI won 42 of the 46 seats in the Senate, and 164 of the 201 seats of the Chamber of Deputies.

85. Although the governing party had the support of the country's largest labor organization, that was not a guarantee of compliance with the privatization initiative, as the case of Argentina showed. In the case of Venezuela, nevertheless, this factor favored the government.

86. Granting workers ownership of 11 percent of the company's shares increased their support.

87. One might also speculate that since the government survived challenges from various fronts for an extended period of time, we are in the presence of a rather insulated state and one with considerable presidential power. Evidence of the latter can be drawn from the fact that despite some initial resistance to CANTV's sale on the part of certain sectors of the governing party and the union, the president was gradually able to achieve broad consensus among key political actors.

88. For data on the competitive provision of services in Malaysia, see Onn 1994, and Ambrose et al. 1990.

89. Li Shui-hua, "Telecommunications Opportunities," *East Asian Executive Report*, 15 April 1986.

90. CT2 systems are a second-generation cordless telephones in which power is boosted to give a range of several miles.

91. Confronted with the inability of transferring ownership to private hands, the government resorted to a reform technique (build, operate, and transfer - BOT) that grants participation to the private sector in the expansion of telecom services, but with the condition that the system will be transferred to the state once it is completed. In this way the government has been able to ease pressures from the business community while simultaneously keeping the opposition in check. This telecom development strategy was initially used in Southeast Asia by Indonesia.

92. *Business Wire*, 15 May 1986.

93. Reform in satellite services was introduced in favor of a company owned by a former military commander, who had excellent connections among political elites, and during a period in which the new military regime had regained most of the political strength that the Chatichai Choonhavan government had lost. Probably the most important strengthening measure for the new regime was the banning of state unions.

94. Growth of long-distance services in the country is an indicator of the expansion of the economy and of the sector itself. Between 1986 and 1990, CAT was the third fastest growing international carrier in the world. See Cowhey and Aronson 1993, Chapter 7. The first two companies were US Sprint and MCI, which through regulatory protection have gained an important share of the huge USA market. Since they are new companies, any minor increase in absolute number of customers appears as a high percentage of growth. Furthermore, the Thai equipment market has grown rapidly, reaching a 1991 value of approximately US$2 billion. See *Asian Business* (November 1991), 62.

7

The Socioeconomic Impact of Reform

Based on the experience of both developing and developed countries, this chapter explores the initial effects that privatization and liberalization of telecom markets have had on consumers, labor, the state, service providers, and equipment suppliers. The analysis covers the period 1989–92 and early reform outcomes are presented and analyzed against the backdrop of preprivatization arguments and expectations.

To attempt an assessment of the early impact of privatization and liberalization constitutes a challenging task because "when one wrestles with privatization in the concrete rather than the abstract, its implications often appear to be complex and uncertain" (Ramamurti 1991, 8). The analysis is further complicated because privatization and liberalization—processes with different roots, features, and goals—tend to overlap and affect each other in a very dynamic way. Thus, complexity and uncertainty are intrinsic to reform outcomes and are unmistakably apparent in the cases studied here.

It is also important to keep in mind that, due to the variety of economic, social, and political changes during the last decade in certain of the less developed countries (LDCs) studied here, one should be careful when attributing socioeconomic effects to telecom reform. There are certain economic factors—such as structural adjustment programs, economic liberalization, new local and foreign direct investments, repatriation of capital, decreased inflation, rapid growth of capital markets, and so forth—that could have easily influenced transformations in the cases under study and could have distorted what appears to be causal correlation between telecom reform and certain outcomes in the sector.

CONSUMERS

One of the most powerful arguments advocates of privatizing telecom systems had was that the private sector was better equipped—in capital, technology, and management expertise—than the state to provide a wide array of reliable, sophisticated services. Entrepreneurial efficiency—a quality invariably associated with the private sector—would facilitate rapid network expansion towards the achievement of universal services.

Those who opposed privatization feared that the retreat of the state from the provision of services would invariably mean a sharp increase in tariffs of basic services, victimizing residential cosumers. Furthermore, they have questioned the prediction that private firms would operate more efficiently, achieving rapid network expansion and better service quality. Traditionally, political and economic incentives have not engendered efficiency in private firms.

Initial outcomes present a mixed picture. As advocates predicted—the network has expanded considerably in most countries; however, the improvement has come—as opponents expected—at the cost of skyrocketing tariffs. As for quality of services, in the short term there was no clear indicator to evaluate it consistently.

Service Penetration

Privatization of telecommunications systems and the introduction of commercial principles in the provision of services seem to have had a positive impact in the expansion of the public network. The commercial drive of the new companies and important changes in their income-investment cycle point to improvements in telephone penetration rates. This has come about for two reasons. First, privatization or corporatization changes the traditional investment patterns of state-owned telecommunications enterprises (SOTEs). In the past, most LDC governments, struggling with a chronic shortage of capital, used highly profitable telecommunications to subsidize other public-sector operations. As a consequence, substantial telephone company earnings were siphoned into the national treasury, with only a small portion reserved for new investments. For example, in 1987 TELMEX contributed US$500 million to the Mexican National Treasury. Yet it received only US$150 million to finance its operations and invest in network development.[1] Now private and regulated, TELMEX has control over its earnings and has a total autonomy over its invesment policies. It committed US$2.5 billion in investments during its first year,[2] and it has contractual obligations to expand investment to US$12 billion over five years.[3]

Second, since new private companies are profit-maximizers, there is an incentive for them to consolidate their market position and establish precedence over future competitors by expanding operations as much as possible.[4] This logic is clearly apparent in Chile, where the opening of the telecom market has led Compañía de Teléfonos de Chile (CTC) and Empresa Nacional de Telecomunicaciones (ENTEL) Chile to adopt aggressive expansion strategies.[5] In CTC, while the average line-growth rate was 5.3 percent from 1972 to 1988, line penetration jumped to 25.7 percent in 1990 (Agurto 1991, 219). CTC planed to double its capacity by 1996 with an additional 750,000 lines in plant, 1.6 million lines in service, and the installation of 15,000 public pay phones.[6]

In countries where the public network is still in its infancy—requiring large sunk capital—there are considerable risks that commercially driven operations will target highly profitable segments with easy-to-provide new technologies—such as cellular systems—that bypass the public network. In Thailand, for example, the government faced formal complaints because Communications Authority of Thailand (CAT) and Telephone Organization of Thailand (TOT) have diverted large investments from planned expansion in the public network to cellular systems.

These changes will affect the expansion of the public network; but as market forces come increasingly to rule the provision of telecommunications, network expansion will depend heavily on the general performance of the domestic economy. Little network expansion can be expected if the local economy is not healthy enough to fuel demand for new services. Further, as the control in the provision of services moves from public to private entities, the fate of network expansion will be closely tied to the effectiveness and strength of regulatory bodies. Because private companies follow profit-maximizing principles, the absence of regulatory controls may lead operating firms to "cream skimming": concentrating on the expansion of services in only the most profitable segments of the market, while disregarding universal service obligations.

Tariff Evolution

Several MDCs have implemented important changes in preexisting tariff arrangements. Traditional subsidy-oriented discriminatory prices have been replaced by a new cost-based pricing. This new tariff policy sharply increased local rates and decreased long-distance and international rates.[7]

Most LDCs have in general followed this pattern. However, in their effort to prepare state-owned telecom companies for sale, some LDC governments raised both local and long-distance tariffs—which had been quite low compared to international standards.[8] Argentina clearly reflects this trend. During the pre-privatization period the government raised both local and long-distance tariffs in order to make ENTel's sale more attractive—and to recover some of the value of tariffs lost to the unprecedented hyperinflation of 1989.[9] The tariff surge affected both local and long-distance users. However, in November 1991 the government allowed a rebalancing of prices that consisted of reducing business tariffs, with an equivalent increase in residential tariffs. In February 1992 the government pressed the companies for further reduction of domestic long-distance tariffs.[10] Although the companies had no contractual obligation to comply with the government demand, they both agreed in exchange for cellular telephone licenses, granted without having to bid for them.[11]

Although tariff increases in several LDCs were a direct consequence of preparing the companies for sale, we should not assume that tariff surges are a function of private or public ownership. To be more precise, tariff cycles are primarily the consequence of changing the principles that govern the provision of public services. In other words, tariffs rise not because a company becomes private, but because telecom services traditionally were not considered a commercial business. Consequently tariffs lagged behind inflation because they were subsidized by the state. When firms (public or private) begin to operate for profit—achieved by tying prices to the cost structure of the business—tariffs tend to increase. A good example of this evolution of tariffs under public ownership is Chile.

As in many other LDCs, telecom tariffs in Chile were set on a political basis, and for that reason they generally lagged behind inflation. Cross-subsidies from long distance to local were the sector's dominant mode of operation. In 1982 the government passed a new General Law of Telecommunications, which established that basic-service tariffs would be based on marginal costs. Although cross-subsidies did not disappear, tariffs rose, keeping pace with inflation and turning the company into a commercial business. In 1987—when the company was still operating under state ownership—new regulations dismantled cross-subsidies. The new law stipulated that tariffs would have to be set on the basis of the long-run marginal cost of each service and geographical area—taking an efficient firm as a base.

Although it is true that commercialization of services—and not ownership change—is what generally produces tariff increases, it is also true that a corporatized and commercialized company in which the state keeps a majority of shares can manipulate tariffs in ways that are unavailable to companies fully controlled by profit-driven private owners. This is the case in Malaysia, where despite the corporatization and commercialization of the former SOTE (Jabatan Telekom Malaysia), tariffs did not increase before or after reform, due to direct government control of the company's pricing policies, facilitated by the government's ownership of approximately 80 percent of the firm's shares.

But not all tariff transformations are a consequence of privatization. Often price fluctuations occur as a result of the liberalization of certain segments of the market and the reconfiguration of telecom traffic generated by new information technologies.

Market liberalization, for example, has led to considerable migration of large users out of the public network. The emergence of more convenient private networks and the lowering of international services rates in some developed countries have considerably altered the profile of users in the public network of many LDCs.[12] In most developing nations the low performance, high costs, and unreliability of the public network drive large users to high-quality, customized, reliable private networks.[13] Since large users usually provide the bulk of earnings for public operators, this exodus to private networks tend to reduce reduce profits for dominant common carriers and increase the cost of providing services to those that remain in the public network.[14]

A second factor affecting public-network costs is the drop in prices of international service in certain industrialized nations—particularly the United States. This important rate reduction has brought about a reconfiguration of long-distance and international telephone traffic in LDCs. International and long-distance callers tend to divert calls through low-rate countries, skipping the long-distance company with which they were supposed to operate.[15] Through small telecommunications firms in the United States—such as International Discount Telecommunications Corporation and Viatel—customers from LDCs are able to connect calls as if they were placed from the United States.[16] This has put pressure on public network operators to lower the prices of long-distance services.[17] However, reducing the price of long-distance service also puts considerable pressure on the companies to try to offset the loss by increasing local services.

Services Quality

Although there is no clear, straightforward evidence of the impact of privatization on the quality of services, it seems that improvements in the sector are more closely related to administrative, financial, and managerial changes within the companies and to the establishment of a competitive environment than to the nature of the companies' ownership—that is, private or public (Luders 1993).[18] Countries such as Malaysia, Chile, and New Zealand offer illustrations of the positive impact of organizational reforms and competitive markets, while Argentina and Mexico reflect the dubious effect of ownership changes.

Malaysia illustrates the impact of organizational reform without privatization. Administrative and operational adjustments in the former SOTE transformed the firm's performance and the quality of services provided without resorting to private participation. The Malaysian state remained the main owner of Syarikat Telekom Malaysia, and its representatives headed the company's executive board. But important changes at the top managerial level (such as hiring executive managers from the private sector to infuse a commercial and rent-seeking spirit into the firm), incentives for labor (such as the participation of workers in the ownership of company shares), and reforms in accounting, procurement, marketing, and billing translated into notable improvements in performance and, more specifically, in the quality of services provided.[19]

New Zealand's restructuring of Telecom Corporation between 1987 and 1990 illustrates competition without privatization. Once the company became a stand-alone, commercial corporation, the government opened all segments of the telecommunications market to widespread competition.[20] Within two years the company had improved its performance remarkably.[21] The clearest indicators were customer service response, installation services, technological innovations, and rates.[22]

In Argentina and Mexico, where privatization of SOTEs has been the dominant mode of reform, improvement in services was linked primarily to improvements in the financial conditions of the companies due to markedly higher tariffs and, therefore, higher revenues and increased investments.[23] Changes in labor regulations have also granted new companies more flexibility in labor management. In all of these cases, changes in tariffs and labor management were carried out by the government and not by new private owners. Therefore, once again we find that improvement in quality of service cannot be attributed to change in ownership.

Possibly some of these changes in SOTEs could not have been achieved without the prospect of privatization or, once the companies were privatized, would have been extremely hard to keep in place given the distorted political incentives of state-owned enterprises (SOEs) managers (Luders 1995). Although the experience of less-developed-country SOEs grants validity to this assessment, in the early stages of reform there was no long-term evidence to prove or disprove any of these arguments.[24] The fact is that, in the short run and under certain market, management, and organizational conditions, ownership has less impact on firm efficiency and performance than has been widely argued.

In sum, while advocates of reform had accurate insights about the good prospects for network expansion under private ownership, the sharp increase in tariffs due to the preparation of SOTEs for sale confirms the ill ease of those who oppose the reform initiative. Finally, evidence for and against improvement in the quality of services after privatization is unclear. However, it seems that positive changes are more strongly linked to organizational reform and the introduction of competition than to change in ownership.

LABOR

Prior to the sale of SOTEs, there was little disagreement that transfer of public firms to private hands would involve sizable layoffs of personnel. Furthermore, unions argued that trends to enforce "labor flexibilization" policies—which implied a considerable loss of labor rights—would be accelerated under a private regime. And they cast serious doubts on the future income and economic situation of employees. Initial reform outcomes have confirmed some of these forecasts—such as the curtailment of pre-existing labor rights—but they have refuted others—such as job losses and income deterioration.

Employment and Income

The prospect of transferring a state-owned company to private owners have systematically created the fear that the change will immediately bring unemployment. Much of those widespread fears were based on long-standing arguments that one of the main roles of companies in the public sector was to buffer unemployment problems by hiring people in excess—a sort of veiled unemployment program. Layoffs of tenured personnel were also expected as a means of reducing the power of unions, through which public-sector employees had presumably gained excessive fringe benefits, high salaries, and too much participation in the companies' decision making process. All these factors made it difficult for managers to achieve efficiency, competitiveness, and independence from workers' interests in their decision making. The solution to most of these problems was, according to some reformist views, the reduction of personnel and curtailment of benefits and rights.

Although many of these arguments were supported by evidence from a large number of SOEs—mostly, but not only, in developing countries—privatization of SOTEs in most cases has not brought massive personnel layoffs. In both Mexico and Argentina the privatized companies retained the majority of their labor forces,[25] and in Chile although there was a considerable reduction of workers the process was linked to the search for efficiency within the public sector and not directly related to the sale of the telecom companies.[26] In Southeast Asia, the privatization of Jabatan Telekom Malaysia (JTM) also reflects this general pattern.[27] The complete workforce of JTM was transferred to the new company (STM) under a five-year stability guarantee.[28]

Three interrelated factors—monopoly conditions, government requirements of job stability, and a high market growth rate—seem to explain the low impact that privatization has had on job stability in the telecom sector of LDCs. First, in most cases governments have granted new owners a relatively extended period of exclusivity (monopoly) in the provision of basic services, which constitute the bulk of the business in LDCs. In exchange, governments have required—through legislation—that the new owners retain most of the labor force of the former SOTE.

Monopoly in the provision of most services has reduced the pressure to cut labor costs in a liberalized environment, and it has made it easy for the new firms to comply with government requirements. Those firms, on the other hand, whose monopolies were dismantled and who face markets dominated by harsh competition have considerably reduced their personnel. This is the experience of companies such as British Telecom (BT) and New Zealand Telecom Corporation (NZTC) which, in striving to maintain competitiveness, dismissed massive numbers of employees.[29]

Finally, there is a certain uniqueness about labor stability in the telecom sector. It seems that in a growing industry—such as telecom—retaining employees is not as much a burden as it is in declining industries—like airlines—which, when privatized, often undertake massive layoffs.[30]

Unemployment was not the only threat posed by privatization. Based on the experience of Chile and Thailand, many predicted that privatization would also bring salary deterioration for telecom workers.[31] Despite this well-grounded fear, SOTE privatizations have resulted in important economic benefits for the companies' employees, the most important of which is access to the ownership of shares in the new private companies and salary improvements.[32] This financial bonanza has largely dismantled labor resistance in privatized firms.

In Chile, for example, the government provided telephone workers with a financial package through which 84 percent of the company's workers bought 6.4 percent of CTC shares.[33] The Mexican government also granted a special low-interest loan to TELMEX workers, which allowed them to acquire 4.4 percent of the new private firm.[34] In Argentina, the Program of Shared Ownership (*Programa de Propiedad Participada*) specifically required that 10 percent of a privatized company's stock goes to its employees. In Asia, Syarikat Telekom Malaysia created the "Executive Share Option Scheme" which reserved 5 percent of the company's capital for the firm's executive staff, and a similar offering was created for all other employees (Onn 1993).

In contrast to their relative job stability and improved economic status, workers have lost important labor rights and social benefits. These detrimental changes are evident in the new labor legislation generated during the privatization process.

Labor Rights

In an effort to regain economic growth LDC governments have tried to implement what has been loosely labeled "labor market flexibilization." The goal is to dismantle most preexisting labor rights to provide the productive system with cheap labor under unrestricted conditions. The rationale supporting labor flexibility links economic globalization with domestic labor conditions. In an increasingly global economy, such as the present one, capital and production capabilities have few limitations on international movement. Global investors in search of competitiveness will tend to migrate to sites in which production cost is low and conditions are receptive to foreign capital. Labor is a key factor influencing both variables. On the one hand it can provide low production costs through low salaries. On the other hand, it can boost or diminish productivity according to working habits of the labor force and number and activism of unionized workers. In a global economy, unattractive labor conditions are likely to generate capital flight. In their competition to lure international capital most LDCs have started to bend their traditionally welfare labor policies to adjust to the demands of global investors. And, as the search for fresh capital grows, so does the pressure for more attractive labor-management conditions.

It is in this context that preexisting labor rights in most countries have been curtailed and transformed during the privatization process. More specifically, in the case of SOTEs privatization, the renegotiation of labor contracts, aimed at the introduction of important reforms, was both a prerequisite imposed by investors for taking over the company and a response to some of the conditions established by governments, such as job stability.

Some of these reforms are related to a variety of labor issues ranging from job security to labor input in the company's decision-making process. The preexisting contractual commitment not to lay off workers, for example, has been erased from the new labor contracts. At the same time temporary hiring has become part of the new agreements granting managers considerable rights to hire and fire workers for short periods of time. Managers have also gained considerable leeway to transfer workers within the company—an event that was highly restricted in the past. There had been also a consolidation of job description and salary ranges, and new programs to increase labor productivity and output efficiency. On other matters, meetings and assembly rights were curtailed, reducing sharply what used to be the lifeblood of the labor movement. Finally, the mechanism by which labor participated in decisions concerning the adoption of new technologies in the workplace has been dismantled.

These trends were clearly present in both the Argentine and the Mexican privatizations. In Argentina the pre-existing collective contract (*Convenio Colectivo*) of the Argentine telecommunications worker signed during the last Peronist government (1973–1976), was replaced by a new one signed in May 1991.[35] In Mexico, the pre-existing agreement was replaced by a new collective contract (*Convenio de Concertación*) which also incorporates a large number of "labor flexibilization" issues.

Labor is one sector in which SOTE privatization has generated unexpected outcomes. Contradicting widespread assumptions, telecom workers have retained prior levels of employment after reform, and most workers now enjoy the economic bonanza of ownership in the company and better salaries. The downside of reform is that in most countries workers have lost many of the rights and social benefits that they enjoyed under a public-sector regime.

THE STATE

The potential consequences of telecom reform for the state have generated conflicting views, serving to support or attack privatization initiatives. Reform advocates have argued that privatization would bring important new revenues to the public treasury in the form of regular taxes paid by the new private operators, and would end the fiscal drain created by money-losing SOEs.[36] Opponents hold that SOE privatization means a loss of control over a crucial sector of the economy (such as telecommunications), a reduction of state revenues, and, when enterprises are sold to foreign firms, a negative effect on external accounts. Early evidence drawn from privatized SOTEs shows mixed outcomes.

Fiscal Accounts

The fiscal impact of SOTE sales is determined by variations in state's revenues due to tax reform, and by the remaining balance in external accounts due to debt reduction and profit remittance abroad. Privatization opponents claim the state will lose not only existing and potential profits from the would-be-privatized SOTE, but also important revenues accrued through direct and indirect taxes.[37] At first glance the argument appears valid, since in some LDCs the government earned profits from taxes or telephone services. In Mexico, for example, more than 90 percent of local and approximately 60 percent of domestic long-distance tariffs were indirect and direct taxes. In Argentina telephone taxes amounted to 30.4 percent.

But tax reform has been different in each country. In Mexico, traditional telephone taxes were incorporated into tariffs, but a new tax on TELMEX revenues was created. Studies of TELMEX's privatization have concluded that "the fiscal impact of the reform was essentially zero—government tax revenues changed only marginally. Reductions in indirect tax revenues [have been] compensated by increased corporate income tax payments" (Tandon and Abdala 1992, 40).

In Argentina, on the other hand, no new telephone tax was created; therefore, ENTel's privatization had a negative impact on the state's revenues. According to studies of reform in the Argentine telecom sector, "with privatization the government gives up collecting the telecommunication indirect tax, and that more than outweighs the increased revenue from the value-added and the corporate tax." The conclusion clearly is that "the government comes out as a loser," (Abdala 1992a, 83) even when projected in the long term, under possible high-growth scenarios (Gerchunoff 1992, 276).

The impact of privatization on external accounts is less clear. Due to the short span of time since the sale of SOTEs, only some projections of possible trends exist, and these will depend largely on the trade-off between savings on the external debt and remittances abroad by new foreign owners and shareholders.

In the case of Mexico, for example, Tandon considers that, "if there is one negative efect with regard to the TELMEX sale, it is that, because such a high proportion of the ownership is foreign, a large fraction of the total benefits have leaked abroad" (Tandon and Abdala 1992, 41). The World Bank estimates that foreign investors have gained approximately 90 percent of the total welfare gain drawn from the TELMEX sale. In this regard, Mexico can be viewed as a Latin American stereotype, since most other SOTE privatizations in the region also show a high level of foreign involvement.

In other cases, like Argentina, the trade off for an extremely high level of foreign participation is presumably a quantity of foreign debt canceled in the transaction. The sale of the first 60 percent of ENTel was a debt-equity swap— an exchange of debt papers in lieu of cash for an interest in the public utility company.[38] The state earned only US$214 million in cash, but it erased US$5 billion in principal from Argentina's US$54 billion external debt. It remains to be seen if this financial transaction will, in the long run, have a positive impact on the country's external sector.

Political Power

Telecommunications privatization removed one of the state's important political tools that civil servants, SOE managers, politicians, union leaders, and the military had used to shape social policy and, in many cases, to enhance their political careers or gain personal economic benefits. While the benefits of privatization are diffusely and thinly spread among SOTE buyers, financial institutions, and certain groups of customers, the cost is heavily borne by state's agents, such as politicians, SOEs managers and employees, and other state organizations.

In most LDCs the provision of telephone service, the repair of damaged equipment, and preferential customer services were tied to political or economic networks. Customers wait several years to get connected to the network, repairs take months or even years, unfair billing was rampant, and there was no institutionalized consumer protection. These serious deficiencies in service turned the ability and power to solve them into a scarce and valuable asset. Those who, due to their state-level connections, could intercede used that ability and power as a tool to gain political and economic benefits. Therefore, the loss of control of telecom resources through privatization carried a heavy price for these actors previously related to the SOTE.

At the institutional level the impact on state control was related to the state's ability to regulate the sector. Early events after privatization show that while some countries have been able to enforce reforms in the level of tariffs and the pricing regime, others have failed to do so. In Argentina, for example, the new private carriers refused to align their tariffs with the general guidelines of a new economic plan implemented by the government in April 1991 (Verbitsky 1991, 261). The experiences of Malaysia and Mexico show, instead, that privatization does not necessarily imply a weakening in tariff control. In Mexico, only six months after privatization the government authorized an 11.7 percent increase in tariffs to offset inflation. Thereafter, the Salinas administration granted increases below the inflation rate. In Malaysia, the Mahatir government kept a tight control over tariffs, and despite strong pressures from the executive board of STM to restructure and raise tariffs, rates did not change from 1985 to 1992.[39]

In sum, effects of recent telecom reform on state-level finances and politics vary among cases and issues. The only consistent pattern for most cases is the weakening of state actors' control over the sector.

SERVICE PROVIDERS

In the same way that there was considerable consensus that privatization would have negative consequences for labor, there was agreement about the significant benefits that private owners could gain from entering telecom markets in LDCs. The difference with the labor forecast is that while for workers several of these assumptions did not come true, in the case of service providers early outcomes have confirmed initial expectations.

Arguments about potential benefits arose from the fact that LDCs that pursued state reform were generally pressed to sell by fiscal and economic constraints. This, along with an overflow of privatization offers in the international market, granted investors the required leverage to demand optimum conditions for their investments. Large unsatisfied demand in a market with high growth potential would enhance the investment prospect. Early outcomes have confirmed this prediction. New private telecom firms have earned considerable profits and accessed—in optimal conditions—markets with prosperous futures.

Although new owners as a whole have gained from these positive results, some of them have benefited even more than others. In several privatization cases the buying consortium comprised members of the international financial community. In their case, the advantage is not only substantive profits but also the swap of low-value debt papers for a high performance company and the control of a technology crucial to their business operations.

Hegemony in Profitable Markets

Traditionally LDCs were considered risky for foreign investment. In the second half of the 1980s a variety of socioeconomic reforms and important political changes began to create institutional guarantees that lured foreign capital into the domestic economy of several LDCs. In the telecommunications sector, this "backing" offered to new investors often took the form of protected monopolies lasting for several years. In fact, this regulatory shield against competition made LDCs a more secure place to invest in telecommunications than the highly competitive markets of developed nations.[40]

In LDCs such as Argentina, Mexico, and Malaysia, the existence of captive and unsatisfied markets brings unexpected high profits to the new companies. Perhaps the best example is TELMEX, which reported net profits of US$2.2 billion for fiscal year 1991—an increase of 78 percent over the same period in the previous year—and US$2.6 billion for 1992. The company became in 1991 the second most profitable telecom enterprise in the world, surpassed only by British Telecom. Syarikat Telekom Malaysia, showed a similar trend with net incomes growing from US$203 million in 1990 to US$360 million in 1991.[41] Sales for the company grew 60 percent between 1987 and 1990.[42]

Besides large profits from the sale of services, the new operating companies have reaped profits from successful flotation of shares in local and international stock exchange markets.[43] With value of shares increasing, the economic conglomerates, which initially bought company shares at relatively low prices, saw their capital value in the business expand sharply. In late 1990, a consortium constituted by France Telecom, Southwestern Bell, and the Mexican Grupo Carso bought TELMEX's AA shares, which consisted of only 20.4 percent of the company's capital but accounted for 51 percent of the voting shares. The price was US$2.03 per share. In July 1991, the Mexican government successfully sold 16.5 percent of the remaining shares on the stock exchange.[44] By May 1992 the price of TELMEX shares had risen 237 percent from their initial value, and the company was appraised at twenty-five times its 1988 value.[45] In Argentina, the flotation of 30 percent of ENTel's shares (those remaining after the sale of 60 percent of the company to two private consortiums) met with a similarly positive public response.[46] The Argentine government anticipated earning approximately US$500 million from the sale. However, intense demand increased the initial estimated value fourfold, and the public ultimately paid a total of US$2 billion for the offering.[47]

Privatized telecom firms' outstanding performance in capital markets has often turned them into the business with the highest market value in their own countries.[48] Furthermore, in cases such as TELMEX, the boost granted by the flotation of shares placed the company into the number one firm in the developing world in terms of market value, while Telefónica and Telecom and CTC ranked within the top twenty-five.[49]

Besides significant profits, telecom firms that became owners of telecom systems in LDCs enjoyed the benefits of an expanding international market for their operations. Most privatized SOTEs in the developing world were purchased by European and North American telecom firms.[50] For many of these foreign operators, privatization was a safety valve to escape from saturated domestic markets at home (at least in regard to expansion of basic services). In these companies' countries of origin—the United States, France, Italy, Spain, and so forth—telephone penetration had reached 80 to 90 percent of the households, while a typical LDC had achieved service in only 20 percent of its households. Unsatisfied demand has remained consistently high in most LDCs. In Argentina, for example, pending requests for new connections have been steady at 45 percent of all lines in operation during the thirty years prior to privatization.[51] Further, as the domestic economies of some LDCs improve and open up to international trade, demand for long-distance telecommunications services rises, leading to substantial profits for foreign investors. Southwestern Bell's profits on its investment in TELMEX in 1991, for example, exceeded its profits from all operations in the United States (Ramamurti 1995, 30).

However, if high profits and unsatisfied demand are important in the short run, the position that new private operators acquire when they enter the market is far more important in the long run.[52] Most conglomerates that recently bought privatized SOTEs in LDCs were granted a monopoly for a limited period of time in the local market.[53] This will probably give them a hegemonic position for a period much longer than initially established in the contracts.

Precedence and consolidation of early entrants in the domestic market point to potential difficulties for future competitors. Early entry is particularly important in markets such as telecommunications that are based on the establishment of networks. To operate in such markets it is necessary to achieve compatible technical standards and a detailed knowledge of the network. Early entrants have competitive advantages, because latecomers must make their equipment compatible with the existing technological features of the network and develop a difficult-to-achieve technical knowledge of the network.[54]

The weakness of LDC governments in regulating and controlling the operation of private carriers and the particular configuration of the consortiums that acquired the SOTEs—generally comprising foreign telecom firms, domestic economic conglomerates with powerful lobbying capability, and sometimes foreign creditors of the country—deepens even further the tendency to create a noncompetitive market.[55]

The dominant position of new private telecom companies, coupled with extremely weak state control, not only affects the future entry of competitors into the market, but it also induces arbitrary corporate behavior menacing the continuity of "common carrier" principles and the prospects of network interconnection.[56] Finally, it is doubtful whether LDC governments, which face economic hardship, will be willing to threaten the commercial strength and business allure of companies that loudly touted their infant domestic capital markets. The outlook for state control of the private telecom companies' commercial behavior is unclear, and the likely options are not particularly encouraging.

FINANCIAL INVESTORS

The international financial community played a crucial role in some LDC telecommunications reforms. In Argentina, for example, the influential presence of international banks and financial institutions was linked to the prominent role assigned to debt-equity swaps in the sale of ENTel. As a consequence, the company that provides services in the southern region comprised eighteen international banks and financial institutions, which controled 82 percent of the consortium's shares. In Chile, the privatization of CTC caught the attention of Australian financier, Alan Bond, who, through successive purchases, acquired control of half of the company.

Those financial institutions that participated directly in the purchase of SOTEs and those that, although absent from the privatization deal, were international creditors of the LDC states are clear winners in privatization. For those who participated directly in privatization programs, gain came in the form of a swap of greatly undervalued debt papers for assets and shares in a business with a bright future. Argentina's creditors, for example, turned over to the Argentine government debt bonds valued in secondary markets at approximately US$0.14 each. The state accepted them at their face value of US$1.00 per bond. Moreover, in the past the state held ENTel's deposits, amounting to an annual average of US$1 billion. Following the transfer, these deposits were handed over to the private banks that made up the telecom consortiums. Finally, the financial firms, now owners of ENTel, profited from the general increase in the company's shares on the stock market.[57]

Those who did not participate directly in the privatization of SOTEs, but who held debt bonds, were rewarded by the financial spillover effects generated by the increasing of value of debt bonds in secondary markets. Following the Argentine case we find that when the government announced ENTel's privatization, Argentine debt papers were traded in secondary markets at US$0.12 per bond. Emphasis on debt-equity swap as the preferred financial mechanism for the sale of the SOTE sent the value of debt papers up twenty points in a few days. By the time ENTel was transferred to the private sector, Argentine debt papers were traded at approximately US$0.35 per bond.

Besides economic advantages, participation in the ownership of telecommunications networks gives the international financial community direct control over a key asset in their business operations. Telecommunications systems have become the nervous system of national and global finance. Dependency on fast, cheap, and reliable telecommunications services is so great it has led to the establishment of private global networks, such as SWIFT,

FEDWIRE, CHIPS, CHATS, and CHAPS.[58] The centrality of tele-communications occurs as much in LDCs as in industrialized nations. For example, since 1987 the Argentine Banks Association (ADEBA) pressured the government to shape the telecommunications system to respond better to its needs.[59] Further, until the late 1980s Citibank and American Express were the only two corporations in the country that acquired government permission to install and operate an international private data network.[60]

EQUIPMENT SUPPLIERS

The equipment industry was the first segment of the telecommunications market opened to competition. As with most market-driven policies, it was thought that liberalization would bring new incentives for technological innovation, lower prices, and greater efficiency. Privatization led to expectations that market forces would expand even further as traditional monopsonies were dismantled and dominant carriers were free to purchase from any provider in the market. Equipment companies with the best products at the best prices would drive out inefficient producers. On the contrary, however, in the early postprivatization stages equipment purchasing in the developing world showed that many new telecom companies did not follow bona fide market practices. Although pure market principles still did not govern LDC firms, liberalized procurement decisions nevertheless had a considerable impact on the reduction of prices paid for products.

Postprivatization Procurement

Equipment liberalization worldwide has brought important changes in the relative and absolute shares that different companies hold in the global market.[61] Many of these changes are based on price and product quality differentiation, that is, on market mechanisms. Yet in most LDCs, equipment liberalization in its early stages did not resulted in this type of dynamic. Political factors appear to override the logic of the market, making the equipment markets extremely unpredictable.

In Argentina political considerations clearly played a role in the procurement decision of new private telecom companies. Argentine equipment liberalization and ENTel's privatization threatened the stability of the two dominant equipment suppliers, Equitel and Pecom Nec.[62] However, after a year and a half of private ownership the situation did not change much. The new private companies still purchase most of their equipment from local firms—to which they have added a third supplier related to one of the operating companies—and there were no signs of major shifts from this pattern in the short term.[63]

A similarly politicized procurement dynamic was present in Malaysia, where market principles fall prey to political considerations (Kennedy 1992). The privatization of Jabatan Telekom Malaysia had, among other goals, the removal of political criteria from company decision making to enhance its commercialization. However, five years after corporatization the company's equipment procurement decisions were still "trapped" in Malaysia's political networks. The most likely reason was that despite corporatization the state was still deeply involved in the control of the company and, therefore, key decisions continued to be crafted at the highest levels of the government. Often "common sense" corporate and market principles were marginalized on behalf of "common sense" political decisions.

Such was the case in April 1992, when the Malay finance minister, Datuk Seri Anwar Ibrahim, was embroiled in a huge political scandal that almost drove him to resign. The private company, Syarikat Telekom Malaysia, opened to public bidding a contract for an ambitious project to install four million new digital lines in the country.[64] Scandal erupted when the finance minister intervened to secure a large share of the market for one of the bidders, the French company Alcatel Alsthom. This company was acting in tandem with the local Foundation Yayasan Bumiputra Pulau Pinang, an institution of which Anwar was president until just prior to assuming his government post. The foundation was affiliated with the governing political party, United Malay National Organisation (UMNO).[65]

Despite the failure of market principles to overcome politics, the privatization of SOTEs had an important impact on the service sector by lowering the price of equipment. In Argentina, for example, Telecom and Telefónica were paying less than half the price of what ENTel used to pay for equipment. Although Mexico's privatized TELMEX renegotiated contracts with its traditional equipment suppliers—Alcatel-Indentel and Teleindustrias Ericsson—studies predicted savings on TELMEX's capital expenditure that ranged from 25 to 50 percent, without any reduction in the rate of network expansion. These forecasts were based on TELMEX's aggressive efforts to negotiate better terms from its traditional equipment suppliers. The company has also added AT&T to its list of traditional suppliers to compete with Alcatel and Ericsson.

This change could have spillover effects on the price of telecom services since it diminishes operating costs for dominant carriers. Yet, these benefits for consumers are only "potential" since, according to the market structure in which each company operates, cost reduction might be transferred to consumers in the form of lower tariffs or could be assimilated by the company in the form of earnings.

In short, although privatization brought a reduction in the price of telecom hardware, the evidence from procurement experiences of privatized firms in LDCs puts in question the widely accepted economic assumption that liberalization and privatization would radically transform the profile of the telecom equipment market in LDCs. In the early stages of reform, new private firms still selected their equipment providers based predominantly on political and nonmarket criteria.

CONCLUSION

As the preceeding summary analysis has shown, there is no straight, unilateral answer to what has been the impact of telecom privatization and liberalization in LDCs. Complexity and mixed results are in evidence in most countries. Analysis is further complicated by the convergence of market liberalization and structural economic transformations. A comparative approach has been used in an effort to overcome the diversity and peculiarities among the cases examined. By seeking a dominant thread in countries that reformed their telecom sectors, differences and similarities can be transcended, providing the following general provisional assessments of the impact of telecom reform in LDCs.

Consumers of telecom services have been affected differently according to which type of service they use (local, long distance, or international). The dismantling of long-distance and international-to-local cross-subsidies, for example, has considerably increased rates for local users while reducing rates in relative terms for long-distance users. In general, the transfer to the private sector has improved the availability of capital for new investments. Further, new private companies, driven by profit-maximization and their efforts to dominate in the local market before more liberalization takes place, have increased network expansion and diversification of services. However, some LDC networks are in their infancy, and hence still require large sunk capital. This has led the dominant carrier to divert investment into easy-to-install and profitable new services—such as cellular—targeting a selected segment of the market and reducing their commitment to universal service obligations.

Labor, for its part, came out better than originally expected. In most countries government requirements for employment stability, paired with the monopoly granted to the new private firms (which are operating in a rapidly growing industry) have secured most SOTE jobs. Furthermore, workers have unexpectedly become shareholders in the new private firms, thus gaining a variety of economic and political benefits. But they have also lost a variety of labor rights gained under earlier public-service regimes.

Also as predicted, the consortiums that have bought SOTEs comprise one of the groups most favored by LDC telecom reforms. Due to the level of unmet demand in LDC telecom markets and because of the introduction of commercial principles in the sector, new private telecom companies have earned large profits in their initial operations and have successfully floated shares in local and international stock exchange markets. Further, they have entered high-growth markets under very advantageous conditions—that is, legal monopoly on most services. Early entrance in the business and the existence of weak regulatory agencies have proven to be an excellent opportunity to establish de facto monopoly control in current and soon-to-be liberalized segments of the market.

As part of the acquiring consortiums, international banks and financial corporations have also benefited significantly from SOTE privatization. Some countries accepted debt papers as payment for their telecommunications companies. Those financial institutions that participated directly in such privatization deals were able to swap low-value debt for an attractive business.

privatization deals were able to swap low-value debt for an attractive business. Moreover, by becoming owners of telecom service companies these financial groups participate in the control of a sector that is key to their own business operations. Those not directly involved in the sale, but who held LDC debt, enjoyed spillover effects with the increase in the value of their bonds in secondary debt markets.

Finally, contrary to carefully considered forecasts, equipment suppliers faced a murky and unpredictable market profile in which politics affected procurement decisions as much as it did in the past. The only clear consequence of privatization for equipment vendors was that the dismantling of monopsonies has pushed them to drop equipment prices considerably.

The material presented here draws on a rich collection of data on early trends in telecom reform in LDCs. However, this information grants us only a preliminary, provisional assessment of the socioeconomic impact of these transformations. More detailed analysis will be needed to accurately evaluate the implications of this unprecedented phenomenon in the field of communications in developing societies.

NOTES

1. The other telecom operator, Dirección General de Telecomunicaciones, transferred to the central administration US$100 million and received back only US$30 million for operations and new investments.

2. TELMEX's first-year operating profit totaled US$2.3 billion. The company expressed confidence that it will be able to generate 70 to 80 percent of the funds needed for future investment internally.

3. In Venezuela, the new private owners of CANTV spent US$500 million throughout 1992, increasing fivefold the average yearly investment of the company compared to when it was under state control. In Chile, the availability of new funds gained through privatization allowed the company to expand internally. This, in turn, led to output diversification into nonregulated, value-added services and also to improved productivity, which generated more funds internally and allowed further expansion into long-distance and other new services. According to assessments of the World Bank study, this impressive investment-expansion cycle would have been mostly absent under a publicly owned business (Galal et al. 1992b).

4. However, the dismantling of cross-subsidies—if not replaced by other financial mechanisms—could discourage service expansion in rural and non-profitable areas of the country. As companies become profit-oriented businesses, development of services tend to concentrate in the most economically attractive segments of the market. In Thailand, for example, in 1989 rural users accounted for only 10 percent of Telecommunications Organization of Thailand (TOT) earnings. Yet, that same population absorbed 40 percent of the company's expenses. Paul Handley, "Progress by Numbers," *Far Eastern Economic Review*, 23 March 1989, 83–84.

5. Similar trends are reported in the now-private Syrikiat Telekom Malaysia. From the time of its establishment as a private company in 1987, it has increased

telephone penetration in the country from 6 main lines per 100 people to more than 10 lines per 100 in 1991.

6. If this occurs, the company will have expanded its stock of installed lines in service 160 percent by 1996 (Galal et al. 1992b, 44).

7. In the United States, for example, following the divestiture of AT&T, local telephone rates rose by 53 percent, while long-distance and international charges plunged by 40 percent. This tariff restructuring benefited a limited number of users. According to 1988 figures, only 10 percent of residential users spend more than US$25 a month on long-distance calls, while only 14 percent of business users spend more than US$50 (Horwitz 1992).

8. For political and social reasons telecommunications tariffs, like many other public services, were highly subsidized by central governments.

9. For details on the evolution of tariffs in Argentina prior to the sale of ENTel, see Chapter 4.

10. Estimates claimed that this tariff reduction would entail a loss of approximately US$145 million for each company—calculated as a net present value of the reduction over a five-year period.

11. Tariff reforms in Mexico followed similar patterns. Consumers benefited from a general decline of tariffs—in real terms—until January 1988, when the government announced a sharp price increase. In January 1990 there was an important new price upgrade for the purpose of making the company more financially attractive for privatization. Although tariffs rose for most services— local services went from 8.69 current Mexican pesos to 100 per minute, domestic long distance went from 420 to 841 pesos per minute, and the annual service rent rose from 50,640 to 85,080 pesos—it is important to highlight that the increase was dramatically greater for local than for long-distance services, and that international services benefited from a drop in rates—international tariffs (U.S. outbound) dropped from 2,017 current Mexican pesos to 1,781 per minute.

12. In developed countries, such as the United States, the emergence of private networks quickly became evident in the mid-1980s. While in the first years of the decade 100 percent of the investments in telecommunications were from public network operators, by 1986 more than one-third of all U.S. spending on capital facilities was by individuals and firms other than common carriers (Crandall 1989).

13. In Venezuela, for instance, the government opened private satellite networking to users and new-services providers. Within two months, 140 businesses had registered. In Brazil, where market liberalization—but not SOTE privatization—is driving reforms, the government has allowed business and residential users to build their own private networks. This regulatory reform has resulted in tenders for half a million lines in the first year.

14. In the United States, for example, more than 50 percent of the common carriers' income is provided by only 3 percent of the users (Noam 1991). In Mexico the proportion is similar.

15. The merging of computers and telecommunications, paired with an exploding practice of avoiding control of regulators and operating companies, led to new challenges for governments and service providers. For a detailed analysis of the political, social, and economic problems raised by technological innovation and the merging of various segments of the communications market, see Drake 1993.

16. In countries like Argentina, a large number of businesses routed their international and domestic long-distance calls through the United States by using

these services. In this way a party calling from Buenos Aires to the north of Argentina routed its call through Miami or New York and then back to Argentina. Some companies have reported up to a 60 percent saving on their telephone bills thanks to this maneuver. Romeo Medina, "Teléfonos: La Espera Sigue," *Clarin*, November 1991.

17. In Argentina, long-distance tariffs were reduced 10 percent in September 1993 due to this situation.

18. Rolf Luders has shown very convincingly that the nature of ownership does not affect the company's internal efficiency. He believes, however, that due to the political constraints placed on SOEs, in the long run they will sacrifice efficiency to respond to political demands of the state.

19. For example, the waiting time for new-service connection was drastically reduced, cutting the waiting list from 200,000 to 50,000 customers. The time for repairing failures in the network and damaged customer-premise equipment (CPE) also dropped, and the efficiency levels of calls has improved. Changes in the billing system diminished errors and enhanced the company's image (Woon 1990, 78).

20. In mid-1992, New Zealand was still the country with the world's highest level of telecom competition.

21. In 1990 Telecom Corporation was sold to a consortium led by the U.S. firm Bell Atlantic.

22. While in 1987 it took an average of forty days to get a telephone installed, by 1989 the company installed new services in forty-eight hours. Residential users also saw dramatic improvements in response to service inquiries and complaints. While only 25 percent of the network was digital in 1988, the new commercially oriented firm quickly upgraded the system. James Colin, "Ringing the Changes," *Far Eastern Economic Review*, 19 October 1989, 57.

23. Contradicting early indicators of service improvement, public-opinion polls conducted in Argentina in May 1991 reflect the frustrated expectations of most users. For the majority of respondents (66 percent), there was no difference between the service provided by the new private companies and those previously provided by ENTel. For 21 percent of the respondents, service was worse than before, while only 8 percent believed there had been improvements (Estudios y Políticas 1991). A similar trend can be seen in Mexico where, during the first eight months of privatized operations, the Office of Consumer Protection (Profeco) received 40,872 complaints regarding the poor quality of TELMEX services, overcharges, charges for services not provided, poor customer relations, and so forth. This represents a 30 percent increase in complaints from 1990, when TELMEX was still run by the state.

24. Based on the impact of telecom reform in selected developed and developing countries, Sinha (1991) has concluded that the privatization and competition introduced in the sector "have not been associated with significant improvements in telecommunications performance." For LDCs he argues in favor of increased government investment, rather than privatization and liberalization.

25. Some categories of TELMEX employees have even benefited from privatization. According to a study of the Mexican telecom labor sector, it was expected that, by the late 1980s, technological innovation and the fiscal crisis would leave 10,000 of the 13,000 telephone operators without jobs. Early indicators of this were present in 1989 when the labor force was reduced through attrition by 1.6 percent, with retiring workers not being replaced. However, the

condition imposed on new owners to retain workers protected, at least for a while, those jobs that were previously at risk (Dubb 1991).

26. During this period public-sector employment in Chile dropped by 39 percent (Hachette and Luders 1993).

27. Prior to the sale, the government offered a well-remunerated early retirement program to the company's employees. In response, almost 400 of the 28,724 company employees dropped out of JTM, while approximately 200 remained in the Department of Telecommunications (now in charge of policies and regulations for the sector) and the remaining employees were transferred to the new private company, Syarikat Telekom Malaysia.

28. Although the period expired in 1992, there have not been massive layoffs. JTM has grown in such way that existing personnel was indispensable for adequate business operations and, unless technological innovation renders labor unnecessary, it does not appear that there will be any major change in the near future. In Argentina and Chile, growing business and labor stability requirements in the privatization contracts have kept the companies' personnel at approximately the same level as before privatization.

29. *Electronics Weekly*, 20 May 1992.

30. The case of Aeroméxico is a good example in this regard. For further details on this see Tandon et al. 1992.

31. A study carried out for the National Commission for Employment Policy of the U.S. Government on the Chilean case confirmed this trend concluding that: (a) "private contractors generally pay lower wages than do the government agencies they replace," and (b) "the government usually provides much more generous fringe benefits than do contractors, with the biggest disparity being in retirement benefits" (Dudek & Company 1988, 3). In Thailand there is a sharp difference between the relatively high salaries earned by public-sector employees and the low ones received by private-sector workers.

32. Labor's ownership status has generated a variety of collateral effects, such as the right to company information that otherwise would have been unavailable to employees, and an unexpected leverage in bargaining arising from the threat that large numbers of workers might simultaneously sell their shares—thus under-cutting stock market performance of the telephone company.

33. By 1989 workers controlled 11.5 percent of the company. Later capital expansion shrunk worker's participation to less than 2 percent of the firms shares. Galal et al. 1992b, and Terol 1993.

34. A loan of US$325 million allowed for the purchase of 187 million type A shares.

35. Convenio Colectivo N° 165/75 was replaced by Convenio Colectivo N° 163/91. The new contract was coincidentaly—or ironically—signed on May 1, 1991, which in Argentina—as in many other countries of the world—is Labor Day.

36. Transferring operations to the private sector would allow the state to concentrate on regulatory efficiency, a crucial role in a period of increasing complexity in the control of information and communications flows.

37. States in LDCs suffer from low tax revenues due to inefficient collection mechanisms, ineffective coercive tools, and endogenous corruption in agencies in charge of tax collection. Many LDCs saw telephone taxes as an easy and secured revenue to compensate for these high levels of fiscal evasion.

38. The main argument in favor of this mode of privatization is based on the fact that by canceling a certain amount of capital debt, the country avoids interest

that it would have paid in the future. However, this mode of privatization has been highly questioned by the opposition because it was carried out in a period in which debt reduction programs dominated the scene in the region.

39. This means that tariffs remained stable since two years prior to the company's privatization.

40. In Japan, for example, shares of the powerful NTT dropped approximately 200 percent between 1988 and 1991 due to increasing competition in the market. In New Zealand, a year following the privatization of Telecom Corporation of New Zealand and the complete liberalization of all segments of the market, the new operators are doubtful that the business can be turned into a profitable investment. In Great Britain, seven years following the privatization of British Telecom, the Labor party, dissatisfied with the performance of the company, started to considered its renationalization. On the other hand, Latin America was viewed by investment consultants as the most promising market of the early 1990s. In a 1991 report by Salomon Brothers on global tele-communications, investors are urged to focus on Latin America. *Spanish News Service*, 23 October 1991.

41. These are pretax incomes because the company was exempt until 1992. "Telekom Malaysia Set for Substantial Long-term Growth," *The Financial Times*, 29 November 1990; and Nick Ingelberecht, "Privatisation Doubles Profits," *Asian Business*, September 1991, 14.

42. In Argentina, it was estimated that the new companies had rates of return over fixed assets that ranged from 24 to 32 percent. A World Bank study estimated that a relatively well-managed telecommunications company in the developing world should have at least a 14 percent average rate of return. Karen Lynch, "World Telecommunications: Wave of Privatisations Sweeps the Globe," *Financial Times*, 7 October 1991, Survey Section, 2.

43. Most privatization in LDCs occurred in two clearly defined stages. The first consisted in the sale of part of the company to economic conglomerates (mostly comprised of foreign telecom companies and local and foreign financial groups). In the second stage, the remaining shares of the company were floated in local and international stock exchange markets. In most of the cases the sale of shares in the stock exchange was strikingly successful, and the governments earned much more than they had expected.

44. These shares were Series L, nonvoting shares, and were worth 2.5 times less than the traditional A TELMEX shares. The Mexican government increased even further the financial profits of the TELMEX consortium by reserving for it 5.1 percent of the capital (series L shares). In this way France Telecom and Southwestern Bell have doubled their participation in TELMEX. Matt Moffett, "Teléfonos de México Makes Promising Start on a Daunting Task," *Wall Street Journal*, 19 February 1992, sec. A, 1a.

45. A record US$5 billion entered Mexico during 1991 in the form of foreign investments. TELMEX was the recipient of half of this total investment.

46. The Chilean CTC was the first LDC telecommunications company to float shares in the international stock exchange. In July 1990 the company sold 110 million shares for US$92.5 million. By the end of that year CTC's shares had risen 45 percent ("Nueva York: Los Nuevos Socios de CTC," *Estrategia*, 12, 601 [July-August 1990]). Syrikiat Telekom Malaysia floated 148 million shares in the Kuala Lumpur Stock Exchange in November 1990. The shares, which initially sold at US$1.80 per unit, rose steadily, so that by July 1991 they were trading at US$4.25 per unit. STM shares were the most active on the KLSE, and were of

such magnitude that in 1991 made the Malaysian market the sixth most important financial market in the world. Ingelberecht, "Privatisation Doubles Profits," 14.

47. The sale was divided in two stages: the state first sold, in December 1991, 30 percent of the Telefónica consortium shares (this 30 percent of the new company's shares is equivalent to 15 percent of ENTel's shares). The state earned US$848 million on that sale. In the second stage the remaining 30 percent of Telecom's shares (or 15 percent of ENTel's shares) sold for US$1.2 billion.

48. From a macroeconomic perspective recent stock flotation of privatized firms' shares has its drawbacks. As pointed out earlier, due to the high level of participation by foreign investors, local economies may be damaged by profit remittance abroad (see section on fiscal impact).

49. *Business Week*, 12 July 1993, 98.

50. In Mexico, the TELMEX consortium was made up of France Telecom (France) and Southwestern Bell (USA). In Argentina, ENTel was bought by Telefónica (Spain), France Telecom (France), and STET (Italy). The Chilean telecommunications system was primarily controlled by Telefónica (Spain). In Venezuela a group led by GTE (USA) that includes AT&T (USA) and Telefónica (Spain) bought CANTV.

51. In Malaysia the market for domestic services grew at 14 percent a year in the late 1980s, while the more lucrative international market expands at 30 percent a year, yet the country still faced waiting lists of 50,000 to 60,000 customers. Michael Taylor, "Good Connections," *Far Eastern Economic Review*, 25 July 1991.

52. As has been accurately highlighted, often "the objective [of incoming investors] is to secure a position of special privilege in entering foreign national markets. The privileged market position then is ensured by the national policies of the countries with respect to such matters as licensing, tax, tariff, currency exchange, capital repatriation, and entry barriers imposed on rivals" (Melody 1991, 29).

53. In some cases, like Argentina, the monopoly guarantee extended up to ten years for most telecom services in the country. In others, like Mexico, the protected market was guaranteed for six years and restricted to basic services.

54. The impact of early entry in the market is clearly illustrated by the highly competitive Mexican cellular telephony market. Cellular services are provided in Mexico City by two companies: IUSACEL and Telcel (this last a subsidiary of TELMEX). They began operations at approximately the same time and with a similar customer profile. Yet after a short period, Iusacel witnessed a halt in the growth of demand and a noticeable migration of customers to the Telcel network. The key to the puzzle was that Telcel (TELMEX), due to its detailed knowledge of the technical features of the public network, had adopted cellular technology highly compatible with the existing technical features of the network. IUSACEL, on the other hand, lacked necessary information, and thus its cellular system required a long time to pair technical protocols of the public network and those of the cellular network. This meant that calls in the Iusacel system took longer and, therefore, were more expensive.

55. In Argentina, for example, both consortia were made up of (1) telecom firms primarily owned by the governments of European countries with which Argentina has strong, long-standing political and economic ties (Spain, Italy, and France); (2) some of the most important international creditors of the Argentine external debt; (3) and large local economic conglomerates with powerful lobbying capabilities.

56. Argentina offers two clear examples of this trend. In 1991, according to the international news agencies operating in the country—Associated Press, France Press, ANSA, EFE, United Press, Deutsche Presse, and Reuters—private telecom companies blocked the flow of news and information, jeopardizing the integrity of the national information system. These agencies, astonished by this consequence of private telecom monopoly, presented formal complaints to the Argentine president and Congress. The second case is reported by the Argentine company Expresión y Medios, to whom Telefónica has denied long-distance access, which the local company was planning to use for teleconferencing. Such discrimination among clients is especially notable since Telefónica grants to Televisión Española the same access that it denies to Expresión y Medios (*La Nación*, 13 August 1991, and Verbitsky 1991, 265).

57. In Chile, Alan Bond, a powerful financier, bought 53 percent of CTC's shares during 1988. He paid US$267 million. Bond headed the business for only a year, during which time the company realized a net income of US$100 million. He then sold his shares to Telefónica de España for US$391 million. In only twelve months Bond gained substantial profits from the firm's operation, as well as earning US$122 million through the sale of his part in CTC.

58. SWIFT stands for Society for Worldwide Interbank Financial Transactions. CHIPS, CHATS, and CHAPS are part of global financial networks with nodes in New York, Tokyo, and London.

59. Due to the peculiar characteristics of this group (economic concentration and powerful political influence) and the nature of their demands (specialized and customized services), governments have acquiesced to their pressures. In Argentina, ADEBA's demands induced the government to set up the "Finantel Project" in early 1988. The initiative was a regulatory reform to privatize and liberalize the provision of telecommunications services in downtown Buenos Aires (where the most powerful financial institutions of the country are located).

60. Diversification of the investment portfolios of international banks is not a simple reaction to debt-equity swap opportunities. On the contrary, such moves reflect a global trend in which large telecom service users and service suppliers integrate. A variety of joint ventures, mergers, consortiums, and absorptions are blurring traditionally well defined boundaries between service providers and service consumers. These structural changes in the makeup of dominant common carriers is heightened by extremely weak state control, and it has important consequences for the development of telecommunications in LDCs. In other words, if certain users are also owners and managers of companies that provide the services, it is not clear what type of services will be developed, at what expense to other services, for the benefit of whom, and at what cost.

61. An executive of Ericsson argues that the global liberalization of the equipment market has meant a 4 percent growth in the company's international market share. "Telecoms: Giants Set for Battle in Asia," *Asian Business* (November 1991): 62.

62. The telecommunications equipment industry in Argentina was dominated for several decades by two branches of transnational companies: Compañía Standard Electric Argentina (CSEA-a branch of ITT), and Equitel (a branch of Siemens). However, in the late 1970s and early 1980s the market was restructured; CSEA was bought by Equitel and a new company, the Argentine-Japanese consortium Pecom Nec, entered the market as the second major equipment provider (Herrera 1989).

63. Some students of the equipment industry have suggested that the answer lies in the realm of politics and intra- and interfirm strategies. Powerful political influences and market precedence of already established equipment suppliers affect the choice of service providers. Representatives of Siemens in Argentina, for example, had strong political ties with the government—President Menem was related to Blas Medina, a political connection of Siemens in Argentina. When these political leverages failed, the German chancellor personally lobbied President Menem to get payments for the company. The other company—Pecom Nec—is made up by one of the most politically powerful local economic conglomerates: the Pérez Companc group. Much of the evolution and stability of the Argentine economy depends on these groups and their financial and political networks. See Acevedo, Basualdo, and Khavisse 1991.

64. The contracts for the project were signed in March 1992 and are worth US$775 million.

65. Doug Tsuruoka, "Minister in a Muddle?," *Far Eastern Economic Review*, 9 April 1992: 55.

Conclusion

The world of telecommunications services in less developed countries (LDCs) underwent a profound transformation in the final years of the 1980s. The transfer of state-owned telecom companies to private owners and the opening of certain segments of the market to competition has radically altered the sector's traditional institutional and economic arrangements. Major changes first occurred in MDCs such as the United States and Britain, where the explosion and diversification of technological innovations, the merger of telecom and computers, and the demands of large corporate users—who sought more sophisticated and cheaper services to compete in an increasingly global and informatized economy—brought pressure for change.

In LDCs, demise of public utilities monopolies—such as telecom—are less tied to technological innovation or economic growth than to the fiscal crisis and economic decline suffered by most developing nations during the 1980s. Economic constraints and the increasingly crucial role of telecom for economic development led LDC governments to carry out sweeping state reforms, which included the privatization and liberalization of telecommunications services.

The medium- and long-term consequences of these reforms are of great importance for LDC development. Due to the multiplier effects of telecom across almost every economic activity, mistakes in the design of new telecom regimes are quickly felt throughout the productive system, affecting a country's ability to compete in the global economy.

In pursuit of fiscal health, renewed economic growth, and improved telecom services, countries have attempted to privatize SOTEs and liberalize key segments of their domestic markets. However, efforts to introduce reforms in the sector have not always reached targeted goals. Some countries have been able to privatize while others have failed to do so. And, while some have been able to liberalize their telecom markets, others have had to renounce their liberalization plans.

Argentina, for example, attempted to privatize ENTel, its national carrier beginning in the early 1980s. Neither the military regime that governed the country from 1976 to 1983, nor the democratic administration that followed from 1984 to 1989, were able to transfer the company to the private sector. Similarly, the governments of Thailand, Colombia, South Africa, and Uruguay failed to privatize their national carriers. Mexico, Malaysia, Chile, Jamaica, and Venezuela succeeded, however, as did the current government of Argentina.

Liberalization of telecom markets has followed similar patterns. Some countries, such as Mexico, Malaysia, and Thailand, have introduced competition in segments of their markets, while others, such as Argentina and Jamaica, recreated a monopoly, but one held privately.

It is intriguing why countries with similar economic profiles, attempting transformations in their telecom sectors at about the same historical moment, reach widely different outcomes. This study argues that an understanding of these outcomes requires an analysis of the political and economic dynamics that surrounded events in each country and the opportunities and obstacles posed by domestic political institutions.

Two variables are crucial to the success (or failure) of privatization: (1) state autonomy from opposition of local interest groups, and (2) cohesiveness of policymakers, or, in its absence, the concentration of power in the head of the executive branch.

Traditionally, a variety of local interest groups—residential users, labor, equipment suppliers, state officials, politicians, and so forth—benefited from preexisting telecom service arrangements. Attempts to reform the sector generally aroused considerable domestic opposition. Insulation of the reform process and the concentration of power in the head of state thus become a key element in controlling that opposition and in assuring the viability of reform initiatives.

The evidence drawn from the cases studied here support this hypothesis. If we look at countries that failed to privatize their SOTEs, such as Argentina (1980–1988), Thailand, Colombia, South Africa, and Uruguay, we find that one or both of these factors are absent. During the Argentine military regime of the early 1980s, for example, the state enjoyed a considerable level of autonomy, but privatization programs emerged, languished, and died due to bureaucratic infighting. The democratic regime that followed lacked insulation from domestic pressures and a centralized state power structure. In Thailand, Colombia, and South Africa it was mainly labor opposition that dismantled privatization programs. And in Uruguay, the opposition of an organized popular movement in an open political system with considerable decentralization of power led to the canceling of the national carrier's sale.

In Argentina (1989), Mexico, Chile, Malaysia, and Jamaica, where privatization was successful, we find a consistent pattern of policy-making insulation and concentration of power in the executive. Venezuela is a puzzle yet to be explored. A ruined economy and troubled political environment gave the Argentine government that came to power in 1989 the necessary conditions to achieve autonomy from local interest-group pressure, while careful political maneuvering gave the president unprecedented power over the national bureaucracy. In Mexico, Malaysia, and Chile, a policy process insulated from domestic political forces and a high concentration of power in head of the government provided no room for maneuver for those opposed to telecom privatization. In Jamaica privatization was implemented almost in secret and went unchallenged due to the "absolutist" power traditionally granted to the party in government.

The experience of these countries reinforces recent arguments about the relation between achievement of reform and distribution of power in the political system, and it renders valuable theoretical insights into the politics of telecom privatization in LDCs.

First, specific country cases highlight the role of political institutions in a process that has been often characterized as predominantly economic. Although telecom privatization evolved somewhat differently in each case, all countries explored in this study point to the politicized nature of the process.

Second, they show that achievement of privatization is strongly linked to the nature of local political institutions, the dynamics between the state and civil society, and the distribution of political power within the state itself. Countries with a long tradition of concentration of power in the executive and of state insulation from civil society—such as Mexico and Malaysia—find a smooth road to reform. Those countries in which states are vulnerable to the pressures and demands of civil society, or which suffer from lack of vertical integration in the state—such as Argentina and Thailand—encounter a rocky trip towards reform and often never reach their destination.

However, as the Argentine case showed, state autonomy or presidential power are not structural factors. They come and go with changes in the economy and the polity of a nation. Hence, new economic and political conditions may give a government—normally unable to carry out controversial reforms—the political tools necessary to implement changes that otherwise would have been impossible.

Third, comparative historical analysis has unveiled strengths and weaknesses in different theoretical approaches that attempt to explain cross-country variations in LDC telecom privatization. The impact of ideas, for example, seems to be crucial in the emergence of reform proposals, but it explains little about the particular paths followed by each country once the reform process is put in motion. Similarly, the difference between presidential and parliamentary systems, which has helped to clarify policy making in other contexts, seems irrelevant since countries with the same political organization (i.e., presidential or parliamentary) behave differently, while countries with different political profiles share similar outcomes.

The work incorporates, instead, theoretical propositions that highlight the role of political actors and institutions—such as interest group coalitions, political parties, Congress, etc. However, the participation and influence of these groups and institutions in the policy-making process are, for two reasons, approached from the perspective of the state. First, since these actors and institutions participated in the reform process, it would be ill-conceived to explain policy formation and transformation from the limited perspective of any one actor. Second, since the state became the central actor and fulcrum for all other political forces, it is appropriate to explore the process from a state perspective.

While domestic politics and the role of political institutions seem central to explaining success or failure in SOTE privatization, the dynamics of telecom market liberalization seems to reflect the workings of other forces. This study contends that privatization and liberalization are intricately linked, yet different, processes. In LDCs the privatization of national carriers deeply affects the well-being of providers, users, and regulators, making it, therefore, a highly politicized process. The liberalization of certain services—often marginal to the bulk of the market—is an event with far fewer social, economic, and political implications.

This difference, however, obscures the close relation that exists between privatization and liberalization. Often, the unleashing of one reform processes brings unpredictable consequences to the other, and vice versa. It is for these reasons that it is important to separate analytically both processes to adequately identify the forces that affect the ability of governments to introduce competition in their telecom markets.

The likelihood of successful liberalization will be affected by the timing of the opening of the market—before, after, or along with privatization. The introduction of competition in selected segments of the market prior to privatization generally encounters dynamics similar to those faced in the sale of SOTEs: local interest groups—mainly related to the national carrier—block the initiative. However, since the stakes are not as high as is the case with the sale of the national telecom monopoly, governments generally find it less difficult to gradually liberalize the sector.

When governments attempt liberalization along with—or following—privatization, the reform dynamics involves new actors—mainly private investors—with different expectations and interests. Since LDCs often pose risky investment environments, governments must improve the profile of the sector to attract and get the commitment of private capitalists. In such cases the prospects for liberalization—if any—are in jeopardy. Private entrepreneurs have often demanded a closed market as a prerequisite for investment. Hence, among those countries that simultaneously pursue privatization and liberalization, some countries give up liberalization to achieve a successful privatization, while others succeed in both objectives: the national carrier is sold and the market is considerably liberalized.

As with privatization, it is intriguing to explore what pushed countries with shared liberalization goals in opposite directions. This work argues that the degree of attractiveness of the local market, and in particular that of telecommunications, is the element that gave some governments—like Mexico's—the needed leverage to protect liberalization programs. Unattractive, risky markets—like Argentina's—created conditions that had to be overcome by offering private investors considerable short-term profits under monopoly conditions.

Another finding of this study is that similar political arrangements (such as closed polities) sometimes respond differently to similar policy initiatives (such as privatization attempts). A comparison of the politics of reform in MDCs and LDCs indicates that institutional responses are strongly affected by the origin or source of new policy proposals.

This study tries to answer why there has been such variation across nations in the adoption of liberalization and the achievement of privatization. It argues that relatively closed political systems (i.e., those in which the state enjoys a considerable autonomy from civil society and presents a significant concentration of power in the executive) are more successful in introducing reform in the sector than more open polities (i.e., those in which the state is vulnerable to pressures from civil society and where political power is dispersed throughout the political system). This assertion opposes the conclusion of studies that have looked at telecom reform in European countries.

Duch, for example, argues that open political systems are more likely to introduce reform in their telecom sector than those with closed, corporate political arrangements. For example, England, an open and participatory polity, has moved further in the reform of its telecom sector than has Germany, which is categorized as a closed, corporatist system. Duch's argument and evidence are convincing. But, how do we explain that in LDCs the opposite political arrangement (i.e., a closed polity with centralized power) is more conducive to the introduction of reform in the sector?

This study argues that one must look at the origin of the forces that pushed for reform. In this regard we find that in most MDCs (and particularly in Europe) telecom reform was introduced into the public agenda by large corporate users. The call for liberalization and privatization thus came from outside the state apparatus. In such cases, an open, participatory system is more receptive to reform than would be a closed one. In LDCs, the state is the one that initiates telecom reform and it generally confronts considerable opposition in civil society. In polities where the policy-making process is closed to the broad participation of civil society, the opportunities for reform are greater than in cases where the system is open to considerable influence by an array of political actors.

Successful reforms in LDCs were generally achieved by insulated states with high concentration of political power—which forced changes despite domestic opposition. This could lead to the conclusion that privatization was a policy benefiting a small, governing elite and its supporters. However, initial outcomes of privatization are nuclear and benefits seem to be distributed in unpredictable ways. A survey of the initial impact of reform shows that users, for example, have been affected in diverse ways. All countries explored here are heading toward a cost-based pricing system (tariffs for each segment of the market will be based on the costs of providing a particular service). In general, the transition from cross-subsidy to cost-based pricing mechanisms tends to benefit long-distance users (generally large businesses) and punish local ones (generally residential customers). The development of network expansion is also mixed. Telephone penetration has improved, mainly, because new private telecommunications enterprises are profit maximizers, completely controlling profits for reinvestment, which often aim to expand the market. Yet, the disappearance of long-distance subsidies shrinks financial resources that otherwise would be available for improvement and enlargement of the public local network. And the emergence of profitable new technologies (such as cellular telephony) that largely bypass the public network further diverts investment. Finally, preliminary data indicate that it is organizational reform and establishment of competitive markets that affect service quality. Ownership change *per se* is less of a factor.

Labor has been affected by reform in unexpected ways. Initially, no massive lay-offs occurred in the telecom sector, and workers have gained access to property rights over a limited number of shares in the new companies. Yet, privatization resulted in the loss of important labor rights gained after years of political struggle. The loss of these rights, along with the reduction of the number of unionized workers, has affected the legitimacy and political presence of the labor movement.

In regard to the impact on the role of the state, effects of reform initially have varied according to the cases considered. Loss of revenue from telephones hurt some states—such as Argentina—but had a neutral impact on others—such as Mexico. The strong presence of foreign investors has negatively affected the external accounts of most LDCs, because of the likelihood of profit repatriation. The sale of SOTEs also weakened the control of state agents over the sector. In general terms, state officials have lost an important tool to shape social policy. At the level of the individual, SOE managers, civil servants, union leaders, politicians, and the military will suffer from the dismantling of a business that helped them to enhance their professional careers, and, in some cases, to gain personal economic benefits.

According to the initial data telecommunications service suppliers and the financial institutions that participated in the purchase of privatized SOTEs are among the main beneficiaries of the reform process. Due to the levels of unsatisfied demand and the increase in telephone rates, new private operators have generally earned large profits. This attractive financial scenario has been enhanced by the increased value of shares floated in international stock exchange markets. Finally, most of the new private companies have moved from saturated domestic markets at home to new markets with high-growth potential. In this they have the advantage of early entry, giving them time to consolidate monopolistic control over markets that are planned for liberalization in the near future.

Finally, developments in the equipment industry have surprised most observers. Despite predictions about increased market-driven procurement due to reform, few changes have occurred in the profile of domestic suppliers of hardware, except for improved equipment prices. In the early postprivatization period, dominant suppliers still selected their equipment providers mainly based on political considerations rather than economic ones. Although wide generalizations cannot be made about the sector at this time, it is undeniable that political factors will affect the procurement of new private firms in LDCs for quite some time.

Although the early socioeconomic impact of telecom reform has unclear and mixed patterns, this study has shown that the privatization of SOTEs and the liberalization of markets have a much more consistent profile. Evidence from the comparative analysis of the cases shows that, while the introduction of competition calls for an attractive domestic market that would give local governments enough leverage to bargain with potential investors, the opening of the economy to private ownership calls for a closing of the polity to widespread participation.

References

Abdala, Manuel A. "Distributional Impact of Divestiture in a High Inflation Economy: The Case of Entel Argentina." Ph.D. Dissertation, Boston University, 1992a.

_____. "The Regulation of Newly Privatized Firms: An Illustration from Argentina." Unpublished manuscript. Córdoba, Argentina, September 1992b.

Acevedo, M., Eduardo Basualdo, and Miguel Khavisse. *Quién es Quién: Los Dueños del Poder Económico*. Buenos Aires: Página 12, 1991.

Adler, Emmanuel. *The Power of Ideology: The Quest for Technological Autonomy in Argentina and Brazil*. Berkeley: University of California Press, 1987.

Agurto, Renato. "Sector Telecomunicaciones." In *Soluciones Privadas a Problemas Públicos*, ed. Cristian Larroulet. Santiago de Chile: Fundación Libertad y Desarrollo, 1991.

Aharoni, Yair. *The Evolution and Managment of State Owned Enterprises*. Cambridge: Ballinger, 1986.

_____. "On Measuring the Success of Privatization." In *Privatization and Control of State-Owned Enterprises*. ed. Ravi Ramamurti and Raymond Vernon. Washington, D.C.: The World Bank, 1991.

Ahmad, Zakaria Haji, ed. *Government and Politics of Malaysia*. Singapore: Oxford University Press, 1987.

Allison, Graham T. *Essence of Decision: Explaining the Cuban Missile Crisis*. Boston: Little, Brown and Company, 1971.

Almond, Gabriel. "The Return to the State." *American Political Science Review* 82 (September 1988).

Ambito Financiero. 9 February 1988; and 21 July 1990.

Ambrose, William, Paul Hennemeyer, and Jean Paul Chapon. *Privatizing Telecommunications Systems.* Washington, D.C.: International Finance Corporation, 1990.

Arango de Maglio, Aída. "Radicalismo y Empresas Públicas (1983/1989)." *Realidad Económica,* no. 97 (1990): 29–54.

Aronson, Jonathan, and Peter F. Cowhey. *When Countries Talk: International Trade in Communications Services.* Cambridge: Ballinger, 1988.

Asian Business. September 1991; and November 1991.

Banco Mundial. *Informe sobre el Desarrollo Mundial.* Washington, D.C.: Banco Mundial, June 1991.

Barrera, Eduardo. "Telecommunications in Industrial Enclaves: The Maquiladora Industry on the United States-Mexico Border." *Research Reports of the Center for Research on Communication Technology and Society.* Austin: University of Texas, Austin, 1990.

Baur, Cynthia. "Rethinking Privatization, Liberalization, and Deregulation: The Case of Argentine Telecommunications." Unpublished manuscript. San Diego: University of California San Diego, 1991.

Beca, Raimundo. "Privatization, Deregulation, and Beyond: Trends in Telecommunications in Some Latin American Countries." In *Global Telecommunications Policies: The Challenge of Change,* ed. Meheroo Jussawalla. Westport: Greenwood Press, 1993.

Becher, Ernst. *Restructuring of Telecommunications in Developing Countries: An Empirical Investigation with ITU's Role in Perspective.* Geneva: International Telecommunication Union, 1991.

Bennett, Douglas C., and Kenneth E. Sharpe. "Agenda Setting and Bargaining Power: The Mexican State vs. Transnational Automobile Companies." *World Politics* , no. 32 (October 1979).

Berg, Elliot, and Mary M. Shirley. "Divestiture in Developing Countries." *World Bank Discussion Papers,* no. 11 (1987).

Bergendorff, Hans, Torsten Larsson, and Ruben Naslund. "The Monopoly vs. Competition Debate." *Telecommunications Policy* (December 1983): 297–307.

Bergsman, Joel, and Wayne Edisis. *Debt-Equity Swaps and Foreign Direct Investment in Latin America.* Washington D.C.: International Finance Corporation, 1988.

Berting, Jan, Felix Geyer, and Ray Jurkovich, eds. *Problems in International Comparative Research in the Social Sciences.* Oxford: Pergamon Press, 1979.

Block, Fred. "The Ruling Class Does Not Rule: Notes on the Marxist Theory of the State." *Socialist Revolution* 7, no. 3 (May–June 1977): 6–28.

Bocco, Arnaldo, and Naum Minsburg, eds. *Privatizaciones: Reestructuración del Estado y la Sociedad.* Buenos Aires: Ediciones Letra Buena, 1991.

Boneo, Horacio, ed. *Privatización: Del Dicho al Hecho.* Buenos Aires: El Cronista Comercial, 1985.

Business Week. 23 July 1990; and 12 July 1993.

Candoy-Sekse, Rebecca. "Techniques of Privatization of State-Owned Enterprises: Inventory of Country Experience and Reference Materials." *World Bank Technical Paper* 3, no. 90 (1988).

Canitrot, Adolfo. "Teoria y Práctica del Liberalismo: Política Antinflacionaria y Apertura Económica en la Argentina 1976–1981." *Estudios CEDES* 3, no. 10 (1988).

Cárdenas de la Peña, Enrique. *El Teléfono*. México, D.F.: Secretaría de Comunicaciones y Transportes, 1987.

Cardoso, Fernando H., and Enzo Faletto. *Dependency and Development in Latin America*. Berkeley: University of California Press, 1979.

Cavarozzi, Marcelo. "Political Cycles in Argentina since 1955." In *Transitions from Authoritarian Rule: Latin America*, eds. Guillermo O'Donnell, Phillippe C. Schmitter, and Laurence Whitehead. Baltimore: Johns Hopkins University Press, 1986.

Centeno, Miguel Angel. "The New Científicos: Technocratic Politics in Mexico, 1970–1990." Ph.D. Dissertation, Yale University, 1990.

Centro de Economía Internacional. "Argentina Economic Report." *Argentina Economic Report* 1, no. 1 (1992).

Chilcote, Ronald H. *Theories of Comparative Politics: The Search for a Paradigm*. Boulder: Westview, 1981.

Clarín. 2 June 1980; 6 August 1982; 28 June 1985; 13 June 1987; 22 December 1989; 22 April 1990; 3 October 1990; November 1991; 21 September 1992.

Coloma, Germán, Pablo Gerchunoff, and Maria Rosa Schappacasse. "Empresa Nacional de Telecomunicaciones." In *Las Privatizaciones en la Argentina*, ed. Pablo Gerchunoff. Buenos Aires: Instituto Torcuato Di Tella, 1992.

Communications International, August 1990.

Cornelius, Wayne A., and Ann L. Craig. *The Mexican Political System in Transition*. La Jolla: Center for U.S.-Mexican Studies, 1991.

_____. *Politics in Mexico: An Introduction and Overview*. La Jolla: Center for U.S.-Mexican Studies, 1989.

Corona, Rosanna. "Teléfonos de Mexico, S.A. de C.V." *Interamerican Development Bank Working Document Series*, no. 18 (1992).

Cowan, Gray L. *Privatization in the Developing World*. New York: Greenwood Press, 1990.

Cowhey, Peter F., and Jonathan D. Aronson. *Managing the World Economy: The Consequences of Corporate Alliances*. Washington D.C.: Council of Foreign Relations, 1993.

Cowhey, Peter F., Jonathan D. Aronson, and Gabriel Székely, eds. *Changing Networks: Mexico's Telecommunications Options*. La Jolla: Center for U.S.-Mexican Studies, 1989.

Cowhey, Peter F. "The Political Economy of Telecommunications Reform in Developing Countries." Paper presented to The World Bank Seminar on "Implementing Reforms in the Telecommunications Sector—Lessons from Recent Experiences." Washington, D.C., April 1991.

Crandall, Robert W., and Kenneth Flamm, eds. *Changing the Rules: Technological Change, International Competition, and Regulation in Communications.* Washington, D.C.: The Brookings Institution, 1989.

Crandall, Robert W. "Fragmentation of the Telephone Network." In *New Directions in Telecommunications Policy*, ed. Paula R. Newberg. Durham: Duke University Press, 1989.

Crozier, Michel. *Cómo Reformar el Estado: Tres Países, Tres Estrategias: Suecia, Japón y Estados Unidos.* Mexico, D.F.: Fondo de Cultura Económica, 1992.

Dahl, Robert. *Who Governs? Democracy and Power in an American City.* New Haven: Yale University Press, 1961.

Datar, Kiran Kapur. *Malaysia: Quest for a Politics of Consensus.* New Delhi: Vikas, 1983.

De Leon, Omar. "Una Privatización Bien Programada." *TelePress* 2, no. 7 (March–April 1992): 28–34.

Derthick, Martha, and Paul J. Quirk. *The Politics of Deregulation.* Washington, D.C.: The Brookings Institution, 1985.

Devlin, Robert, and Martine Guerguil. "América Latina y las Nuevas Corrientes Financieras y Comerciales." *Revista de la Cepal*, no. 43 (April 1991): 23–50.

Deyo, Frederic. *Beneath the Miracle: Labor Subordination in the New Asian Industrialism.* Berkeley: University of California Press, 1989.

Diario Oficial, 29 October 1990; and 10 December 1990.

Di Tella, Torcuato. "An Introduction to the Argentine System." In *Political Power in Latin America: Seven Confrontations*, ed. Richard R. Fagen and Wayne A. Cornelius. Englewood Cliffs: Prentice-Hall, 1970.

Donikian, Luis, Raul V. Arri, Vito Di Leo, and Roberto Varone. *Teléfonos: De la Política Nacional al Saqueo Privatista.* Buenos Aires: Foetra, 1990.

Drake, William J. "Asymmetric Deregulation and the Trasnformation of the International Telecommunications Regime." In *Asymmetric Deregulation: The Dynamics of Telecommunications Policy in Europe and the United States*, ed. Eli Noam and Gerard Pogerel. Norwood, N.J.: Ablex, 1993a.

_____. "Territoriality and Intangibility: Transborder Data Flows and National Sovereignty." In *Beyond National Sovereignty: International Communication in the 1990s*, ed. Kaarle Nordenstreng and Herbert I. Schiller. Norwood, N.J.: Ablex, 1993b.

Drake, William J., and Kalypso Nicolaidis. "Ideas, Interest, and Institutionalization: 'Trade in Service' and the Uruguay Round." *International Organization* 46, no. 1 (Winter 1992): 37–86.

Drake, William J., and Lee McKnight. "Telecommunications Standards in the Global Information Economy: The Impact of Deregulation and Commercialization." *Project Promethee Perspectives* 5 (1988): 14–20.

Dromi, Roberto J. Reporte a la Comisión Bicameral para la Privatización de Empresas Públicas del Congreso de la Nación, Buenos Aires, September 1990.

Dubb, Steve. "Trozos de Cristal: Modernization and Union Politics in Teléfonos de México." Unpublished manuscript. University of California, San Diego, 1991.

Duch, Raymond M. *Privatizing the Economy: Telecommunications Policy in Comparative Perspective.* Ann Arbor: The University of Michigan Press, 1991.

Dudek & Company. *Privatization and Public Employees.* Washington, D.C.: National Commission for Employment Policy, 1988.

East Asian Executive Report, 15 April 1986.

ECLAC. *Changing Production Patterns with Social Equity.* Santiago, Chile: United Nations, 1990.

Economic Intelligence Unit. "Venezuela." In *Venezuela, Suriname, Netherlands Antilles: Country Profile, 1992–93.* London: Business International Limited, 1992.

_____. "Thailand." *EIU Country Report.* London: Business International Limited, 1989.

_____. "Malaysia," *EIU Country Profile, 1986–91.* London: Business International Limited, 1992.

El Cronista Comercial. 21 October 1990.

El Día. 22 December 1990.

El Diario de Caracas. 22 October 1991.

El Nacional. 26 February 1989; 24 March 1989; 10 September 1989; 18 October 1990; and 22 December 1990.

El País. 14 June 1990.

Electronics Weekly. 20 May 1992.

Elixmann, Dieter, and Karl-Heinz Neumann, eds. *Communications Policy in Europe.* Berlin: Springer, 1990.

Empresa Nacional de Telecommunicaciones. "Informe del Proceso de Reestructuracion de las Telecomunicaciones en la Republica Argentina." 1990.

Encarnation, Dennis J., and Louis T. Wells, Jr. "Sovereignty En Garde: Negotiating With Foreign Investors." *International Organization* 39, no. 1 (1985): 47–78.

Entelequia. no. 23, Enero-Febrero 1990.

Esman, Milton J. *Administration and Development in Malaysia: Institution Building and Reform in a Plural Society.* Ithaca: Cornell University Press, 1972.

Estudios y Políticas. "Nueva Telefonía." *Estudios & Políticas Newsletter,* no. 10 (July 1991).

Evangelista, Matthew. "Issue-areas and Foreign Policy Revisited." *International Organization* 43, no. 1 (Winter 1989).

Evans, Peter B. *Dependent Development: The Alliance of Multinationals, State, and Local Capital in Brazil.* Princeton: Princeton University Press, 1979.

Evans, Peter B., Dietrich Rueschemeyer, and Theda Skocpol, eds. *Bringing the State Back In.* Cambridge: Cambridge University Press, 1985.

_____. "Transnational Linkages and the Economic Role of the State: An Analysis of Developing and Industrialized Nations in the Post-World War II Period." In *Bringing the State Back In*, ed Peter Evans, Dietrich Rueschemeyer, and Theda Skocpol. New York: Cambridge University Press, 1985.

_____. "The State as Problem and Solution: Predation, Embedded Autonomy, and Structural Change." In *The Politics of Economic Adjustment*, ed. Stephan Haggard and Robert Kaufman. Princeton: Princeton University Press, 1992.

Evans, Peter B., and Dietrich Rueschemeyer. "The State and Economic Transformation: Toward an Analysis of the Conditions Underlying Effective Intervention." In *Bringing the State Back In*, eds. Peter B. Evans, Dietrich Rueschemeyer, and Theda Skocpol. Cambridge: Cambridge University Press, 1985.

Fagre, Nathan, and Louis T. Wells, Jr. "Bargaining Power of Multinationals and Host Governments." *Journal of International Business Studies* (Fall 1982).

Fajnzylber, Fernando. *Unavoidable Industrial Restructuring in Latin America*. Durham: Duke University Press, 1990.

Fanelli, José Maria, Roberto Frenkel, and Guillermo Rozenwurcel. "Growth and Structural Reform in Latin America: Where We Stand." *Cuadernos CEDES*, no. 57 (1990).

Far Eastern Economic Review. 23 March 1989; 27 July 1989; 19 October 1989; 15 February 1990; 25 July 1991; 9 April 1992.

Fernández Christlieb, Fátima. *Avatares del Teléfono en México*. Mexico, D.F.: Teleindustria Ericsson, 1991.

Ferreira Rubio, Delia, and Matteo Goretti. "Gobernar por Decreto." *Poder Ciudadano* (August 1992).

Fischer, Frank, and Carmen Sirianni. *Critical Studies in Organization and Bureaucracy*. Philadelphia: Temple University Press, 1984.

Fonnegra, Gabriel, and Nelson Osorio. *La Subasta de Telecom*. Bogota: Ediciones Tormenta Tropical, 1992.

Fontana, Andrés. "Fuerzas Armadas e Ideologia Neoconservadora: El Redimensionamiento del Estado en la Argentina (1976–1981)." In *Privatización: Del Dicho al Hecho*, ed. Horacio Boneo. Buenos Aires: El Cronista Comercial, 1985.

Foreman-Peck, James, Alfred Haid, and Jurgen Muller. *The Spectrum of Alternative Market Configurations in European Telecommunications*. Berlin: Newcastle, 1988.

Foster, Christopher D. *Privatization, Public Ownership and the Regulation of Natural Monopoly*. Oxford: Blackwell, 1992.

Fowler, Mark S., and Aileen Amarandos Pisciotta. "Privatization as an Objective: Telecommunications and Regulatory Reform." In *Latin America's Turnaround: Privatization, Foreign Investment, and Growth*, ed. Paul Boeker. San Francisco: ICS Press, 1993.

Francés, Antonio. *Aló Venezuela: Apertura y Privatización de las Telecomunicaciones*. Caracas: IESA, 1993.

_____. "The Privatization of Venezuelan Telecommunications." In *The Privatization of Infrastructure in Developing Countries: Lessons from Latin America*, ed. Ravi Ramamurti. Baltimore: John Hopkins University Press, Forthcoming 1995.

Frank, Andre Gunder. *Dependent Accumulation and Underdevelopment.* London: Macmillan, 1978.

Freeman, Orville L. *The Multinational Company: Investment for World Growth* (New York: Praeger, 1981).

Frieden, Jeffry A. "Third World Indebted Industrialization: International Finance and State Capitalism in Mexico, Brazil, Algeria, and South Korea." *International Organization* 35, no. 3 (Summer 1981): 407–431.

FUCADE. "Evolucion de las Comunicaciones Durante el Primer Año de Gobierno del Sr. Presidente Carlos Menem." Unpublished manuscript. Instituto de Analisis de Políticas Públicas, Buenos Aires, 1990.

Galal, Ahmed, Leroy Jones, Pankaj Tandon, and Ingo Vogelsang. *Welfare Consequences of Selling Public Enterprises: Synthesis of Cases and Policy Summary.* Washington, D.C.: The World Bank, 1992a.

Galal, Ahmed, with Raul E. Saez, and Clemencia Torres. "Chile: Compañía de Teléfonos de Chile." In *Welfare Consequences of Selling Public Enterprises: Case Studies from Chile, Malaysia, Mexico, and the U.K.*, ed. Ahmed Galal, Leroy Jones, Pankaj Tandon, and Ingo Vogelsang. Washington, D.C.: The World Bank, 1992b.

Galal, Ahmed. "Does Divestiture Matter?: A Framework for Learning from Experience." *The World Bank Policy, Research, and External Affairs Papers*, no. 475 (1990).

_____. "Public Enterprise Reform: A Challenge for the World Bank." *The World Bank, Policy Research, and External Affairs Working Papers*, no. 407 (April 1990).

Garcia, Aníbal. "Ineficiencia, Deuda Externa y Privatización." *Realidad Económica*, no. 89 (1989): 34–51.

Garner, Maurice R. "Public Enterprise in Thailand." In *Public Enterprise and the Developing World*, ed. V. V. Ramanadham. London: Croom Helm, 1984.

Garutti, Humberto C. "La Privatización del Servicio de Telecomunicaciones en la Argentina." Tercera Reunion de la Comisión Técnica Permanente I: Servicios Públicos de Telecomunicaciones, Montevideo, Uruguay, April 1990.

Gerchunoff, Pablo, ed. *Las Privatizaciones en la Argentina.* Buenos Aires: Instituto Torcuato Di Tella, 1992.

Gereffi, Gary. *Industria Farmaceutica y Dependencia en el Tercer Mundo.* Mexico, D.F.: Fondo de Cultura Economica, 1986.

Givorgi, Carlos A. "Estudio de un Programa para la Expansion del Servicio de Telecomunicaciones." *Estudios* 8 (1985): 203–228.

Glade, William, ed. *Privatization of Public Enterprises in Latin America.* Washington, D.C.: ICS Press, 1991.

Goldin, Javier, Alfredo Peña, and Miguel Alberto Sánchez. "Reforma del Estado y Empresas Públicas." *Realidad Económica*, no. 92 (1990): 55–91.

Goldstein, Judith. "The Impact of Ideas on Trade Policy." *International Organization* 43, no. 1 (Winter 1989): 31–71.

Goldstein, Judith, and Robert O. Keohane. "Ideas and Foreign Policy." Unpublished manuscript. Stanford University, June 1991.

González Arzac, Alberto R. "Aerolineas, ENTel y la Inspección General de Justicia." *Realidad Económica*, no. 97 (1990): 55–63.

González Fraga, Javier. "The Argentine Privatization in Retrospect." In *Privatization of Public Enterprises in Latin America*, ed. William Glade. San Francisco: ICS Press, 1991.

Gourevitch, Peter. *Politics in Hard Times: Comparative Responses to International Economic Crisis*. Ithaca: Cornell University Press, 1986.

Government of Argentina. "Conditional Offer of Argentina Concerning Initial Commitments." Proposal presented to the Group of Negotiations on Services of the Uruguay Round Multilateral Trade Negotiations of the GATT. Geneva, July 1991.

Government of Malaysia, Economic Planning Unit. *Guidelines on Privatization*. Kuala Lumpur: Prime Minister Department, 1985.

_____. *Privatization Masterplan*. Kuala Lumpur: Prime Minister's Department, 1991.

Government of Malaysia, Ministry of Public Enterprises. "Privatisation in Malaysia." In *Privatisation in Developing Countries*, ed. V.V. Ramanadham. London: Routledge, 1989.

Grieco, Joseph M. *Between Dependency and Autonomy: India's Experience with the International Computer Industry*. Berkeley: California University Press, 1984.

_____. "Foreign Investment and Development: Theories and Evidence." In *Investing in Development: New Roles for Private Capital?*, ed. Theodore H. Moran. Washington, D.C.: Overseas Development Council, 1986.

Grindle, Marrilee S., and John W. Thomas. *Public Choices and Policy Change: The Political Economy of Reform In Developing Countries*. Baltimore: Johns Hopkins University Press, 1991.

Hachette, Dominique, and Rolf Luders. *Privatization in Chile: An Economic Appraisal*. San Francisco: International Center for Economic Growth, 1993.

Haggard, Stephan. *Pathways from the Periphery: The Politics of Growth in the Newly Industrializing Countries*. Ithaca: Cornell University Press, 1990.

Haggard, Stephan, and Robert Kaufman. *The Politics of Economic Adjustment*. Princeton: Princeton University Press, 1992.

_____. "Democratic Transitions and Economic Reform." Paper presented at the Southern California Workshop on Economic and Political Liberalization. University of Southern California, Los Angeles, May 1993.

Hall, Peter A., ed. *The Political Power of Economic Ideas: Keynesianism Across Nations*. Princeton: Princeton University Press, 1989.

Hamilton, Nora. *The Limits of State Autonomy*. Princeton: Princeton University Press, 1982.

Headrick, Daniel R. *The Invisible Weapon: Telecommunications and International Politics 1851–1945.* New York: Oxford University Press, 1991.

Helm, Dieter, and George Yarrow. "The Assessment: The Regulation of Utilities." *Oxford Review of Economic Policy* 4, no. 2 (1988): 1–31.

Henck, Fred W., and Bernard Strassburg. *Slippery Slope, The Long Road to the Breakup of AT&T.* New York: Greenwood Press, 1988.

Hernández Juárez, Francisco. "El Nuevo Sindicalismo," *Nexos*, March 1991.

Herrera, Alejandra. *La Revolución Tecnológica y la Telefonía Argentina.* Buenos Aires: Ed. Legasa, 1989.

Hewison, Kevin. *Power and Politics in Thailand.* Manila: JCAP, 1989.

Hill, Alice, and Manuel A. Abdala. "Regulation, Institutions and Commitment: Privatization and Regulation in the Argentine Telecommunications Sector." *The World Bank Working Papers.* The World Bank, Washington, D.C. 1994.

Hills, Jill. *Deregulating Telecoms: Competition and Control in the United States, Japan, and Britain.* Westport: Quorum Books, 1986.

Hirsh Ganievich, Carlos. "Alternativas para las Telecommunications en México." Ph.D. Dissertation, Universidad Nacional Autonoma de México, 1995.

Hobday, Michael. *Telecommunications in Developing Countries: The Challenge from Brazil.* London: Routledge, 1990.

Holt, Robert T., and John E. Turner. *The Methodology of Comparative Research.* New York: The Free Press, 1970.

Horwitz, Robert B. *The Irony of Regulatory Reform: The Deregulation of American Telecommunications.* New York: Oxford University Press, 1989.

_____. "The Ownership Regulation of Parastatals: The Future of South African Electricity and Telecommunications Industries in Light of International Experience." Paper presented at the Economic Trends Research Group Conference. Cape Town, South Africa, June 1992.

_____. "The Politics of Telecommunications Reform in South Africa." *Telecommunications Policy* 16, no. 4 (May –June 1992): 291–306.

_____. "South African Telecommunications: History and Prospects." In *Telecommunications In Africa*, ed. Eli M. Noam and Raymond W. Akwule. Forthcoming.

Huber, Peter. *The Geodesic Network: Report on Competition in the Telephone Industry.* Washington D.C.: U.S. Department of Justice, 1987.

Hukill, Mark A., and Meheroo Jussawalla. "Telecommunications Policies and Markets in the ASEAN Countries." *Columbia Journal of World Business* (Spring 1989).

Hukill, Mark A. "Telematic Infrastructure and Investment in the ASEAN Countries." Ph.D. Dissertation, Univeristy of Hawaii, 1990.

Huss, Torben. *FDI and Industrial Restructuring in Mexico.* New York: UN Center on Transnational Corporations, 1991.

Hymer, Stephen. *The Multinational Corporation: A Radical Approach.* Cambridge: Cambridge University Press, 1979.

Ikenberry, John. "Conclusion: An Institutional Approach to American Foreign Economic Policy." *International Organization* 42 (Winter 1988).

Independent Commission for Worldwide Telecommunications Development. *The Missing Link.* Geneva: International Telecommunications Union, 1984.

Institute for Information Studies. *Universal Telephone Service: Ready for the 21st Century?* Washington, D.C.: Institute for Information Studies, 1991.

Inter-American Development Bank. *Economic and Social Progress in Latin America: 1991 Report.* Washington, D.C.: Johns Hopkins University Press, 1991.

International Telecommunication Union. "Documents (vol. 1 & 2)." *Proceedings from the American Regional Telecommunication Development Conference.* Acapulco, Mexico, April 1992a.

_____. *International Telecommunications and Development.* Geneva: ITU, 1986.

_____. *Yearbook of Common Carrier Telecommunication Statistics.* Geneva: ITU, 1992b.

Isahak, Daud bin. "Meeting the Challenges of Privatization in Malaysia." In *Restructuring and Managing the Telecommunications Sector*, ed. Bjorn Wellenius, Peter A. Stern, Timothy E. Nulty, and Richard D. Stern. Washington, D.C.: The World Bank, 1990.

Jasperson, Fred, and Juan Carlos Ginarte. "External Resource Flows to Latin America: Recent Developments and Prospects." *IDB Development Policy Research Papers.* Washington, D.C.: Interamerican Development Bank, 1992.

Jervis, Robert. *Perception and Misperception in International Politics.* Princeton: Princeton University Press, 1976.

Jessop, Robert. *State Theory: Putting the Capitalist State in its Place.* Cambridge: Polity Press, 1990.

Jones, Leroy P., Ingo Vogelsang, and Pankaj Tandon. "Public Enterprise Divestiture." In *Politics and Policy Making in Developing Countries*, ed. Gerald M. Meier. San Francisco: ICS Press, 1991.

_____. *Selling Public Enterprises: A Cost-Benefit Methodology.* Cambridge: MIT Press, 1990.

Jussawalla, Meheroo, and D. M. Lamberton, eds. *Communication, Economics and Development.* New York: Pergammon Press, 1982.

Jussawalla, Meheroo, Tadayuki Okuma, and Toshihiro Araki, eds. *Information Technology and Global Interdependence.* New York: Greenwood Press, 1989.

Jussawalla, Meheroo, and Mark D. Lofstrom. "The Nexus Between Telecommunications Technology, Telecommunications Regulatory Policy, and Labor Law and Its Effect on the Division of Labor in Information Economies." Paper presented at the XV Pacific Telecommunications Conference. Honolulu, Hawaii, January 1993.

Katz, Jorge, and Bernardo Kosacoff. *El Proceso de Industrializacion en la Argentina: Evolución, Retroceso y Prospetiva.* Buenos Aires: Centro Editor de América Latina, 1989.

Katzenstein, Peter. *Between Power and Plenty: Foreign Economic Policies of Advanced Industrial States.* Madison: University of Wisconsin Press, 1978.

Kennedy, Laurel B. "Liberalization, Privatization, and the Politics of Malaysian Telecommunications Policy." Association for Asian Studies Annual Conference. April 1992.

Kikeri, Sunita, John Nellis, and Mary Shirley. *Privatization: The Lessons of Experience.* Washington, D.C.: The World Bank, 1992.

King, Robin A. "Toward a Theory of Multi-Player Macro-Economic Policy Under External Debt Crisis: Mexican Debt and Adjustment Policy, 1982–1990." Ph.D. Dissertation. University of Texas, Austin, 1991.

Kingdom of Thailand, Office of the Prime Minister. *Thailand in the 80s.* Bangkok: Muang Boran Publishing House, 1984.

Kobrin, Stephen J. "Testing the Bargaining Hypothesis in the Manufacturing Sector in Developing Countries." *International Organization* 41, no. 4 (Autumn 1987).

Krasner, Stephen. *Structural Conflict: The Third World Against Global Liberalism.* Berkeley: University of California Press, 1985.

Kuczynski, Pedro-Pablo. *Latin American Debt.* Baltimore: Johns Hopkins University Press, 1988.

Kuhlmann, Federico Antonio Alonso, and Alfredo Mateos. *Communicaciones: Pasado y Futuro.* Mexico: Fondo de Cultura Económica, 1989.

Labardini de Madrazo, Adriana. "The Privatization of Teléfonos de México S.A. de C.V.: The End of the Monopoly?" Unpublished manuscript. Columbia University, New York, 1990.

La Jornada. 8 December 1990; 9 April 1992; 23 July 1993.

La Nación. 22 May 1989; 2 October 1990; 13 August 1991; 6 April 1992.

Langdale, John. "Competition in Telecommunications." *Telecommunications Policy* (December 1982): 283–300.

Larroulet, Cristián V., ed. *Soluciones Privadas a Problemas Públicos.* Santiago de Chile: Editorial Trineo, 1991.

Lee, Barbara W. "Should Employee Participation Be Part of Privatization?" *The World Bank Policy, Research, and External Affairs Papers*, no. 664 (1991).

Lent, John A. "Telematics in Malaysia: Room at the Top for a Selected Few." In *Transnational Communications: Wiring the Third World*, ed. Gerald Sussman and John A. Lent. London: Sage, 1991.

Leong, Choon Heng. "Late Industrialization Along with Democratic Politics in Malaysia." Ph.D. Disseration, Harvard University, 1991.

Levy, Brian, and Pablo T. Spiller. "Regulation, Institutions and Economic Efficiency: Promoting Regulatory Reform and Private Sector Participation in Developing Countries." Research Proposal. Washington, D.C., The World Bank, February 1991.

Lewis, Paul H. *The Crisis of Argentine Capitalism*. Chapel Hill: University of North Carolina Press, 1990.

Lichtensztejn, Samuel. "Inversión Extranjera Directa por Deuda Externa: ¿Freno o Impulso de la Crisis en América Latina?" In *Crisis Financiera y Mecanismos de Contención*, ed. Carlos Tello Macías and Clemente Ruíz Durán. Mexico, D.F.: Fondo de Cultura Económica, 1990.

Littlechild, Stephen C. Report to the Secretary of State Regulation of the British Telecommunications' Profitability. London: Department of Industry, February 1983.

Luders, Rolf. "Did Privatization Raise Enterprise Efficiency in Chile?" In *Economic and Social Impact of Privatization in Latin America*, ed. William Glade. Boulder: Westview Press, forthcoming 1995.

Luis, Luis R. "Why Privatize in Latin America?" *Latin Finance* (March 1991).

Lukes, Steven. *Power: A Radical View*. Hong Kong: Macmillan Education Ltd, 1974.

Machinea, José Luis. "Stabilization Under the Alfonsín Government: A Frustrated Attempt." *Documentos CEDES* 42 (1990).

MacIntyre, Andrew J., and Kanishka Jayasuriya, eds. *The Dynamics of Economic Policy Reform in Southeast Asia and the Southwest Pacific*. New York: Oxford University Press, 1992.

March, James, and Johan Olsen. *Rediscovering Institutions: The Organizational Basis of Politics*. London: The Free Press, 1989.

_____. "The New Institutionalism: Organizational Factors in Political Life." *The American Political Science Review* 78, no. 3 (September 1984).

Martínez, Gabriel. "Regulación de la Industria Mexicana de Telecomunicaciones." In *México y el Tratado Trilateral de Libre Comercio: Impacto Sectorial*, ed. Eduardo Andere and Georgina Kessel. Mexico, D.F.: McGraw-Hill, 1992.

Mattelart, Armand, and Héctor Schmucler. *América Latina en la Encrucijada Telemática*. Buenos Aires: Paidos, 1983.

Maxfield, Silvia, and James H. Nolt. "Protectionism and the Internationalization of Capital: U.S. Sponsorship of Import Substitution Industrialization in the Philippines, Turkey, and Argentina." *International Studies Quarterly* 34, no. 1 (March 1990): 49–81.

McCormack, Arthur. *Multinational Investment: Boon and Burden for Developing Countries?* New York: W. R. Grace & Co., 1980.

McCormick, Patricia K. "Telecommunications Privatization Issues: The Jamaican Experience." *Telecommunications Policy* 17, no. 2 (March 1993): 145–157.

McDonald, Ronald H. *Party Systems and Elections in Latin America*. Chicago: Markham Publishing Co., 1971.

Meier, Gerald M., ed. *Politics and Policy Making in Developing Countries*. San Francisco: ICS Press, 1991.

Melo, José Ricardo. "La Privatización y la Estructura Regulatoria: El Caso de Chile." Paper presented at the Organization of the American States Seminar on "Restructuring the Telecommunications Sector in Latin America." Washington, D.C., May 1991.

Melody, William H. "The Information Society: The Transnational Economic Context and Its Implications." In *Transnational Communications: Wiring the Third World*, ed. Gerald Sussman and John A. Lent. London: Sage, 1991.

_____. "Telecommunication Reform: Which Sectors to Privatise?" Unpublished manuscript. CIRCIT, Melbourne, Australia, 1993.

Menem, Carlos, and Roberto Dromi. *Reforma del Estado y Transformación Nacional*. Buenos Aires: Ciencias de la Administracion SRL, 1990.

Meyer, Lorenzo. "Democratization of the PRI: Mission Impossible?" In *Mexico's Alternative Political Futures,* ed. Wayne A. Cornelius, Judith Gentleman, and Peter H. Smith. La Jolla: Center for U.S.-Mexican Studies, 1989.

Mier y Terán, Carlos. "La Modernización de las Telecomunicaciones en México." Unpublished manuscript. Mexico, D.F.,1991.

Mier y Terán, Carlos, and Alejandro López Toledo. "Structural Change in Mexican Telecommunications." Unpublished manuscript. Mexico, D.F., May 1991.

Miliband, Ralph. *The State in Capitalist Society*. London: Weidenfeld & Nicolson, 1969.

Milne, Robert S., and Diane K. Mauzy. *Politics and Government in Malaysia.* Vancouver: University of British Columbia Press, 1978.

Milner, Helen V. *Resisting Protectionism: Global Industries and the Politics of International Trade*. Princeton: Princeton University Press, 1988.

Minoli, Daniel. *Telecommunications Technology Handbook*. Boston: Artech House, 1991.

Mitrani, Christian J. P. "Lessons of Privatization from Argentina." Paper presented at the Association of the Bar of the City of New York Conference on "Lessons of Privatization in Latin America." New York, June 1991.

Mody, Bella, and Jorge Borrego. "Mexico's Morelos Satellite: Reaching for Autonomy?" In *Transnational Communications: Wiring the Third World*, ed. Gerald Sussman and John Lent. London: Sage, 1991.

Molano, Walter. "A Comparative Analysis of the Process of Privatization in the Southern Cone of Latin America: The Case of Telecommunications." Ph.D. Dissertation, Duke University, 1995.

Molinar Horcasitas, Juan. *El Tiempo de la Legitimidad: Elecciones, Autoritarismo y Democracia en México*. México, D.F.: Cal y Arena, 1991.

Mora y Araujo, Noguera y Asociados. "Opinión sobre la Privatización de Entel." Unpublished manuscript. Buenos Aires, November 1990.

Moran, Theodore H. *Investing in Development: New Roles for Private Capital?* Washington, D.C.: Overseas Development Council, 1986.

Moran, Theodore H., ed. *Multinational Corporations: The Political Economy of Foreign Direct Investment*. Lexington: Lexington Books, 1985.

Morell, David, and Chai-Anan Samudavanija. *Political Conflict in Thailand: Reform, Reaction, Revolution*. Cambridge: Oelgeschalager Gunn & Main Publishers, 1981.

Mosco, Vincent. "Toward a Theory of the State and Telecommunications Policy." *Journal of Communication* 38, no. 1 (1988): 107–124.

Mueller, Milton. *International Telecommunications in Hong Kong: The Case for Liberalization.* Hong Kong: The Chinese University of Hong Kong, 1992.

_____. "Universal Service in Telephone History: A Reconstruction." *Telecommunications Policy* (July 1993): 352–369.

Mulleady, Ricardo T. *Breve Historia de la Telefonía Argentina (1886–1956).* Buenos Aires: 1956.

Muzaffar, Chandra. *Challenges and Choices in Malaysian Politics and Society.* Penang, Malaysia: Aliran Kesedaran Negara, 1989.

Nankani, Helen. "Techniques of Privatization of State-Owned Enterprises: Selected Country Case Studies." *World Bank Technical Paper* 2, no. 89 (1988).

National Telecommunications and Information Administration. *Telecommunications Infrastructure Study for the Kingdom of Thailand.* Washington, D.C.: NTIA, 1991.

National Economic and Social Development Board, Government of Thailand. *The Seventh National Economic and Social Development Plan (1992–1996).* Bangkok: Office of the Prime Minister, 1992.

_____. *The Sixth National Economic and Social Development Plan: 1987–1991.* Bangkok: Office of the Prime Minister, 1987.

Neher, Clark D. *Southeast Asia: In the New International Era.* Boulder: Westivew, 1991.

Netl, J. P. "The State as a Conceptual Variable." *World Politics* 20 (1968).

Newberg, Paula R., ed. *New Directions in Telecommunications Policy.* Durham: Duke University Press, 1989.

Newfarmer, Richard S., ed. *Profits, Progress, and Poverty: Case Studies of International Industries in Latin America.* Notre Dame: University of Notre Dame Press, 1985.

Newman, Karin. *The Selling of British Telecom.* London: Holt, Rinehart and Winston, 1986.

New York Times. 13 November 1990.

Noam, Eli M. "Network Pluralism and Regulatory Pluralism." In *New Directions in Telecommunications Policy*, ed., Paula R. Newberg. Durham: Duke University Press, 1989.

_____. "Private Networks and Public Objectives." In *Universal Telephone Service: Ready for the 21st Century?* ed., Annual Review of the Institute for Information Studies. Washington, D.C.: Institute for Information Studies, 1991.

_____. "The Public Telecommunications Network: A Concept in Transition." *Journal of Communication* 37, no. 1 (Winter 1987).

_____. *Telecommunications in Europe.* New York: Oxford University Press, 1992.

Nohlen, Dieter, and Mario Fernández, eds. *Presidencialismo versus Parlamentarismo: América Latina.* Caracas: Nueva Sociedad, 1991.

Noll, Roger G. *Reforming Regulation*. Washington, D.C.: The Brookings Institutions, 1971.

_____. "The Future of Telecommunications Regulation." In *Telecommunications Regulation Today and Tomorrow*, ed. Eli M. Noam. New York: Harcourt Brace Janovich, Publishers, 1983.

_____. "The Political and Institutional Context of Communications Policy." In *Marketplace for Telecommunications: Regulation and Deregulation in Industrialized Democracies*, ed. Marcellus Snow. New York: Longman, 1986.

_____. "Telecommunications Regulation in the 1990s." In *New Directions in Telecommunication Policy*, ed. Paula R. Newberg. Durham: Duke University Press, 1989.

Nordlinger, Eric A. *On the Autonomy of the Democratic State*. Cambridge, MA: Harvard University Press, 1981.

North-South Center. "Basic Human Needs and the Democratic Process in Latin America." *North-South Issues II*, no. 2 (1993).

Oakeshott, Robert. "The Beginnings of an Employee-Owned Sector." In *Privatization and Ownership*, ed. Christopher Johnson. London: Pinter Publishers, 1988.

O'Donnell, Guillermo A. *Modernización y Autoritarismo*. Buenos Aires: Paidos, 1972.

O'Donnell, Guillermo A., Philippe C. Schmitter, and Laurence Whitehead, eds. *Transitions from Authoritarian Rule*. Baltimore: Johns Hopkins University Press, 1986.

OECD. *The Telecommunications Industry: The Challenges of Structural Change*. Paris: OECD, 1988.

_____. *Universal Service and Rate Restructuring in Telecommunications*. Paris: OECD, 1991.

Offe, Claus. *Contradictions of the Welfare State*. London: Hutchinson, 1984.

Ohmae, Kenichi. *The Borderless World: Power and Strategy in the Interlinked Economy*. New York: Harper Perennial, 1991.

Olson, Mancur. *The Logic of Collective Action: Public Goods and the Theory of Groups*. Cambridge: Harvard University Press, 1965.

Onn, Fong Chan. "The Malaysian Telecommunications Services Industry: Development, Perspective, and Prospects." *Columbia Journal of World Business* (Spring 1989).

_____. "Malaysia." In *Pacific Basin Telecommunications: An Evolutionary Approach*, ed. Eli M. Noam, Seisuke Komatsuzaki, and Douglas A. Conn. New York: Oxford University Press, 1994.

Oszlak, Oscar, ed. *Teoría de la Burocracia Estatal*. Buenos Aires: Paidos, 1984.

_____. "La Reforma del Estado en la Argentina." *Documentos CEDES* (1990).

_____. "Formación Histórica del Estado en América Latina: Elementos Teórico-Metodológicos para su Estudio." *Documentos CEDES* (1978).

Peres Núñez, Wilson. *Foreign Direct Investment and Industrial Development in Mexico*. Paris: OECD Development Center, 1990.

Peres Núñez, Wilson, and María Amparo Casar. *El Estado Empresario en México: Agotamiento o Renovación?* Mexico, D.F.: Siglo Veintiuno Ed., 1988.

Pérez de Mendoza, Alfredo. "Teléfonos de México: Development and Perspectives." In *Changing Networks: Mexico's Telecommunications Options*, ed. Peter F. Cowhey, Jonathan D. Aronson, and Gabriel Szekely. La Jolla: Center for U.S.-Mexican Studies, 1989.

Pérez Escamilla, Juan Ricardo. "Telephone Policy in Mexico: Rates and Investment." In *Changing Networks: Mexico's Telecommunications Options*, ed. Peter F. Cowhey, Jonathan D. Aronson, and Gabriel Szekely. La Jolla: Center for U.S.-Mexican Studies, 1989.

Petrazzini, Ben A. "Foreign Direct Investment in Latin America's Privatization." In *Latin America's Turnaround: Privatization, Foreign Investment, and Growth*, ed. Paul Boeker. San Francisco: ICS Press, 1993.

_____. "Labor: A Post-Privatization Assessment." In *Economic and Social Impact of Privatization in Latin America*, ed. William Glade. Boulder: Westview Press, forthcoming 1995.

Philip, George. "Public Enterprise in Mexico." In *Public Enterprise and the Developing World*, ed. V. V. Ramanadham. London: Croom Helm, 1984.

Pipe, Russell G. Report prepared for the International Telecommunications Union on Trade of Telecommunications Services: Implications of a GATT Uruguay Round Agreement for ITU and Member States, Geneva: ITU, May 1993.

Prizzia, Ross. *Thailand in Transition: The Role of Oppositional Forces*. Honolulu: University of Hawaii Press, 1985.

Puthucheary, Mavis. "The Administrative Elite." In *Government and Politics in Malaysia*, ed. Zakari Haji Ahmad. Singapore: Oxford University Press, 1987.

Rahim, Syed A., and Anthony J. Pennings. *Computerization and Development in Southeast Asia*. Singapore: The Asian Mass Communication Research and Information Centre, 1987.

Ramamurti, Ravi, and Raymond Vernon, eds. *Privatization and Control of State-Owned Enterprises*. Washington, D.C.: The World Bank, 1991.

Ramamurti, Ravi. "The Privatization of Teléfonos de México." "The Privatization of Venezuelan Telecommunications." In *The Privatization of Infrastructure in Developing Countries: Lessons from Latin America*, ed. Ravi Ramamurti. Baltimore: John Hopkins University Press, Forthcoming 1995.

_____. "Why Are Developing Countries Privatizing?" *Journal of International Business Studies* 23, no. 2 (Second Quarter 1992): 225–249.

Rebella, Jorge. "Uruguay Dice No a la Privatización." *TelePress* 2, no. 12 (January–February 1993): 22–26.

Reich, Robert B. *The Work of Nations: Preparing Ourselves for 21st–Century Capitalism*. New York: Vintage Books, 1992.

Remmer, Karen L. "Democracy and Economic Crisis: The Latin American Experience." *World Politics* 42, no. 3 (April 1990): 315–335.

Riggs, Fred W. *Thailand: The Modernization of a Bureaucratic Polity.* Honolulu: East-West Center, 1966.

Rock, David. *Argentina 1516–1982: From Spanish Colonization to the Falklands War.* Berkeley: University of California Press, 1985.

Rogozinski, Jacques. "Privatization of State-Owned Enterprises in Mexico: The TELMEX Case." Paper presented at the Association of the Bar of the City of New York Conference on "Lessons of Privatization in Latin America." New York, June 1991.

Ronfeldt, David. "Prospects for Elite Cohesion." In *Mexico's Alternative Political Futures,* ed. Wayne A. Cornelius, Judith Gentleman, and Peter H. Smith. La Jolla: Center for U.S.-Mexican Studies, 1989.

Rose, Richard. *Do Parties Make a Difference?* London: Macmillan, 1980.

Rosenberg, Emily. *Spreading the American Dream: American Economics and Cultural Expansion, 1890–1945.* New York: Hill and Wang, Inc., 1982.

Ross, Prizzia. *Thailand in Transition: The Role of Oppositional Forces.* Honolulu: University of Hawaii Press, 1985.

Rourke, Francis E., ed. *Bureaucratic Power in National Policy Making.* Boston: Little, Brown and Company, 1986.

Salomon Brothers. "American Depositary Shares Representing 100,000,000 Shares of Series A Common Stock," Prospectus, July 1990.

Salomon Brothers. "Strategic Investors' Perspectives on Telecommunications Privatization in Latin America." Paper presented at the Institute of the Americas' Second International Conference on Privatization in Latin America. La Jolla, April 1991.

Sartori, Giovanni. *Parties and Political Systems: A Framework for Analysis.* New York: Cambridge University Press, 1976.

Saunders, Robert J., Jeremy J. Warford, and Bjorn Wellenius. *Telecommunications and Economic Development.* Baltimore: Johns Hopkins University Press, 1994.

Savage, James. *The Politics of International Telecommunications Regulation.* Boulder: Westview, 1989.

Schiller, Dan. *Telematics and Government.* Norwood, N.J.: Ablex, 1982a.

_____. "Business Users and the Telecommunications Network." *Journal of Communication* 32, no. 4 (1982b): 84–96.

Schiller, Herbert I. *Who Knows: Information in the Age of the Fortune 500.* Norwood, N.J.: Ablex, 1981.

Schmitter, Philippe, and Gerahard Luhmbruch. *Trends Toward Corporatist Intermediation.* Beverly Hills: Sage Publications, 1979.

Secretaría de Comunicaciones y Transportes de México. "Modificaciones al Título de Concesión de Teléfonos de México, S.A. de C.V." *Diario Oficial* (10 December 1990): 13–40.

_____. *Reglamento de Telecomunicaciones.* Secretaria de Communicaciones y Transportes: Mexico, D.F., 1990.

Secretariat for Commerce and Industrial Development of Mexico. *Legal Framework for Direct Foreign Investment in Mexico.* Mexico, D.F.: Secretariat for Commerce and Industrial Development of Mexico, 1990.

Sharkey, William W. *The Theory of Natural Monopoly.* Cambridge: Cambridge University Press, 1982.

Shirley, Mary. *The Reform of State-Owned Enterprises: Lessons from the World Bank Lending.* Washington, D.C.: The World Bank, 1989.

Shirley, Mary, and John Nellis. *Public Enterprise Reform: The Lessons of Experience.* Washington, D.C.: The World Bank, 1991.

Shugart, Matthew S., and John M. Carey. *Presidents and Assemblies: Constitutional Design and Electoral Dynamics.* Cambridge: Cambridge University Press, 1992.

Sindicatura de Empresas Publicas. "Empresa Nacional de Telecomunicaciones: Informe de Gestión Anual." *SIGEP Annual Reports.* Buenos Aires: SIGEP, 1983–1990.

Sinha, Nikhil. "Choices and Consequences: A Cross-national Evaluation of Telecommunications Policies in Developing Countries." Ph.D. Dissertation, University of Pennsylvania, 1991.

Skocpol, Theda. "Bringing the State Back In: Strategies of Analysis in Current Research." In *Bringing the State Back In,* ed. Peter Evans, Theda Skocpol, and Dietrich Rueschemeyer. Cambridge: Cambridge University Press, 1985.

Skocpol, Theda, and Margaret Somers. "The Uses of Comparative History in Macrosocial Inquiry." *Comparative Studies in Society and History* 22 (1980).

Skocpol, Theda, ed. *Vision and Method in Historical Sociology.* Cambridge: Cambridge University Press, 1984.

Smelser, Neil J. *Comparative Methods in the Social Sciences.* Englewood Cliffs, N.J.: Prentice-Hall, 1976.

Smith Barney & Co. "TELMEX." Unpublished manuscript. Mexico, D.F., June 1991.

Smith, D. G., and D. C. Pitt. "Open Network Achitecture: Journey to an Unknown Destination." *Telecommunications Policy* (October 1991): 379–394.

Smith, Peter H. *Argentina and the Failure of Democracy: Conflict Among Political Elites, 1904–1955.* Madison: University of Wisconsin Press, 1974.

_____. *Labyrinths of Power.* Princeton: Princeton University Press, 1979.

Smith, Peter, and Gregory Staple. "Telecommunications Sector Reform in Asia: Toward a New Pragmatism." *The World Bank Discussion Papers,* no. 232. The World Bank, Washington, D.C. 1994.

Snow, Marcellus S. *Marketplace for Telecommunications: Regulation and Deregulation in Industrialized Democracies.* New York: Longman, 1986.

Sonnenschein, Mabelle, and Patricia Yokopenic. " Privatization of Telecommunications: The Strategic Investor's View." "The Privatization of Venezuelan Telecommunications." In *The Privatization of Infrastructure in Developing Countries: Lessons from Latin America,* ed. Ravi Ramamurti. Baltimore: John Hopkins University Press, Forthcoming 1995.

Spanish News Service. 23 October 1991.

Spiller, Pablo. "La Economía Política de Regulaciones a las Industrias: Un Informe con Implicaciones para el Estudios de Regulaciones en Paises en Desarrollo." *Estudios de Economía* 15, no. 3 (December 1988).

Spiller, Pablo T., and Cezley I. Sampson. "Regulation, Institution and Commitment: The Jamaican Telecommunications Sector." Unpublished manuscript. University of Illinois and University of West Indies, June 1992.

Stallings, Barbara, and Robert Kaufman. *Debt and Democracy in Latin America.* San Francisco: Westview, 1989.

Steinfield, Charles. "The Role of Users in Shaping Telecommunications Policy in the United States." Paper presented to the Academic Network for European Telecommunications, Workshop on the Role of Users in Telecommunications. Paris, May 1993.

Stone, Alan. *Wrong Number: The Break Up of AT&T.* New York: Basic Books, 1989.

Suárez del Cerro, Alejandro. "Futuro de las Telecomunicaciones en la Argentina." *Revista Argentina de Política, Economía y Sociedad* 3 (1984): 91–107.

Sussman, Gerald, and John A. Lent, eds. *Transnational Communications: Wiring the Third World.* London: Sage, 1991.

Székely, Gabriel. "Mexico's Challenge: Developing a New International Economic Strategy." In *Changing Networks: Mexico's Telecommunications Options,* ed. Peter F. Cowhey, Jonathan Aronson, and Gabriel Székely. La Jolla: Center for U.S.-Mexican Studies, 1989.

Takano, Yoshiro. "Nippon Telegraph and Telephone Privatization Study: Experience of Japan and Lessons for Developing Countries." *World Bank Discussion Papers,* no. 179 (1992).

Tandon, Pankaj, and Manuel Abdala. "Mexico: Teléfonos de México." In *Welfare Consequences of Selling Public Enterprises: Case Studies from Chile, Malaysia, Mexico, and the U.K.,* ed. Ahmed Galal, Leroy Jones, Pankaj Tandon, and Ingo Vogelsang. Washington, D.C.: The World Bank, 1992.

Tanoira, Manuel. "Cómo el Socialismo Arruinó a la Argentina y Cómo la Privatización Puede Revitalizarla." *Contribuciones* (October–December 1988): 43–52.

Telephony. 23 April 1990.

Temin, Peter, and Louis Galambois. *The Fall of the Bell System: A Study in Prices and Politics.* Cambridge: Cambridge University Press, 1987.

Terol, Luis. "Development of the Telecommunications Sector in Chile and its Role Within the Pacific Basin." Paper presented at the XV Pacific Telecommunications Conference. Hawaii, January 1993.

Terragno, Rodolfo H. "Privatizar Para Que El Estado Controle Mejor." *Nueva Sociedad,* no. 104 (November–December 1989): 144–154.

Teske, Paul E. *After Divestiture: The Political Economy of State Telecommunications Regulation.* New York: State University of New York Press, 1990a.

_____. "The Political Demand for and Supply of Deregulation." Paper presented at the Annual Conference of the American Political Science Association. San Francisco, August 1990b.

Testler, Mario. *La Telefonía Argentina: Su Otra Historia*. Buenos Aires: Ed. Rescate, 1990.

_____. *Un Siglo de Telefonía*. Buenos Aires: Empresa Nacional de Telecomunicaciones, 1981.

The Financial Times. 26 March 1990; 29 November 1990; and 7 October 1991.

The Economist. 23 February 1985.

Tiempo Nuevo. 16 May 1989.

Todaro, Michael. *Economic Development in the Third World*. New York: Longman, 1981.

Torre, Juan Carlos. "Building Democracies in Hard Times: The Current Latin American Experience." Unpublished manuscript, Buenos Aires, 1992.

Trimberger, Ellen Kay. *Revolution from Above: Military Bureaucrats and Development in Japan, Turkey, Egypt, and Peru*. New Brunswick, N.J.: Transaction Books, 1978.

Tucker, Hyde. "The Benefits of Telecom Privatizations: The New Zealand Experience." Pacific Telecommunications Conference. January 1991.

Ure, John. "Corporatization and Privatization of Telecommunications in ASEAN Countries." *Pacific Telecommunications Review* 15, no. 1 (September 1993): 3–15.

Urricochea, Fernando Sady. "Colombia: Privatización Tiene Pocos Defensores." *TelePress* 2, no. 7 (March–April 1992).

U.S. Department of Labor: Bureau of International Labor Affairs. *Privatization in Latin America*. Washington, D.C.: U.S. Government Printing Office, 1989.

U.S. Office of Technology Assesment. *Critical Connections: Communication for the Future*. Washington, D.C.: U.S. Printing Office, 1990.

Verbitsky, Horacio. *Robo para la Corona*. Buenos Aires: Editorial Planeta, 1991.

Vickers, John, and George Yarrow. *Privatization: An Economic Analysis*. Massachussets: MIT Press, 1988.

Vogelsang, Ingo, with Manuel Abdala, Christopher Doyle, and Richard Green. "United Kingdom: British Telecom." In *Welfare Consequences of Selling Public Enterprises: Case Studies from Chile, Malaysia, Mexico, and the U.K.*, ed. Ahmed Galal, Leroy Jones, Pankaj Tandon, and Ingo Vogelsang. Washington, D.C.: The World Bank, 1992.

Vuylsteke, Charles. "Techniques of Privatization of State-Owned Enterprises," *World Bank Technical Papers*. Washington, D.C.: World Bank, 1988.

Waisman, Carlos H. *Reversal of Development in Argentina: Postwar Counterrevolutionary Policies and Their Structural Consequences*. Princeton: Princeton University Press, 1987.

_____. "Argentina's Revolution from Above." In *The New Democracy in Argentina*, ed. Edward C. Epstein. New York: Praeger, 1992.

Wall Street Journal. 15 February 1990; 22 March 1990; 19 February 1992.

Waterbury, John. "The Heart of the Matter? Public Enterprises and the Adjustment Process." In *The Politics of Structural Economic Adjustments*, ed. Stephan Haggard and Robert Kaufman. Princeton: Princeton University Press, 1992.

Wellenius, Bjorn. "Beginnings of Sector Reform in the Developing World." In *Restructuring and Managing the Telecommunications Sector*, ed. Bjorn Wellenius, Peter A. Stern, Timothy E. Nulty, and Richard D. Stern. Washington, D.C.: The World Bank, 1989.

Wellenius, Bjorn, Peter A. Stern, Timothy E. Nulty, and Richard D. Stern, eds. *Restructuring and Managing the Telecommunications Sector.* Washington, D.C.: The World Bank, 1990.

Williamson, John, ed. *The Political Economy of Policy Reform.* Washington, D.C.: Institute for International Economics, 1994.

Williamson, John, ed. *Latin American Adjustment: How Much Has Happened?* Washington, D.C.: Institute for International Economics, 1990.

Wilson, David. *Politics in Thailand.* Ithaca: Cornell University Press, 1962.

Wint, Alvin G. "Telephone Privatization in a Small Country: Jamaica." "The Privatization of Venezuelan Telecommunications." In *The Privatization of Infrastructure in Developing Countries: Lessons from Latin America*, ed. Ravi Ramamurti. Baltimore: John Hopkins University Press, Forthcoming 1995.

Woldenberg, José, and Carlos Garcia, eds. *Sindicalismo Mexicano de los 90.* Mexico, D.F.: Friedrich Ebert Stiftung, 1990.

Wolhers de Almeida, Marcio. "Reestructuracao, Internacionalizacao e Mudancas Institucionais das Telecomunicacoes: Licoes das Experiencias Internacionais para o Caso Brasileiro." Ph.D. Dissertation, Universidade Estadual de Campinas, Brasil, 1994.

Woon, Toh Kin. "The Liberalization and Privatization of Telecommunications: The Malaysian Experience." In *Privatization and Deregulation in ASEAN and the EC: Making Markets More Effective*, ed. Jacques Plekmans and Norbert Wagner. Singapore: ISEAS, 1990.

World Telecoms Research. 30 March 1990.

Wynia, Gary W. *Argentina in the Postwar Era: Politics and Economic Policy Making in a Divided Society.* Albuquerque: University of New Mexico Press, 1978.

_____. *Argentina: Illusions and Realities.* New York: Holmes & Meier, 1986.

Xelhuantzi López, María. *El Sindicato de Telefonistas de la República Mexicana: Doce Años (1976–1988).* Mexico, D.F.: Lito L. de México, 1989.

Yoon, Jinpyo. "Formation and Transformation of the Modern State: A Comparative Study of the Nature and Role of the State in Indonesia, Thailand, and Vietnam." Ph.D. Dissertation, University of South Carolina, 1990.

Index

About the Author

BEN A. PETRAZZINI is Assistant Professor, Department of Information and Systems Management, the Hong Kong University of Science and Technology. His research on telecommunications reform in developing countries was awarded the 1993 Pacific Telecommunications Council Research Prize.

ISBN 0-275-95294-0

90000>

9 780275 952945

HARDCOVER BAR CODE

EAN

DATE DUE

Inc. 38-293